HUMAN RIGHTS IN INDIA:
ISSUES AND CHALLENGES

Human Rights in India

Edited By

Aftab Alam

Raj Publications

New Delhi - 110002 (INDIA)

Human Rights in India: Issues and Challenges

2012

ISBN 978-81-86208-10-6

Published by : **Raj Publications**
108, 4855/24 Ansari Road
Daryaganj, New Delhi - 110002
Tel. : 011- 23250939, 9811010939
Email- rajpublications@yahoo.co.in

Laser Typesetting : Aarati Computers, Delhi-110 009

Printed at : Balaji Offset, Delhi

Printed in India

Contents

Preface

This book deals with the important subject of Human Rights which has been the crucial element of Philosophical, Social and Political debates in the second half of the twentieth century and, will probably also constitute a dominant discourse of the twenty first century. While there is increasingly widespread concern for universal respect and observance of human rights, grossviolation of internationally recognised norms continue unabated in almost all parts of the world. India is no exception to this. Though in large parts of the world we boast of a democratic set-up with a comprehensive charter of rights enshrined in the constitution, protected by an independent Judiciary, yet large scale violation of Peoples' rights has become a routine affair. Cases of human rights violation in India are innumerable, repetitive, enduring and have almost become a permanent feature of the state system. The present volume is a modest attempt to highlight some of these issues which deserve special attention and also offers suggestions for improving the existing conditgions. The book covers a wide range of issues like human rights violation of Women and Children, of Dalits and Minorities and of Refugees. It also deals with human rights abuses in pre-trial detention and covers the issue of environmental degradation and human rights. It also gives insight into the human rights situation in North-east India. The book also provides a historical perspective of the conceptual evolution of human rights and endeavours to unfold the controversies gathering around its universality and its misuse by the West as a diplomatic tool for establishing their hegemony over the Third World.

For now I want simply to express my deep gratitude to

individuals for the help, guidance and encouragement I have received. The main credit in this endeavour undoubtedly goes to the contributors who despite their pressing commitment, extended their whole hearted support and cooperation witghout which it would not have been possible for me to shoulder this responsibility. I owe my deep debt of gratitude to all of them. I wish to place on record my appreciation and gratitude to my teacher, guide, and colleague Prof. M.A.Kishore, Currently Chairman Department of Political Science and Coordinator Human Rights Programme, Aligarh Muslim University, who has been main motivating source behind the completion of this volume. I may also put on record Shri Mohan Sing-Member of Parliament and Dr. Surya Narayan Singh for their love, motivation and manifold help. Very sincerely, I owe heartfelt thanks to all my friends and colleagues for their valuable assistance, encouragement and pleasant association. Finally, I am also thankful to Mr. Pawan Kumar Goel of Rajaaaa Publication, Delhi for taking keen interest in this project and bringing this volume in a very short time but in an elegant manner.

Aligarh **Aftab Alam**

Contributors

1.	**Aftab Alam**	Teaches Political Science at the Aligarh Muslim University.
2.	**Jayanti Alam**	Former Senior Programme Officer, Indian Social Institute, Freelance Writer, New Delhi.
3.	**K.I. Vibhute**	Professor in Law, University of Pune, Maharashtra.
4.	**Kunja Medhi**	Professor in Political Science, Gauhati University, Assam.
5.	**M. Afzal Wani**	Reader in Law, Aligarh Muslim University, Aligarh.
6.	**Mamta Rao**	Lecturer in Law, Rani Durgawati University, Jabalpur, M.P.
7.	**Md. Shadan Zeb Khan**	Lecturer in Political Science, Aligarh Muslim University, Aligarh.
8.	**Md. Zafar Mahfooz Nomani**	Lecturer in Law, Aligarh Muslim University, Aligarh.
9.	**Mohiuddin Ahmad Farooqui**	Doctoral Fellow in Law, Aligarh Muslim University, Aligarh.
10.	**Nadeem Mohsin**	Executive Director, Institute for Neglected Child and Juvenile Justice, New Delhi.

11.	**Parul Modi**	Senior Advocate, High Court of Gujrat, Ahmadabad.
12.	**P.D. Mathew, S.J.**	Editor, Legal News & Views, New Delhi.
13.	**Ravi Kiran Jain**	Senior Advocate and the President, The People Union for Civil Liberties, U.P.
14.	**Subhram Rajkhowa**	Reader in Law, Gauhati University, Assam.

1

Introduction

Emerging Dimensions of Human Rights

Aftab Alam

The concept of human rights has assumed importance globally during the past few decades. Ever since the proclamation of the Universal Declaration of Human Rights, the term human right has gained currency. Human rights have been the crucial element of philosophical, social and political debates in the second portion of the twentieth century. They will probably also constitute a major discourse of the twenty first century. While there is increasingly widespread concern for universal respect and observance of human rights, gross violation of internationally recognised norms continue unabated in almost all parts of the world. Countless people around the world suffer hunger, disease and lack of opportunity, there being denied the enjoyment of the most basic economic, social and cultural rights as well as civil and political rights, which is of paramount importance for full realization of human dignity and for the attainment of legitimate aspiration of every individual. The challenge of violation of human rights faces the mankind in its stark nakedness. The challenge is global, concern universal and the issue is basic.

In a developing society such as ours where around 50 per cent of the people are living below poverty line and around

70 per cent of the people are illiterate and large number of men and women are living a life of want and destitution, misery and suffering, this subject assumes much greater importance. Despite much hype and holloa a vast number of Indian masses continue to live indignified and uncongenial life. Most of the fundamental human rights and fundamental freedoms enshrined in the Indian Constitution have remained paper aspirations, which compel many to rethink about India's commitment and seriousness to these issues. There is wide gap between rhetoric and reality and sometimes human rights appear more or less a myth in India.

Although, the ideal of human rights may tend to be universal, the response to the issues of human rights vary according to the kind of society and the stage of national development that relates to the system of human right. Further some nation may be genuinely interested about the issue of human rights, for others certainly it has become useful diplomatic tool. Many leaders from the South feel that issue of human rights has been politically manipulated by the powers of North specially by the USA, as a means of exercising domination over the Third World countries.

What are Human Rights ?

Although much has been written and pronounced about human rights through the centuries, yet one would still be hard put to define the term. But again as one author has aptly remarked—"Human rights may be difficult to define but impossible to ignore." Human rights is a dynamic concept and endeavours to adopt itself to the needs of the day. For this reason, the definition and understanding of the term depend much on the condition and opinions prevailing in the given society at a given time and it attains new dimension with the march of history. Since the socio-economic environment with which the question of human rights is intrinsically bound up, keep changing, so do the form and content of human rights. Hence, what constitute human rights cannot be spelt out, in absolute terms for all times and all situations.

Inspite of the complications involve in defining human rights attempts are made to comprehend it. To put it simply, human rights constitute those very rights which one has precisely because of being a human. To have a human rights one need not to do anything special than be born a human being. In their basic meanings, human rights are claims of the individual for such conditions as are essential for the fullest realization of the innate characteristic which nature has bestowed him/her with as a human being. They are inherent in our nature and without which we cannot live as human beings. Human rights pertain to all persons and are possessed by everybody in the world because they are human beings. They are not earned, bought or inherited nor are they created by any contractual authority. Differences of sex, race, language and colour do not change these rights. Nor do the differences of property, social origins, political ideals or religious beliefs. Every one regardless of who they are and what they do or think, is born with human rights. The colour of the skin may be white or black, the level of mental make-up may be high or low, the way of life of a people may be modern or primitive, to the core the essential reality of all belonging to the species of human race cannot be dismissed by any stretch of imagination.

Human Rights are essential for full development of human personality and for human happiness. They are indispensable for physical and mental upliftment of the human race. These rights are inalienable because the enlightened conscience of the community would not permit the surrender of these rights by any person even of his own volition. These rights are inviolable because they are not only vital for the development of human personality but also because without them men would be reduced to the level of animals. These rights are expression of what is a life minimally worth living and are based upon primary material and immaterial necessities of life. Of course there cannot be single opinion about quality of life minimally worth living, about primary necessities of life and thus about human rights. But still some rights must be regarded as fundamental like right to life with dignity, right to freedom of conscience and of course right to minimal means of subsistence. Human rights are based on mankind's increasingly demand for a decent and civilized life in which the inherent dignity of each human being will receive respect and protection.

Saga of Human Rights

There is no doubt that the term "Human right" is a twentieth century phraseological invention. However, the idea of the inalienable rights of man is much older and infact was often articulated by poets, philosophers and politicians since antiquity. The genesis of human rights is the utopian concept of natural rights traceable from the days of the Greeks or even earlier. The doctrine of natural rights rests on a belief in "Nature", as the original creating force which gave to every man the power of finding by reason the right principles on which to organise his life. Natural right refers to some conditions, situation or conduct that is right, as opposed to being neutral or wrong for human beings. For example, if we have the natural right to be free, then being free is right, not wrong for us by nature.

In the medieval period, which stretch from 13th century to the Peace of Westphalia (1648), encompassing the period of Renaissance and the decline of feudalism, certain basic changes in the beliefs and practices of society were witnessed because people felt the idea of human right as a general social need and reality. It was during this period when resistence to religious intolerance and political-economic bondage began, the real foundation of human rights were truly laid. The Magna Carta (1215), the Petition of Rights (1628), and the English Bill of Rights (1689) were proof of increasingly popular view that human beings are endowed with certain eternal and inalienable Rights.

However, the modernist conception of natural rights took real shape only during 17th and 18th century. The scientific and intellectual achievements of the 17th century - the discoveries of Galileo and Newton, the materialism of Hobbes, the raitionalism of Rene Descartes and G.W. Leibniz, the pantheism of Spinoza, the empiricism of Francis Bacon and John Locke – encouraged a belief in natural law and universal order. During the 18th century, the so called Age of Enlightenment, a growing confidence in human reason and in the perfectability of human affairs led to its more comprehensive expression in the writings of English philosopher John Locke and the works of Montesquieu, Voltaire and Rosseau. John Locke, the father of modern liberalism argued in detail, mainly in writing associated with the Glorious Revolution (1688), that certain rights like right to life, liberty and property self-evidently pertain to individuals as human beings because they even existed in the "state of nature" before humankind entered into civil society. He further argued that while entering into civil society through contract humankind surrendered to the state only the right to enforce these natural rights and not the rights themselves. He also cautioned that if state fails to protect these rights people also have a right to revolt against state. The liberal philosophers though belonged to varied current of thoughts had a common supreme faith in reason and vigorously attacked religious and scientific dogmatism, intolerance, censorship, and social-economic restraints. They also sought to discover and act upon universally valid principles based on law of nature, human reason, civil society and of course inalienable rights of man.

The teachings of these liberal thinkers had a profound influence on the Western world of the late 18th and early 19th century. Together with the practical example of England's revolution of 1688 and the resulting Bill of Rights, the liberal intellectual ferment provided the rationale for the wave of revolutionary agitation that then swept the West, most notably in North America and France. The American Declaration of Independence (1776) stated: "We hold these truths to be self-evident that all men are created equal, that they are endowed by (their) creator with certain inalienable rights; that among these are Life, Liberty and the Pursuit of Happiness." Similarly the French Declaration of the Rights of Man (1789) emphasised that "men are born and remain free and equal in rights," which are "Liberty, Property, Safety and Resistance to Oppression." It defined 'liberty' so as to include the right to free speech, freedom of association, religious freedom, and freedom from arbitrary arrest and confinement.

The most important factor which attributed to the development of the notion of natural or human rights during this period was indeed the failure of rulers to respect the principle of freedom and equality. In the words of Maurice Cranston it was infact political absoluteness which prompted men to claim their rights which were denied to them.

Despite practical success in France and England the idea of human rights as natural rights was not without its detractors. The doctrine of natural rights with the passage of time became less and less acceptable to philosophical and political liberals due to its frequent association with religious orthodoxy and its abstract nature. What is more important that the doctrine of natural rights came under powerful philosophical and political attack not only from leftists but from liberals also.

Without much doubt the most serious philosophical blow to natural rights theory came particularly from Edmund Burke David Hume and Jermy Bentham. Conservative Burke and Bentham questioned the very basis of the doctrine. They held the view that we can never know the nature of man, and thus we can never identify human rights. For if human nature is impossible to identify or if no such idea as the nature of something can be meaningful, so that human nature does not exist such that we could know it – then the rights that people have because they are human beings, i.e., by virtue of their humanity, human nature, cannot be identified. They further condemned the doctrine out of fear that public affirmation of natural rights would lead to social upheaval. Despite believer in natural law they expressed doubt that the rights of man could be derived from it. They criticized the Declaration of Rights of Man as "Monstrous fiction" of human equality.

Bentham one of the founders of Utilitarianism was more critical. He asserted that "right is the child of law," from real laws come real rights but from imaginary laws, from law of nature, come imaginary rights". He goes on to the extent of calling it (natural rights) as "simply nonsense, natural and imprescriptible rights, rhetorical nonsense, nonsense upon stilts." This assault upon natural law and natural rights further intensified and broadened during 19th and early 20th centuries by philosophers like J.S. Mill, Friedrich Karl Von Savigny, Sir Henry Maine and John Austin. Attack on the doctrine was so intense that by the World War I there were hardly any theorist who would or could defend the 'rights of man' along the line of natural law. Thereafter, under the influence of Hegel's idealism and rising European nationalism, the Marxian school of thought emerged. The Marxists, although, did not reject the rights of men altogether but maintained that right derived from whatever source preeminently belong to the communities or whole societies and nations and not only to individuals.

Although the heyday of natural rights proved short, the notion of human rights nonetheless endured in one or other form. But it was not untill the rise and fall of Nazism in Germany that the idea of human rights came truly into its own. After the first world war, the world community for the first time realised the need to establish some institutional mechanism to protect and preserve the rights of man. The establishment of the League of Nations was the first such modest attempt in this direction. However, it should be born in mind that human rights did not find any direct and explicit reference in the *Covenant* of the League of Nations. The League Covenant made an indirect reference to the welfare of the people governed under the mandate Art 22 (1) reads "that the well being and development of such people form a sacred trust of civilization." Art 22(5) made responsible to the mandatory state to maintain such conditions in the territory which will guarantee "freedom of conscience and religion" and "the prohibition of abuses such as slave trade" etc. The contribution of the International Labour Organization under the aegis of the League was equally noteworthy in creating an atmosphere of international involvement in securing fair and humane conditions of labourers.

However, until 1945 international response towards human rights tended to concentrate on remedying particular abuses or on protecting particular groups; it was only after the UN Charter was signed in 1945 that any attempt was made to provide comprehensive protection of all individuals against all forms of injustice and human rights violations. The vague and halting hunger for peace, human rights and social justice expressed in the covenant of League of Nations was transformed into firmer commitments and stronger imperatives in the Charter of the United Nations which stressed the urgency of international cooperation in promoting and encouraging respect for human rights and fundamental freedoms. Commenting on UN Charter, Brownlie observed that "a major achievement of the draftsmen of the Charter was the emphasis of the provisions on the importance of social justice and human rights as the foundation for a stable international order."

Infact the horrors and worst kind of brutalization of human rights in the 2nd world war was the main motivating factor in pursuing the goals of protection of human rights in the post-war period. The United Nations, which arose like a phoenix out of the ashes of the 2nd world war, put utmost stress on promotion and fostering of human rights and basic freedom. The UN Charter was the first international instrument which, in unequivocal *terms* proclaimed "universal respect for, and observance of human rights and fundamental freedoms for all without distinction as to race, sex, language or religion." The Charter made promotion of these rights as one of its basic purposes and obligated member states to take joint and separate action in cooperation with the United Nations for the achievement of this purpose. Thus the UN Charter ushered in a new international law of human rights; until then question of human rights was considered to be a matter between a state and individuals within its territory – a matter of domestic jurisdiction. For the first time in the history of mankind human rights – which every individual could claim as a member of human society – were universalised and internationalised. It was just beginning of a new era and concerted efforts were needed to keep it moving forward towards the desired goal.

The Charter of the United Nations, however, did not define or specify the contents of human rights and this task was left to organisation itself. For this purpose in December 1948, after three years of preparatory work, the UN General Assembly proclaimed the Universal Declaration of Human Rights. The UNDHR was primarily an enunciation of common standard to be adopted by all people and all nations in the promotion and protection of human rights across the globe. It was a yardstick of international standards and a path-finding instrument. It defines specific rights–civil and political as well as economic, social and cultural–with equality and freedom from discrimination as a principal and recurrent theme. It spells out the rights to life, liberty and security of person, to fair trial by due process of law, to freedom of conscience, thought, expression, association and privacy, freedom of movement. It also enumerates such economic, social and cultural rights as the right to equal pay for equal work, right to form and join trade unions, right to rest and leisure, and the right to health care and education and so on.

The UNDHR is not, of course, a perfect or even complete compilation. It must be seen as the beginning of a process, not its end. The Declaration does not include many rights which have become enormously significant since then, such as right to self-determination, and the right to development. These rights have been subsequently embodied in declaration of their own, the formular and format modelled on their precursor, the Universal Declaration.

The Declaration though devoid of legal authority and enforceability it has exercised a profound influence upon the minds of men and practice of states throughout the world. It stirred the moral consciousness as well as the political assertiveness of people in various countries. Various parts of the Declaration have been cited in national constitutions and other international instruments as well as regional treaties and conventions. It has also been invoked and reinvoked by a broad range of decision makers, national and international, judicial and others. Adoption of Declaration was really an event of great significance which launched a new era of hopes and aspirations for human civilization in the protection and promotion of human rights across the globe. Mrs. Eleanor Rosevelt rightly called it the "Magna Carta" of all mankind, as it constitutes a landmark in the history of human rights.

It should, however, be noted that the UNDHR was devoid of legal sanction to compel states to meet the obligation of ensuring observance and implementation of human rights enshrined in it. So to transform the 'principles' into provisions casting binding legal obligation on the part of ratifying states, the General Assembly promulgated in December 1966 International Covenants comprising three instruments : International Covenants on Economic, Social and Cultural rights. International Covenants on Civil and Political Rights; and Optional Protocol to the Covenants on Civil and Political Rights. Besides, over the decades, scores of other instruments dealing with specific rights—rights of stateless person, of the refugees, of women, elimination of all forms of discrimination, and so on have also been proclaimed. All these embody political commitments by signatory states and also provide for the conduct of international relations in the field of human rights and bring the domestic policies in line with international code of ethics. International covenants and instruments are beacon lights showing the path of justice and humanity to the nations. However, what has been traversed so far could be regarded as the initial steps towards a long and arduous journey. Progressive steps forward on this journey call for ceaseless struggle by people in different parts of the world, to ensure that human rights are respected and upheld universally.

Human Rights discourse: West versus Third World

Though the human rights issue is basically universal in nature, it has been politically manipulated by the Western powers as a means of exercising domination over the Third World countries. Political use of the issue of human rights has made the intention of the most western countries sceptic in the eye of the majority of the people of the Third World countries. Most importantly the USA and other countries, which have not been slow to condemn violation of human rights in the third world countries have not only been the worst violators of human rights of these countries but also among the most laggard in respect of signature and ratification of the covenants and conventions on human rights drafted and adopted in or outside the UN. Interestingly, the country which is readily agree to serve the interests of the West, inspite of the large scale violations of human rights therein, is given clean chit. But if a country questions the policies of West and refuse to be a tool in their hand and rejects their model of development, suddenly the issue of human rights is invoked. Does it not lead to think that should the non-western countries need certificate of human rights record from western world? This is a perennial question to deal with.

Frequent recourse to the sanction of human rights in the untenably narrow sense of civil and political ones, accentuates the irony of the situation. The powerful countries of west (particularly the USA) are trying to use their clout in ways palpably harmful to the economic interests of the poor countries. The tendency in the west to link unrelated issues such on labour standards, social conditions and environment to the new trading regimes work to the disadvantage of the developing countries. Ironically, the sanction of human rights is further invoked by the self-appointed policeman of the world – the US to pressurise threshold nuclear power countries to sign the NPT and CTBT, while it and its allies remain free to use nuclear blackmail to secure their strategic objectives. If the history of imperialism is any guide, it is these powerful countries which need to be disciplined first.

It is also worthy to note that the western scholars use academic Jargon rationalising the limited definition of human rights which fits in with the emerging post-cold war US policy of establishing political hegemony over third world countries, justifying control over their economy and polity. Not only that the US is funding to scholars and politicians of third world who offers their service in rationalising American ideology and political and economic interests. India is going to be target of this kind of programme because India is a potential market with its over 200 million middle class population, not only for consumer goods, but also for mass media products. If these facts are any guide one can speculate on a latent political objective behind the current fashion of the frequent use of the terms human rights, democracy etc.

However, our enthusiasm in speculating American hidden agenda must not blind us with the fact that violation of human rights has become every day's affairs in many of the third world countries. Politics of convenience, authoritarianism and repressive state practices, politically motivated ethnic and communal carnages, massive corruption and virtual collapse of any system of accountability have become some of the striking features of the modern state system in the third world. The strategy for third world countries, therefore, should be two fold. At one level they must *unitedly* chalkout their plan to shield themselves against any design of the western intrusion into their sovereign domain and at the other level they should also strive to do away from there evils which have crept into their society and show great respect for the human rights of their own citizens. They must set their own house in order alongwith their crusade against western imperialism. Promoting human rights is a historic process and no country can be exception. If one country or several countries act as a permanent guard of human rights, supervise and attack other countries which can only be watched and have no right to speech, this in itself violates the principle and spirit of human rights.

How Universal are Human Rights ?

Despite the many achievements of the international community in the field of human rights, the question of the universality of human rights versus relativism again revisited against the background of the 50th anniversary of the Universal Declaration of Human Rights. Many scholars and states have contended the view that the Universal Declaration serves as the universally valid standard of human rights and morality to which one country could appeal in making *judgements* about another country or countries with altogether a different culture and tradition. They are of the view that while human rights are universal in nature they must be considered in the context of a dynamic and evolving process of international norm setting, bearing in mind the significance of national and regional particularities and various historical, cultural and religious background. But unfortunately not only do human rights as set forth in the Universal Declaration reveal a strong western bias, but there has been a tendency to view human rights *ahistorically* and in isolation from their social, political and economic milieu. In its White Paper "Human Rights in China," the Chinese government stated that "despite its international aspect, the issue of human rights falls by and large within the *sovereignty* of each state." The Chinese White Paper further states that "the evolution of the situation in regard to human rights is circumscribed by the historical, social, economic and cultural conditions of various nations, and involves a process of historical development. Owing to tremendous differences in historical background, social system, cultural tradition and economic development, countries differ in their understanding and practice of human rights."

The concept of universality of human rights caused sharp differences of opinion among the states during Vienna Conference (June, 1993). Lien Huapiu, the head of the Chinese delegation stated that "one should not and cannot think the human rights standards and models of certain countries as the only proper ones and demand that all countries comply with them. It is neither realistic nor workable to make international economic assistance or even international cooperation conditional on them." Similar view was expressed by the Iranian Deputy Foreign Minister at the Bangkok Regional Conference (March, 1993) - "The political predominance of the group of countries which is temporary by nature cannot provide a license for the imposition of a set of guidelines and norms for the behaviour of the entire international community, especially since these states do not present an ideal, feasible or practical model in theory or practice."

The Malaysian Prime Minister Mohatir Mohammad has been one of the ardent critics of the universality principle. He has long claimed that Human Rights were a western import, inconsisted with Asian values and giving too much emphasis to the rights of the individual. Recently, he called for a review of the UNDHR to reflect the needs of developing countries. He blamed the western society that "these people would rather see people starve than allow for a stable government." The nub of third world criticism of western concept of human rights is that international human rights standard were conceived and formulated largely by westerners, and reflect cultural values that are alien to non-western traditions and that a blanket application of western principles to non-western conditions is unjustifiable. Developing countries further object the western undue emphasis on Civil and Political rights.

They feel that hungary masses in their countries are too concerned with filling their stomachs to concern themselves civil liberties and political freedoms. Further, developing countries must sacrifice freedom temporarily to achieve the rapid economic development that their exploding population and rising expectations demand. And most importantly the West is using human rights as a stalking horse to achieve economic domination over the poorer world.

The objections raised by developing countries are immediately refuted by the west sometimes as a "total lie" and another as "pretext of authoritarianism". The western countries argue that human rights, particularly civil liberties, do not endanger social and economic development or undermine nation building. Protecting citizens from torture by State authorities or imprisonment without trial, permitting freedoms of worship are not incompatible with economic development. The west feels that "fundamental human rights and freedom are universal and are inherent in all human kind. They find expression in constitutions and legal systems throughout the world, they are anchored in the international human rights instruments by which all genuinely democratic *states* are bound.....The principle transcends national political systems." The West argue that what the UNDHR offers are guiding precepts to be fleshed out in all societies regardless of their political, legal, economic or social systems, or their philosophies or values.

There is no doubt that principle of universality concerning human rights laid down by the international community must be respected. However, the universality principle must be combined with concrete situation in different countries. Due to different historic background, cultural traditions and social and economic level of development, countries are different in implementing the principle in terms of content and forms, approaches and steps. We cannot simply denounce the views subscribed by non-western states and scholars merely by labelling it "a tactic move to justify deviation from the universal standards" or "pretext for violating international human rights" or "an alibi for authoritarianism". It is normal phenomenon that there are different opinions over human rights in international society. There is no harm in accomodating different opinions, as it will also ensure universality.

Respect and observance of human rights are always conditional upon economic conditions of respective states. Unfortunately, this fact is often ignored by the Western scholars and states. Any discourse on human rights situation in the Third World countries would be incomplete unless it takes into account prevailing economic condition. According to UN statistics, the world's total population is about 5.7 billion, with 4.9 billion living in developing countries and about 1.3 billion living in hunger. Poverty has been one of the most potent cause of the violation of human rights in third world countries. Poverty undermines human dignity and without human dignity there is no human right. If unprejudiced, one can easily understand a simple argument: one can enjoy human right only after one manages to live on. The Civil and Political rights are neither meaningful nor feasible in conditions of want and destitute. When there is a grim struggle for existence, many of the principles of human rights appear to be impractical and devoid of merit. When employment itself is scarce, insistence on payment of minimum wages, abolition of child labour, abolition of bonded labour etc. appear to be constraints in getting employment. For a poor man, if his child could earn any amount, it is an addition to his income and will keep the pot boiling. He is unable to see any merit in the virtues of universal education and prevention of child labour.

If human rights are really universal, it implies entitlement of world's resources to satisfy, to start with, the most basic want of hunger. Normatively, suffering on this account anywhere in the world should be the concern of the world community everywhere. But irony of the situation is that if millions of people are dying in many states of third world due to hunger, many rich countries of the west are dumping huge quantities of food grains in the sea as a price stabilisation measure and huge amount in these countries are spent on nutritional needs of dogs and cats. Are the lives of poor masses of the third world are more worthless than cats and dogs of the west? Similarly, the current emphasis on environmental problem is shared world wide. But there appear to be some subtle attempts to compel the already poor third world countries to invest in environmental protection measures so that the affluent countries do not suffer in terms of competition on account of such investment in their countries.

Indivisibility and Interdependence of Human Rights

One of the most strident objections made by Third

World countries against Universal Declaration is that it lays greater emphasis on civil and political rights than on economic, social and cultural rights. The balance of Declaration, according to critics is somewhat upset "because it does not properly examine social, economic and cultural rights." Similarly in the developed Western countries the emphasis has always been on civil and political rights and human rights are sought to be equated only with civil and political rights. It is believed in many third world countries that it was on the insistence of the United States that originally proposed as one document, the International Covenant of Human Rights had to be *split* into two because the US did not want to see the same force given to implementing economic and social rights. Hence, more stringent monitoring and implementation procedures were agreed for civil and political covenant (ICCPR), including an Optional Protocol which provides international machinery for individuals to use in making a complaint about the violation of any of the rights covered in ICCPR. But unfortunately no such mechanism was tried for to ensure the implementation of social and economic rights which needed more for Third World countries.

Thus we see that the protection of economic and social rights compared to the civil and political rights at both national and international level has been weak and irregular. Very often social and economic rights are considered as aspirational and non-justiciable. There is also fallacious thinking that negative rights which gather around our liberties are more important than positive rights that evolve from basic needs. The reason for Western emphasis (undue) on civil and political rights seems to be that having attained a fairly high stage of development in material and economic resources, the social and economic rights did not find much preoccupation in their minds and their concerns were largely confined to civil and political rights. The socio-economic condition being totally reverse in the Third World countries their priority must be different from the West. Majority of the developing countries are reeling in extreme poverty, ignorance, illiteracy, mal-nutrition, disease and suffering and in the prevailing situation civil and political rights loose much of its relevance.

However, the West's unwillingness to recognise and give proper weight to economic and social rights is itself a distortion of universal human rights. What is now needed is a renewed and woder recognition of the interdependence and indivisibility of all human rights – civil and political as well as social, economic and cultural. It is a matter of satisfaction that there are in fact optimistic signs that the inter-relationships between political freedoms and economic and social development are being increasingly recognised. The Vienna World Conference on Human Rights (June 1993) realised this need and stated in no unclear/less certain terms that all human rights are "universal, indivisible and interrelated." The Vienna Declaration stressed that economic and social rights are as important as civil and political rights. The Vienna Declaration tried to set at rest the debate between the primacy of civil and political rights on one hand and economic and social rights on the other. The divide between the two sets of rights was in fact a product of the cold war with the West pushing for civil and political rights and East insisting on economic, social and cultural rights. Indeed, acceptance at Vienna by the developed countries the importance and validity of economic and social rights and interdependence of these rights with civil and political freedoms represents a positive sign.

In simple terms the indivisibility concept is based on the belief that freedom and food both are essential for ensuring the dignity of person. This fact was very much appreciated in the Universal Declaration which declares that human beings to safeguard their dignity should enjoy freedom of speech and belief and freedom from fear and want. There is indeed a close relationship between these two sets of rights and their relationship is so obvious that the International Human Rights Conference in Tehran called by the General Assembly in 1968 declared in a final proclamation : "Since human rights and fundamental freedoms are indivisible, the full realisation of civil and political rights without the enjoyment of social, economic and cultural rights is impossible." The ideas of the Tehran Conference had a profound impact on the Declaration on Social Progress and Development adopted by the UN General Assembly in 1969 proclaiming that "international peace and security on the one hand and social progress and economic development on the other are closely interdependent and, influence each other and it is of cardinal importance to accelerate social and economic progress everywhere, thus contributing to international peace and solidarity."

Another major step in the direction of the recognition of indivisibility concept was the adoption of Resolution 32/130 on "Alternative approaches....for improving the effective enjoyment of human rights" by General Assembly in 1977. This resolution stressed that the approach to be followed by the UN system with respect to human rights should be based on the concept that all human rights are indivisible and equal attention should be given to the promotion and protection of both civil and political, and economic, social and cultural rights. One of the outcomes of this Resolution was the recognition of the link between the realisation of a new international economic order and the promotion of human rights. Another important outcome was the initiation of debate on the right to development which paved the way for the adoption of the UN Declaration on Right to Development in 1986. However, it took almost a decade to General Assembly to adopt this much cherished demand of developing countries of the Third World but alas developed world showed very little interest in passing of this long awaited resolution.

The Declaration on Right to Development ties the realisation of human rights in developing countries to international economic aid for them and gives the people the right to participate in, contribute to, and enjoy economic, social, cultural and political development, in which all human rights and fundamental freedoms can be fully realised. The Declaration which also recognises the concept of indivisibility of human rights, emphasised that the denial of civil and political rights as well as economic, social and cultural rights would constitute a serious obstacle to development. Further, the Declaration also stressed that promotion of one set of rights cannot justify the denial of other human rights. Most importantly the Declaration recognised that the "human person is the central subject of development and should be an active participant and beneficiary of the right to development."

The right to development is one of the most important basic human rights and it constitutes the culminating point of the evolution of the concept of human rights. This super-right, transcends the differentiation of civil and political rights and socio-economic cultural rights. It includes within its ambit both sets of rights. It correctly links the both because with hunger and ill health freedom can have no meaning.

The importance of the indivisibility concept is not restricted to international normative developments, it also provides an effective antidote against efforts to undermine human rights under "trade-off theory." Under this theory many dictators of Third World countries proposed that to achieve development civil and political rights should be atleast temporarily sacrificed. But in reality the ultimate result of this trade-off was denial of civil and political rights as well as impoverishment rather than development. Thus the trade-off theory could only be effectively countered by stressing on the indivisibility concept of human rights.

A question which has become central to the relationship between human rights and development is the issue of political conditionalities. This means that the continuance of development assistance would be dependent on political conditions such as "good governance" and the observance of civil and political rights. The European Council in its one resolution passed on November 28, 1991 emphasised that respect for human rights, the rule of law and the existence of political institutions which are effective, accountable and enjoy democratic legitimacy are the basis for equitable development. It also stressed the safeguarding of human rights as an essential condition for its relations with other states. Similarly, the US House of Representative passed the Burton Bill on June 1992 cutting 24 million dollars of development assistance to Third World countries including India on grounds of poor human rights records. The Canadian House of Commons Standing Committee on External Affairs and International Trade recommended as early as in May 1987 that progress on human rights should be central element of development assistance.

However, the developing countries by and large have resented the link between human rights and aid on the ground that such conditions infringe on their national sovereignty. They see these intercessions in political terms as efforts to appropriate human rights as an instrument in the political and ideological hagemony of the North over the South. The policy of donor countries may appear genuine but inconsistency in its application and selective approach is bound to create doubts and suspicions. And it will also invite strong criticism and rebuff from the developing countries. If the developed countries of the West really want to see their policy being effective it should not only be credible, consistent and non-discriminatory but it also appears to be so. Is the decision to suspend or terminate developmental assistance based solely on human rights considerations or is it more probable that factors such as geopolitical importance, the economic model pursued by the recipient country and the domestic politics of the donor country are likely to influence such decisions? Although no one would allow developing states to use "primacy of development" or "cultural relativism" as a pretext for diluting or derogating from universal human rights but the political use of the concept of human rights by the West could not either be tolerated.

The concept of indivisibility of human rights assumes greater importance in the changed global situation which is dominated by a single development model based on multinational capital and corporation. By and large the experience of countries that have gone through the process of restructuring and privatising their economies has been a negative one. This economic model has contributed to increased inequalities, dismantling of social services with adverse effect on the poor, restrictions on trade union rights, implementation of development projects with negative impact on the local populations, particularly indigenous people and the tendency to centralise the decision making process. However, it is yet to be seen whether the end of the Cold War and *rhetoric* of human rights and good governance can prevent some of the fragrant violations that were witnessed in the past centuries that embarked on restructuring and privatising their economy, whether on their own or on dictate of the North.

Whatever be the current of attitudes and policies of governments, the reality of popular demands of human rights, including both greater economic justice and greater political freedom, is beyond debate. A deepening and widening concern for the promotion and protection of human rights, has now unmistakably woven into the fabric of contemporary world affairs. We have a great opportunity now to make progress in protecting and fully realising the human rights that the architects of the post war settlement so eloquently laid down. The end of the Cold War has been accompanied by a growing recognition that successful sustainable development is impossible where rights are divided and economic and social rights downgraded. Poverty and inequality remain the two great barriers to the realisation of "all human rights for all". Fifty years after signing of the UNDHR, it is more than very necessary to reaffirm, as the Preamble declares, our "faith in fundamental human rights, in the dignity and worth of the human person and in the equal rights of men and women and (determine) to promote social progress and better standard of life in larger freedom."

Human Rights in India: Some Issues

Though in large parts of the world we boast of a democratic set-up with a comprehensive charter of rights written into its constitution protected by an independent Judiciary, and we pride ourselves on observance of the rule of law, large scale violation of individuals' rights has almost become a permanent feature. Hardly any day passes when we do not witness one or other types of human rights violations of women and children, of lower caste and otherwise disadvantaged communities, of religious and ethnic minorities, and of workers. These violations range over whole conspectus of human rights, civil and political rights, as well as social and economic.

There are mass killings and widespread disappearances, torture, wide displacement of communities from traditional abode; arbitrary detentions and extensive censorship of thought and expression. Cases of human rights violation in India are innumerable, repetitive, enduring and have almost become a permanent feature of the state system. The state is a major culprit, brutalising whole population, but massive violations also take place in and through civil society sometimes with connivance of the state and frequently reflecting feudalistic and patriarchal dimension of culture. Justice V.R. Krishna Iyer writes that "India with all its thousands of years of cultural heritage and Vedic vintage, has not been able to assure to its people even a pretence of the preamble's grand undertaking of justice, liberty, equality and fraternity to every citizens."

However, the notion of human rights is not new for India which can claim to be one of the oldest civilizations of the world, where the modern democratic ideals had been their way of life under their enlightened emperors. India can boast of having rulers like Ashoka and Akbar whose concern for the people and their welfare can hardly be over emphasized. Later when India was colonized resistence to foreign rule manifested in the form of demand for fundamental freedoms and civil and political rights for the people. The freedom struggle in India when viewed in its historical perspective is also found to be a, struggle for human rights. As early as in 1895 the Swaraj Bill inspired by B.G. Tilak emphasised the importance of human rights. In the Delhi session of December 1918, Indian National Congress included the principles of self-determination as one of the basic rights of human beings. Madras Congress of the INC in 1927 demanded incorporation of Declaration of fundamental rights in any future constitutional frame work. Lahore Congress of 1930 declared freedom from foreign rule as a fundamental right.

The famous resolution on "Fundamental Rights and Social Change" was adopted by the Indian National Congress at the Karachi session on March 29, 1931. The Karachi Resolution envisaged the future constitution of free India providing for classical freedoms and equality, non-discrimination, religious neutrality of the state, adult suffrage, as well as right to free primary education, living wages for workers under healthy conditions of work, freedom from serfdom, prohibition of child labour and social security system for old age, sickness and unemployment. There was wide public acceptance with such thinking concerning fundamental human rights and freedom. These were perhaps the powerful factors in ensuring that the Constitution of India when it came into being, based itself on an emphatic articulation of essential human rights.

Promulgation of the constitution by the people of India in January 1950 was the culmination of India's long struggle for fundamental freedom and human rights. The Preamble, Fundamental Rights and the Directive Principles together provide the basic human rights for people of India. Democratic socialism spelt out in the Preamble and the Directive Principles is meant to provide the context in which the fulfilment of Fundamental Rights has to be achieved. Fundamental Rights contained in Part III are essentially civil and political rights which are declared supreme under Article 13 of the constitution and as such are judicially enforceable. While Directive Principles of State Policy contained in Part IV are by and large social and economic rights which as per Article 37 of the constitution, are not enforceable in courts of law but, nevertheless, fundamental in the governance of the country.

After independence and adoption of a constitution which contained in it a long list of people's rights including civil and political and economic and social right, it was hoped by millions of poor people in India that now they would get the chance to improve their lot under the guidance and protection of democratic government. Pandit Nehru voiced the hopes of people : "I trust that the constitution itself will lead us to real freedom that we have clamoured for and real freedom in turn will bring food to our starving people, clothing for them, housing for them and all manners of opportunities of progress."

Now the question arises how far the dream of the founding fathers has been realised in India in its 50 years of journey after independence? It is pertinent to discuss whether the concept of human rights enshrined in the Indian constitution is really being honoured or not. This needs thorough examination of working of political process, institutional structure, development process and the condition of the man who is the base component of the entire system. Though this examination is beyond the scope of this paper but a cursory look at the whole situation would certainly lead to disappointment. Constitutional goal of socio-economic justice has become mirage. Directive Principles have been transformed into 'Decorative Principles of State Policy'. Inspite of claimed rapid economic development half of the population in India still live in miserable and pathetic condition. People are still dying due to starvation in some part of the country. Half of the people are illiterate and equal number of them are living below poverty line. Managing two times meal is still dream for many and difficult task for others. In absence of basic necessities of life, talking of human rights appears to be cruel joke for them. We must be mindful of the fact that inspite of constitutional safeguards an statutory provisions evils like untouchability and other social discriminations are still prevalent in many part of the country. In many areas S.C. & S.Ts and down trodden are not allowed to go to the place of worship. What is more shameful that even today these people in some part of the country are not allowed to pass nearby the houses of land lords wearing shoes or Chappals. We cannot ignore the fact that there can neither be human freedom nor respect for human dignity till socio-economic rights are not protected.

The situation is not better on civil liberties front. This also represents a very gloomy picture. Civil liberties and fundamental freedoms of the people are often violated by the state machinery and by those who hold money and power in the society. The use of force and coercive method is normally used by police and bureaucracy in their dealing with the people. While the criminals and anti-social elements are left scot-free, innocent people are often harassed and some time killed in the name of law and order. Secret trials, incognito witness, presumption of guilt, hearing in unknown places and far away states, draconian refusal of bail and restriction on appeals and shoot-at-sight with no habeas corpus remedy and other Star Chamber processes, preventive detentions, sound-proof – sight-proof system of law with a hands-off mandate to human rights and a total blackout of the rule of law – this subjects not only the terrorists but all citizens indiscriminately to a regime where decencies of justice are outlawed. Despite the non-derogable rights available to the people, state has used the device of national emergency to rob humans of their right to life and like core rights.

Moreover the condition of Minorities, Dalits, Women and Children are even worse in India. Women represents the most vulnerable section of the society inspite of their celebrated and privileged position as referred to by the ancient Indian scriptures. Women are treated as unequal by society for genetic sin of her discriminated sex. She suffers gender devaluation at home, at work, in literacy, in matrimony, in inheritance and allied rights, in economic opportunity, public life and power process. The gender violence is common and takes many forms across culture, race and class. According to a recent data given by the Ministry of Women and Child Development, there is one rape every 54 minutes, one molestation every 26 minutes, one kidnapping or abduction every 43 minutes, one dowry death every one hour 42 minutes, one act of cruelty every 33 minutes, and one criminal offence against women every 7 minutes. These statistics do not take into account domestic violence which is believed to be the most common yet least reported crime. With more than 500 cases of rape reported every year sexual crimes against women have assumed dangerous proportions. Women are reluctant to report such incidents for fear of serious reprisals from offenders, societal ostracism, damaging marriage prospects, bringing shame to the family and being victimised. The woman's dignity is most vulnerable in caste and communal wars, women become the soft targets and are made to face physical and psychological violence. There are numerous example when the caste animities are avenged at the cost of women. They are raped, humiliated, harassed and tortured. A decade ago Chief Justice of Guwahati High Court in his Judgment in "A Police Gang – Rape Case" observed : "It is really unfortunate that in this year of 1988 when we have crossed four decades of our independence and Constitutional guarantees, our woman folk and amongst them also the poor down-trodden are still treated as vegetables to provide tastes to the sex lust for resourceful males."

The primary reason why women are subjected to intimidation and violence is their subordinate status in a male dominated patriarchal society. It is considered a male privilege to legitimise gender hierarchy within the family and the use of violence against women. Thus there is need for better protection through stringent legislation and policy and reform in criminal justice system. Education and legal awareness widens a woman's perspective, lends confidence to stand up to the oppressor, and if need be take recourse to the courts for redressal. There is need to make an all out attempt to reorient the society and transform social ethos, educate people about concept of women's dignity and the need to treat women as a human being and individual and a person demanding and needing respect and dignity.

There are other rightless groups such as the suppressed, oppressed Dalits. Inspite of the untouchability being abolished, provision for reservation in jobs and legislation and special protection in criminal justice system neither their is any spectacular change in their condition nor violation of human rights against them has disappeared. Instead atrocities against them have increased including their women. Widespread atrocities and all-round discrimination against Dalits and the ruthless attempts to suppress them whenever they try to assert their rights pose the problem of denial of human rights to a substantial section of our population. The violence against Dalits takes many form. Most common are murder, rape, grievous hurt, arson and other types of offences. Atrocities on Dalits are not new but what is new in the situation today is that now atrocities and violence against them are carried out in an organised and concerted manner and almost with impunity. More pervasively, there is denial of civil rights provided under law and the Constitution. Reality today is that Dalits are not allowed to enjoy these rights rather they are prevented from exercising these rights. During the elections, they are prevented from voting in many villages, or if they exercise their franchise at their free will against the dictates of the landlords, they are physically assaulted, their properties destroyed and they are even murdered in some places. What is more important that the state which is supposed to create the necessary conditions to enable the weaker sections to exercise their rights and protect them when they are attacked often behave in a manner which helps only the oppressors and exploiters. They also suffer from a number of social disabilities. For centuries, they have been segregated from the mainstream of society. Evil practice of untouchability is still prevalent in many parts of the country and especially in the rural areas. In many village they cannot still draw water from the common village tank. Going on a bicycle in front of a Brahmin's house is still a crime in rural areas. In many tea-shops in the villages Dalits have no entry. Even if they are served they have to sit in a separate place and to wash the glasses after drinking. In some villages they are not allowed to take out marriage processions without permission from the caste Hindu landlords. There are a large number of places where they are not allowed to use certain public thorough fares. In short they are discriminated against in every sphere of life. In these circumstances there is no other way left for the suffering people except to rally unitedly and fight and defend their rights. A sense of resistance to injustice and oppression should grow among the Dalits. Ultimately it is their united will and determination to fight and defend their rights which will help them in achieving their goal of social equality. Besides all progressive forces, right thinking people and all those who believe in social justice and social equality should come to the aid of the Dalits in their struggle against atrocities and social oppression.

Abuse of Child Rights is another area which requires our special attention. We should not forget that the children also have rights like other human beings, to be respected with regard to their integrity, dignity, interest and opinion. But significantly enough children in India are deprived of even the basic human rights due to them, as they ought to be in any civilized society. Human rights violations of children are numerous and of various types. It is shocking to learn that about a million babies, out of 21 million born every year in India are abandoned soon after their birth due to various socio-economic pressures. We are guilty of many crimes and errors but our worst crime is abandoning our children. The problem of child labour in India is an alarming one and constitutes egregious violation of children's rights. India continues to be in the stranglehold of child labour even after five decades of planned development. The fact remains that these are around 20 million child labourers in India working in various hazardous and non-hazardous industries. Driven by the poverty of their parents, they are working for long hours in miserable conditions and most unhealthy environment, denied nutritive food and deprived of elementary education. The sad plight of there innocent children remain an untold story and offshoot of unequitable socio-economic ambience. Child rape and child prostitution is another dimension of violation of child rights and dignity. There are various reported incidents when girls have been raped by their fathers. This is a kind of custodial rape that has not so far received adequate attention from the social activists. Because of silence born of fear and shame this kind of child abuse continues for years without any punishment and without any relief to child. There are violations in various ways of the basic rights of the children, but nothing is more than exploiting them sexually and engaging them in prostitution. Using children to satisfy an adult's sexual needs is something so cruel and mean that it does not exist even in the animal kingdom. Besides govt's concerted efforts general people should be sensitised to children's merciless exploitation and child abuse to put an end to the violation of child rights. Much more attention requires to be given to children's needs for health care, games and recreation and much harsher punishment needs to be given to those who sexually abuse the child.

Minorities in India are another disadvantaged group whose human rights are frequently violated in one or other ways. Minorities who are numerically weak and enjoy inadequate share in power are subjected to discrimination exclusion by the dominant majority especially when they assert their right to distinct identity and are not prepared to get assimilated. Inspite of the fact that India is party to several international covenants and declarations which particularly deal with minorities rights and Constitutional safeguard, practical experience of minorities has been quite narrowing. Their general educational backwardness, poverty, low representation in political institutions and government services and recurrent riots testify to it. Communal violence has been the most serious problem faced by the minorities from very beginning which causes large scale violations of their many rights. Regardless of which side starts the riot, the minorities are generally the relative losers in terms of lives lost and property destroyed. Communal violence resulting in extensive destruction of lives and property of the Muslim minority continues unabated. Problem of violence against Christian is a recent phenomena. What is even more perturbing that in many cases police and other law enforcing agencies have been guilty of active or passive connivance, complicity or participation in rioting against the vulnerable minorities. This fact was recently highlighted by the Srikrishna Commission on the Mumbai Communal Riots of 1992-93 : "the built in bias of Police forces against Muslims became pronounced." A Tamil Nadu PUCL report spoke of the nexus between a section of the local police and the Hindu fundamentalist forces in the Coimbatore riots of November 1997. "The manner in which the Police indulged in senseless killing would shame even hardened criminals" it said. Thus there is urgent need to protect the rights of minorities which can be done by ensuring their adequate representation in all walks of life and police and law enforcing agencies. State should take special care for their education, employment and overall upliftment in cooperation with NGOs and members of minority groups. This is not merely a humanitarian task, but the very interests of the country's development and national advance require such cooperation and help from all progressive and democratic sections. As long as a considerable section of our people is forced to live a life of utter misery and is denied even the basic rights granted to them in constitution, there cannot be any national progress in the real sense. Such a situation will act as a drag on the country's forward march.

2

The Emerging Human Rights Situation in India : In the Context of Recent Socio-Political And Economic Changes

Ravi Kiran Jain

On 15th August, 1947 when we the people of India became independent the Constituent Assembly was already engaged in the task of framing a Constitution for us.

The teeming millions of this country were suffering from deprivation, exploitation and social and economic injustices for centuries under a colonial rule when we enacted the Constitution. It is these teeming millions who are the architects and founding fathers and mothers of the Constitution. The people of this country who gave to themselves the Constitution at that time were semistarved, semi naked, illiterate and deprived of basic Human Rights. We the people in our Constitution made a promise to ourselves to build a new socio-economic and political order in which people would enjoy real justice social, economic and political. This was a document of hope. It was promisory Constitution. A promise for future. It was meant to give to the poorest of the poor the promised justice, social, economic and political and to the meekest of the meek, the dignity of brother citizens.

There was a promise contained in the preamble and part IV in Directive Principles of State Policy. The promise contained was to be redeemed by legislators we would elect, the judges we would select and the executive we would nominate.

Directive Principles exhort the state to ensure that citizens have an adequate means of livelihood, that the operation of the economic system and the ownership and control of the material resources of the country subserve the common good, that the health of the workers, including children is not abused and that special consideration be given to pregnant women. Workers, both agricultural and industrial are to have a standard of living that allows them to enjoy leisure and social and cultural opportunities. Among the primary duties of the state is the raising of the level of nutrition and the general standard of living of the people. The principles express the hope that within ten years of the adoption of the Constitution, there will be compulsory primary education for children up to the age of fourteen years. The other provisions of the Principles seek equally to secure the renovation of Indian society by improving the techniques of agriculture, husbandry, cottage industry, etc.

It was expected that we should have achieved these objectives within a reasonable time, say within two decades or roughly say by 1970.

But there has been a breach of faith by those who were elected by us to redeem this promise. Since 1971 we have allowed politicians to define the national agenda, be it Garibi Hatao, Su-raaj, or social justice. No other nation in the world has been held to ransom by politics and politicians as relentlessly as India has been. And all along, we have depended upon our politicians to represent us, seeking false comfort in the thought that we are, after all, the largest democracy in world.

Till 1989, the people in this country had an urge, an impatient urge to participate in events and processes that could shape their lives. This urge was manifesting itself consistently and persisted as a regular feature from 1947 till 1971 in all walks or life.

In 1971 corruption started in public life. In 1967 elections there were large number of M.Ps. and M.L.As., who had won election without spending much money. Politics was an instrument of public service and a person in politics had to respond to the aspirations and impatient urge of the people of this country. In 1971 money was dumped in the elections with a false slogan 'Garibi Hatao'.

The peoples' urge was marred and sought to curb during emergency, but it re-emerged with greater force in 1977. Till 1989, poverty, unemployment, right to work, corruption high prices, etc. were issues and there was an impatience in the people but if it had been properly nurtured in the national frame work, it could have become a source of tremendous vitality and innovation for the creation of a dynamic and just society. But that impatience of the people was marred by the impatience of those who were in the waiting to come into power. Development must be woven around people, not people around development and it should empower the citizens with an awareness of the issues to participate in the development and politics and not to make them share the corruption of the politicians.

We have raw materials and natural resources of all types in abundance and this country is perhaps the only one where we have skilled labours of all types, like potters, weavers, shoe makers, carpanters, candle stick makers and so on, and also unskilled labour. This skilled and unskilled labour was to be brought up and engaged in building up a prosperous social order by using our raw material and natural resources by a sustainable development.

The sustainable development is the key to a social order based on equality, prosperity and security. It is a process in which development can be sustained for many generations to come. The phenomenon provides for improving the quality of both the human life and nature's surroundings. It thus aims at harmonising and maintaining the carrying capacity of life supporting eco-system 'Sustainable development' is a development that meets the needs of the present without compromising the ability of the future generations to meet their own needs.

The fundamental norm governing the concept of human rights is that of the respect for human personality and its absolute worth, regardless of colour, race, sex, religion or other considerations. These are essential for other considerations. These rights are essential for the adequate development of the human personality and for human happiness and progress.

That a general election in 1971 was fought and won on the single slogan of 'Garibi Hatao' with huge majority was sympatomatic of the people's expectations. Lack of people's mandate could no longer be invoked to explain inaction. But in 1971 the children of those who were in power started attaining adulthood. Politics ceased to be an instrument of service and started becoming a hereditary profit; oriented huge business and corruption in public life made the things worst. If those in power are corrupt, the relevant consideration for them in taking major policy decisions is not the interest of the country that their own personal narrow interest at the cost of even losing political and economic sovereignty of the country. The people gave a massive mandate to the political leadership to act but the grim reality is that those to whom we elected had not planned for the poor. The super powers took full advantage of corruption in politics in India and with a nexus of corrupt political leadership with those super powers, we followed the western industrial path. Through the instrumentality of World Bank and I.M.F. the corrupt politicians of this country have made us to enter an era of liberalization and globalisation. Now poverty has ceased to be important on the political agenda. It has become a technical matter for experts and planners to handle. The rheotic, however, is being kept alive as it has tremendous appeal for the Vote Bank.

Mr. M.A.O. Oaman, a scientific fellow of Institute for Social Science, New Delhi who is presently co-ordinating research on IMF/World Bank Conditionalities and its Impact on Growth and Social Justice in India has made a recent survey in which he says.

"Look at where we are as nation. 291 million adults are still illiterate and substantial majority of them are females whose capabilities are the key to changing the society. 45 million children were out of Primary Schools in 1995. Nearly one third of children under 16 are forced to child labour. 135 million people are denied access to primary health care, 226 million are without safe drinking water, 640 million lack basic sanitation and so on (see Mehbub-Ul-Haq 1997) 350 million people live below a poverty line which views people only as biological entity and not as a social individual with self respect. Ironically, the same India which houses the largest number of the world's poor, was ranked first in arms india imports among the developing countries."

Mr. Ooman further says :-

"In less than 6 years, the Prime Minister, the Finance Minister, Union Ministers, Chief Minister, senior bureaucrats have gone abroad innumerable times in order to convince the capital of the world that we have given up planning in favour of market medicated regime. Freedom for capital does not mean freedom for people. Living in squalor and misery you have no real freedom of choice. True development essentially in enlarging the capabilities of the people and their choice. Looking back we have failed in this task during the last fifty years of independence."

These visits of Prime Minister, Union Finance Minister, Chief Ministers and Senior bureaucrats created a nexus between corrupt politicians and bureaucrats and the super powers and the result is the acceptance of the policy of Liberalization and reliance on free global market. A key element in the present development strategy is reliance on a 'Free' global market. It needs to be recognized that conceding supremacy to the free-market in economic affairs makes the very concept of a society's development strategy meaningless. For development or lack of it brings in its wake the outcome of the interplay of market forces, too complex, impoundable and un-predictable to be brought within a policy frame. What is produced how, how much and for whom sold out, at what price, all gets determined by free competition in the market and by competitive profitability. Investment also follows the signals put out by market. Thus even at a conceptual level dependence on a free global market does not appear consistent with any definite strategy even for economic development, much less so for development in the full sense of the term.

We take loan from the World Bank even for infrastructure, roads, bridges, etc. Central Government, State Governments and even Local Self Governments take such loans. The result is total dependence upon loan and no desire to build up our own economy in accordance with our necessities. All the institutions at all levels including at the level of Local Self Government have been destroyed. We must come out of it. Otherwise we are bound to be ruined completely.

The Globalisation is nothing but losing our economic and political sovereignty by entering into unequal treaties like GATT and becoming member of W.T.O. There are clauses in these Treaties that our Parliament will have to enact laws in tune with some of it's provisions and if our Parliament does not do so the W.T.O. can take cross retalitory measures. We are not free to decide what to export, or import. The consequence is that we can never even imagine of having an economy of self reliance. These unequal treaties suit either the developed countries who have surplus production, or those under developed countries who have an economy of self restraint like China. It does not suit our country where there is scaricity of certain consumer items but still we want to adopt the western consumer culture.

Market hunger of Americans and their blind admiration for the glamorous life at the expense of World's happiness has been demonstrated and remonstrated in a book "On Third World Legs" by a well known author Willson who says in that book about United States of America.

"This country consumes more than 40% of the world's production of natural resources with about 6% of the population, a disparity that is both practically and morally indefensible."

This globalisation is creating unemployment, recession, scarcity of raw materials and a haphazerd industrial growth and making this country economically bankrupt and it has put us in the cobweb of multinationals with total loss of sovereignty, both political and economic, on account of liberalization and globalisation of W.T.O.

The people's Commission on GATT consisting of Mr. Justice V.R. Krishna Iyre, Mr. Justice O. Chinnappa Reddy, Mr. Justice D.A. Desai, Mr. Justice Rajendra Sacchar submitted its report in which it came to the conclusion, after hearing large number of eminent experts and organizations who made their submissions to that commission that the treaty constituted a 'Surrender of India's sovereignty' and was inimical to the fundamental rights of the citizens guaranteed under the Constitution.

Although on account of twin social diseases, institutional corruption and consumer culture, which have been aggravated by our membership of W.T.O. and loan of World Bank total apathy has been created in the minds of India, yet there are still some people and the organisers left in this country who are mobilising public opinion against this treaty. These include Mr. Justice V.R. Krishna Iyer, Mr. Justice O. Chinnappa Reddy, Mr. Justice D.A. Desai, Mr. Justice Rajendra Sachchar and few organisations like Azadi Bachao Andolan Rabi Ray's Lok Sakti Abhiyan, Sunder Lal Bahuguna's Himalaya Bachao Andolan and Medha Patekar's Narmada Bachao Andolan. U.P., PUCL will make an appeal to all such distinguished citizens and N.G.O's approach National Human Rights Commission by filing petitions and to urge on the inevitable adverse effect of signing of the treaty to become member of W.T.O. on the:

1. Fundamental rights of the citizens of India and specially

the right to food, livelihood, health, self governance and democracy.

2. Sovereignty and integrity of India in as much as sovereignty and integrity is part of the basic structure of the Constitution; and

3. Federal structure of the constitution as a consequence of which the exclusive powers of the State would be lost to the Union without the consultation and consent of the States.

If the N.H.R.C. is satisfied with the submissions, then the Commission may also be persuaded to file a writ petition on behalf of people of the country in the Supreme Court as P.I.L. in exercise of its powers U/S 18(2) of the Protection of Human Rights Act. No doubt judges are not expected to examine the desirability of entering into a particular treaty obligation. That is another matter altogether. But if the direct and inevitable effect of the treaty is that it will infringe fundamental rights. The judiciary has constitutional obligation to interfere. Nor can the judiciary stand by to witness a treaty simply riding rough shod over the very basic structure of the Constitution including, democracy, sovereignty and social justice.

Old timers of our country confine the concept of Human rights only to civil liberties and not the economic social and cultural rights. Mr. Justice H.R. Khanna in a recent article published in March part of AIR has said that Civil Liberty and Human Rights are two faces of the same coin. His whole article is based on the belief and assumption that Human Rights have to remain confined to the question of Civil Liberties only. PUCL Uttar Pradesh begs to differ. In the Indian context, particularly in the context of globalisation at the dictates of W.T.O. and under the debts of World Bank and I.M.F. there has to be an emerging concept of Human Rights which affects the lives and liberty, natural resources and cultural aspects of the people of the country.

The corrupt politicians of this country have also divided

us on caste and communal lines. The human right activists of this country are terribly upset and shocked at the brazen increase of caste and communal violence, atrocities, harassment and hate campaign that has been unleashed by all types of politicians against one community or the other. It suits the arithmetic of all the political parties. There are criminals in the game of power politics in all the political parties. These criminals are encouraging religious fundamentalism which leads to large scale violence like Bombay riots and these days oppression of the Christian minorities in Gujrat and else where in the country.

The National Human Rights Commission in its Annual Report of 1996-97 in the summary of that report and principal recommendations has observed :-

"In recent years there has been growing concern in the country that the process of governance have, on occasion, been corroded by a nexus between criminals, lees then scrupulous political elements and members of the executive lacking in integrity. The deleterious effects on human rights resulting from such a nexus can be gauged from the nature of the petitions received by this Commission. True democracy is built on restraint, on the excise of moderation both by the majority and by minority groups. When such restraint snaps and society yields of ethnic, religious and caste entrepreneurs' who garner support for opportunistic ends even at the cost of inciting violence against those belonging to other groups, the citizens of this country pay the price in the destruction of their right to life and in assaults on the dignity and worth of the human person. It is time that the leadership of this nation untidily turned away from the politics of expedience and established clear Code of Conduct of govern their behaviour".

This shows that the National Human Rights Commission recognizes that corruption in politic, criminalisation of politics, communal and caste politics are issues directly related to questions of violation of Human Rights and the concept of Human Rights can not be confined only to Civil Liberties.

3

Women, "Development" & Human Rights

Jayanti Alam

December 10, 1998 marked the 50th anniversary of one of the most persuasive international documents of our times—the United Nations' Universal Declaration of Human Rights (UDHR). In a world of continuing brutality, impunity and abuse of human dignity and freedoms, the UDHR has been the centerpiece of an ambitious project to promote universal respect and protection of basic human rights worldwide. According to some Third World activists, "in celebrating 50 Years of UDHR we are actually violating the human rights of the non-West, non-developed countries because that is how we are subscribing to that notion of human rights which has been framed and dictated by the post-war imperialist power represented by the US-West Europe Bloc." Very recently we have seen ample proof of that....in how the world body for peace, viz the UNO, has been used as a "tool" by Anglo-American imperialism. (The reference obviously, is to the bombing of Iraq and its innocent people).

There is no escape from this, as the UN list of human rights were initially formulated not to protect and guarantee universal human rights, but with the primary and sole purpose of "containing Communism or the Soviet Bloc", which was growing in both power or influence and geographical expanse.

The idea was to protect the "rights" of the capitalist world vis a vis the economic justice to the "real producers", which the newly established socialist governments were claiming to ensure. It could also have been actually ensured to a not too insignificance extent. In the new democracies of the newly independent countries the elected leaders were taking the place of the colonial rulers.

Rights were defined and granted by these rulers; people did not get them as a matter of their right. In a true democracy, on the other hand, people are born NATURALLY with rights and the people only grant power to their governments, instead of the "small powerful group" called "government" granting power as charity, as if. This is so because human rights are as old as human beings; human rights were born the moment human beings were born. Human Rights thus, are nothing but the "realization/obligation of my OWN PERSON in another person."

On January 27, 1947 the United Nations Human Rights Commission had its first meeting under the chairmanship of Eleanor Roosevelt to create an international bill of rights. (The choice of the word "to create" is noteworthy. The rights--- looking noble--- were carefully worded to clandestinely serve a particular vested interest). Eleanor was a powerful human rights campaigner no doubt, but she was also the wife of the American President. Therefore, she naturally used American State ideals as the template. J.P. Hendricks, then a senior U.S. official and advisor to Ms. Roosevelt, had admitted that the U.S. policy was to make UDHR "a carbon copy of the American Declaration of Independence and the American Bill of Rights."

Originally, there was a three member Drafting Committee, consisting of Ms. Roosevelt, P.C. Chang of China and Charles Malik of Lebanon. To accommodate a hostile Soviet Union, threatening to stay out of the human rights project, she recast this Committee with representatives from Australia, Chile, France, U.K. and the Soviet Union, in addition to the existing members. Inspite of these additions, the Committee was starkly unrepresentative. It did not represent any African or Islamic nation among the total membership of 58. That is why when the UDHR draft came to be debated by the member nations in 1948, 168 resolutions proposing amendments were tabled during the 81 meetings. These countries felt that "it was a Western model applicable in a very different social and cultural context only. It draws primarily from the Western conceptions of individual rights, ignoring the ancient religious values, philosophical traditions and the socio-cultural practices in the Third World societies". Finally 48 States supported and 8 abstained.

But this i.e. overlooking regional/national cultural peculiarity/speciality, perhaps is the real value behind the Human Rights Document. It discounts the social context in favour of an "absolute" human being, unlike the understanding of the nature of the individual within the society, as characterized in most authoritarian religions. What is remarkable about UDHR therefore, is that it does not invoke God, Nature, morality, etc. It talks of "a social and international order in which the rights and freedoms set forth in the Declaration can be fully realized" (Article 28), or of the "duties to the community in which alone the free and full development of his personality is possible" (Article 29). In the Western "natural rights" construct it had transpired that certain rights were inherent in the individual who must be protected against the arbitrary use of State power. Doctrines such as the rule of law, the separation of powers and other theories restraining social and political structures and promoting respect for human dignity seeped into the 18th century dialogues. They, in turn, influenced Declarations like the American (of Independence) in 1776 and the French in 1789.

Ms. Roosevelt comforted the nations in power by assuring them that "the Declaration is not, and does not, purport to be a statement of law or legal obligation"....It was merely "a common standard of achievement". Eight years later, the UN summoned the first international conference on human rights which proclaimed, on December 19, 1968, that the UNDHR "constitutes an obligation for the members of the international community."

Human rights issues today are more difficult and complex and even richer than what they were 50 years ago.

Human Rights are a powerful tool for development provided, of course, the political rights are firmly secured through a democratic process. Otherwise, the ideology of development can be used to suppress human rights and freedoms. True democracy, which instils the right kind of motivation and confidence in the people, can also insulate the State and the people from the opportunistic use of human rights issues by outside powers, who may take advantage of the discontent and dissensions born out of the "development" models evolved and exported by the US imperialist-led West. The pervasiveness of poverty thus gets compounded by the problems of displacement as a result of anti-indigenous people policies, the prime most of which is environmental degradation. In the volatile (Indian) situation of high community "sensitivity" and the struggle for resources, which get scarcer to scarcer, communalism raises its head as a highly disruptive influence. In such circumstances, the ideology of development is made to have greater appeal than human rights because human rights allow no space to any authority or dictum or dictat. Planned and programmed "development", as opposed to "Natural" development cannot be effected without authority and authoritarianism.

Indigenous and tribal peoples usually live in less developed, hinterland areas of the states. Their lands are often the sites of programmes or projects designed to serve the interests of others. History abounds in such instances whereby indigenous or aboriginal peoples lost their land, resources, culture, tradition and even their history and identity. The glaring examples of the Americas and Australasia (where the so-called "Indians" and the Aboriginies" got thoroughly marginalised even geographically!) is anybody's knowledge. The most glaring example in the case of India is the "dispossession" of the original inhabitants (now known as the Dravidians) by the Aryans - a warring tribe from the barren lands of Central Asia who invaded India in search of water and agricultural land and then settled down permanently. They had to create and institutionalize division between the conquered and the conqueror, the ruled and the ruler, (known as the caste system) in order to enforce and stabilize their usurped power. Thus, the original inhabitants (adivasis) not only lost their property and resources, but were forced into compulsory labour little different from slavery. They were also subjected to alien systems of law, administration and culture. They were discriminated in the eyes of law in an obvious manner and sometimes, even exterminated.

The international community has been slow in acknowledging this injustice. In 1957, for the first time, the Indigenous and Tribal People's Convention has been convened. But that was to stabilize the status quo. The Recommendations sponsored by the International Labour Organization hinted that the remedy lay in their assimilation into the culture and way of life of the communities that ruled over them. In other words, the path prescribed was not of individualism of the Western liberal thoughts. But the model of human rights accepted by the wife of the U.S. President, Ms. Roosevelt, was based on that, What an irony!

This approach was however, abandoned in 1989 when the Convention on the Indigenous and Tribal Peoples in Independent Countries recognized the values of their culture, ecology and their dignity as a people. There can be no destruction of Natural environment and no displaced person or refugees if what is put on paper is honoured as pragmatic and beneficial for the entire humanity.

"People should develop along the lines of their own genius and we should avoid imposing anything on them. We should try to encourage in every way their traditional art and culture. Tribal rights in land and forests should be respected. We should try to train and build up a team of their own people to do the work of administration and development. Some technical person from outside will, no doubt, be needed, especially in the beginning. But we should avoid introducing too many outsiders into tribal territory. We should not over administer these areas nor overwhelm them with a multiplicity of schemes. We should rather work through, and not in rivalry to, their own social and cultural institutions. We should judge results, not by statistics or the amount of money spent, but by the quality of human character that is evolved." (Pt. Jawaharlal Nehru, the first Prime Minister of India, 1959). This advice or direction from the politically most powerful person of newly developing India is a commendable thought, considering that it comes out from a leader of the "mainstream". It appears to be in line with the spirit and the Articles of the Constitution--- perfectly democratic and socialistic. But we must not miss the word "try to"; it is the key word and portrays the bad faith with which both our Constitution makers and the political leaders went about. The "special" section of the Directive Principles was carefully charted out with the hidden consensus of "democratic socialism without meaning it." (I call it "special" because no other written Constitution contains the kind of (hypocrisy). In the so long years of "Swaraj", eradication of poverty, illiteracy, untouchability and gender--- inequality--- everything have remained at the level of trying and noble words only. Intentions trudged always on the opposite path. That is why our leaders and the mainstream group talk of privatisation and people's good, secularism and uniformity in the same breath and love for one's own culture, which does not subscribe to that of the mainstream, is branded as anti-national or unpatriotic.

Arthur Koestler said, on the other hand, "the continuous disasters in man's history are mainly due to his excessive capacity and urge to become identified with a tribe, nation, church or a cause, and to espouse its credo uncritically and unenthusiastically, even if its tenets are contrary to reason, devoid of self-interest and detrimental to the claims of self-preservation". It is for reasons such as these that we have created refugees: people who have a "well-founded fear of being persecuted for reasons of race, religion, nationality, membership of a particular social group or political opinion", continues Koestler.

Accordingly, all the adivasis, dalits and some of the religious minorities, who are poor, and women, of all socio-economic categories, are "refugees" in their own lands; ...they are refugees even if they do not have to migrate. They are permanent victims of "planned" neglect and economic under-development, so that they can remain marginalised permanently.

Declaration of the Principles of Indigenous Rights, adopted by the World Council of Indigenous Peoples in 1984, says "the traditions and custom of the indigenous people must be respected by the states and recognized as fundamental sources of law" (Principle 4). Convention on Indigenous and Tribal Peoples in Independent Countries (1989), in its Article 3 says, "indigenous and tribal peoples shall enjoy the full measure of human rights and fundamental freedoms without hindrance or discrimination. The provisions of the Convention shall be applied without discrimination to male and female members of these peoples."

Constitution of India, in Article 29, said, "any section of the citizens...having a distinct language, script or culture of its own shall have the right to conserve the same." Article 46 says, "the State shall promote with special care the educational and economic interests of the weaker sections of the people, and, in particular, of the Scheduled Castes and the Scheduled Tribes, and shall protect them from social injustice and all forms of exploitation." We must specially take note of the fact that there is no mention or intention of "developing" these distinct cultures, nor the mode or methods are prescribed. Secondly, the notion of "weaker sections" is rather vague. It implies, in a very subtle way, that, further one is from the mainstream cultural pattern weaker that individual or the community is (from a true developmental angle).

The urgency of human rights is supported by the emerging concerns for the environment and sustainable growth, which is fundamentally connected with equity and which can only be met through a recognition of basic human needs and new forms of co-operation. Declaration of the United Nations Conference on the Human Environment (Stockholm, 16 June, 1971) says in Principle 1 that "Man has the fundamental right to freedom, equality and adequate conditions of life, in an environment of a quality that permits a life of dignity and well-being..." Universal Declaration of Human Rights says in Article 3 that "Everyone has the right to life", thereby making it clear that right to life has no meaning without the adequate right to environment. After all, before industries and technologies, as a weapon in the hands of the capitalists cum imperialists, started having its sway, human beings were basically and primarily Nature's children. UN General Assembly Resolution on the World Charter for Nature (28 October, 1982) demanded in its General Principle 1 that "Nature shall be respected and its essential processes shall not be impaired." It is not clear from this "noble" statement whether this "concern" from the First World-directed UN General Assembly was for those who are totally dependent on Nature not only for their livelihood but also for their very living and life-pattern. Considering the history of the "moral/peace" positions the UNO takes and has generally taken (the latest being in case of the arbitrary bombing of Iraqi civilians), a true human rights fighter tends to believe that this "principle" was actually to "conserve" (in other words, to control) the Natural environment for their own needs. The Treaty of Rome (Article 130r) and the Constitution of India (Article 48A) sings the same tune. The former proclaims that the "Action by the Community relating to the environment shall have the following objectives: - to preserve, protect and improve the quality of the environment..." and the latter endorses that "The state shall endeavour to protect and improve the environment and to safeguard the forests and wild life of the country". Note that the Indian Constitution once again talks of "endeavour" (trying) and not of any resolution or determination. "Endeavour" allows enough scope for not doing anything at all.

Besides, the mere "protection" or even "improvement" of environment does not necessarily protect and improve the life of those who are completely dependent on it. The protection and improvement can be cleverly tailored and located for the benefit of the vested interests like the timber merchants, pharmaceutical companies and industries seeking raw materials, etc. Thirdly, does human life and livelihood get necessarily safeguarded if forests and wild life are?

The Constitution of Namibia, on the other hand, states (Article 95), "The State shall actively promote and maintain the welfare of the people by adopting inter alia policies aimed at the following : (1) the maintenance of ecosystems, essential ecological processes and biological diversity of Namibia and (2) utilization of living natural resources on a sustainable basis for the benefit of all Namibians, both present and future..." How sincere and comprehensive this statement is. It perceives the real value of Natural environment, i.e. for the sustenance and growth of "all" people - not just those who are directly dependent on Nature. It recognizes that destruction of Nature affects even those who destroy it; over-utilization of Nature may give short-term financial benefits, but should not we think of our future, viz: our own children?

Environmental rights mesh with other sorts of rights in various ways. They are often perceived as conflicting with developmental needs, and the emphasis on development has led, in many countries—both developed and developing, capitalist and socialist—to environmental considerations being neglected because they were assumed to conflict with development. But now, perceptions are changing. Witness the Namibian Constitution's emphasis on sustainable development, i.e. development FOR the people and BY the people. Most of the socialist countries even make statements on environmental protection either as aspiration or as purporting to represent what the state does,-- and not what the state SHOULD do or is bound to do. On the whole, the constitutional statements in this field are at the highest level of generality (and quite a substantial number do not have anything to do with environment at all). At best, the constitutions impose duties upon the state, rather than granting rights to the citizens (like India & Vanuatu).

An Indian journalist recently wrote "India has among

the finest bodies of environmental legislation in the world...most provisions of those laws have either remained on paper or have been mauled completely out of shape during their implementation"...Kenya, for example, has 50 enactments relevant to environmental protection, but "very little of it is applied". Hong Kong has had a substantial body of legislation which has only recently begun to be seriously enforced...Some countries lack the law, some the resources, but all lack the "elusive quality of political will to enforce". The implications of introducing human rights into development are far reaching. "Once human rights are accepted as human, that is universal, human rights obligations reach far beyond national borders. Wide disparities in the opportunities to enjoy human rights thereby become one of the principal challenges in human rights, and the principal challenge in development". (Tomasevski, 1993).

There is a connection, if by no means a rigid one, between inequality and environmental degradation. Ethnic minorities, the old and the very young, women and the poorest sections of society, often (if not always) suffer disproportionately.

While the cities...often the most affluent sectors of developing nations-- suffer from air and noise pollutions and water shortages, it is in the rural areas that the worst effects are felt--- Indigenous people are deprived of their forest homes in Malaysia, for example; tribal people lose their land to dams and reservoirs in India; villages in Bangladesh are flooded; and women, all over, have to walk miles for water and firewood. These dispossessed and displaced suffer the worst environment, or levels of pollution, when they migrate to the cities. Those who dispossess them and vitiate the environment enjoy relatively less pollutions, as they live in less congested localities with the best available civic amenities. They travel in air-conditioned cars, insulated from air pollution, thus generating pollution for those whom poverty forces to commute by bi-cycles or scooters or even on foot...Therefore, strengthening and strict and sincere enforcing of all other human rights, particularly those related to health, livelihood and identity, are absolutely imperative for the conservation of environment and sustainable growth.

Repressive and discriminating practices lead to pervasiveness of ethnic conflict, the humiliations heaped daily on the lower caste communities and on the members of the indigenous and minority peoples They live in constant fears about their lives; civilized life or dignity become impossible. Neither the government nor the dissident forces respect the rights of the civilians, thus disregarding the principles and the rules of humanitarian law. Many are driven to seek refuge abroad. Others live in such abject poverty or deprivation that even the discourse on human rights sounds obscene!...Needless to remind, women and children are the most prominent among the victims of social and environmental discrimination and deprivation. The women and children of the outcastes and the tribals happen to be the worse among the worst. Women tend to be less educated, less nourished and work harder for smaller returns even in developed and rich economies. Eighty percent of refugees are women and children fleeing from persecution and serious amount of deprivation, they are, in general, compelled to live in degrading conditions and without adequate legal safeguards in the land of their asylum also. They manage to get employed in the unorganized sector only—thus getting further exploited.

There are over 15,000,000 refugees in the world today. Women in Australia (otherwise a rich society) constitute 75% of the total number of people living in poverty.

Like always, men take the decision to migrate and they continue to take all other decisions thereafter, even though the burden of managing with meagre income, changed and new livelihood and the "strange" demands of the "new" society is invariably much more on the women. The host government and the society, which usually is not favourable or friendly, tends to be more exploitative to the refugee women because they are exploited by their own men also. Ironically, it is the women who are more capable of providing the best insights into the problems which affect the needs, security and the future of their family and their society. This is a well-researched, well-recognized fact, observable in both tribal and mainstream societies. A Canadian scholar, Prof. Rebecca Cook, observes that ratifications of and reportings on various/sundry human rights declarations "only deals with symptoms". At the heart of discriminations against women lie deep-rooted cultural traditions in both developed and developing countries. Prof. Cook quotes a Sri Lankan lawyer, "in many ways the issues of women's rights have accentuated the constant tension between tradition and modernity. Women have been classically recognized as bearers of tradition from one generation to another." Therefore, "the transformation of their role in society", as a result of human rights, "is seen as an erosion of the foundations of traditional cultures". Women of all ages suffer avoidable premature death, avoidable sickness and avoidable disadvantages in education and economic & social opportunities.

Article 2 of the Universal Declaration of Human Rights says, "Everybody is entitled to all the rights and freedoms set forth in the Declaration, without distinction of any kind, such as race, colour, SEX, language, religion, political or other status." International Covenant on Civil and Political Rights declares in its Article 3 that "the State Parties to the present Covenant undertake to ensure the equal right of men and WOMEN to the enjoyment of all economic, social and cultural rights set forth in the present Covenant." (March, 1976). International Covenant on Economic, Social and Cultural Rights of January, 1976, declares exactly the same thing. The famous CEDAW or the International Convention on the Elimination of all forms of Discrimination Against Women of 1979, "prohibits", in Article 1, any distinction, exclusion or restriction made on the basis of SEX which has the effect or purpose of impairing or nullifying the recognition, enjoyment or exercise by women, irrespective of their marital status, on the basis of EQUALITY of men and women, of HUMAN rights and FUNDAMENTAL freedoms in the political, economic, social, civil or other field." Finally, it is important for all women - refugee, mainstream or tribal to know that as a result of the Communique of

Commonwealth Ministers Responsible for Women's Affairs (London, 1990), the Ministers recognized that "economic equality between WOMEN and men is an important dimension of gender equality and economic ADVANCEMENT of women as well as a basic premise for all human rights and national economic development." They also noted, with regret, that national and international policies and programmes are formulated without regard for gender issues and any number of such declarations and resolutions have no effect and no validity.

While the United Nations Declaration of Human Rights (adopted in 1948) does not explicitly exclude women, it does not elaborate on how the rights set out in this declaration relate to women. It does not talk of the "private sphere", the area in which most violations of women's human rights occur. This separation of women's rights from human rights rendered most violations of women's rights invisible. Bunch wrote in 1995 that the "West-educated, propertied men feared the violations of their civil and political rights in the private sphere" because that would affect their property and privileged position (which is due to property); they were not concerned with the "violations in the private sphere of their home as they were the masters of that territory". He further opines that "private-public" distinction is a "dichotomy largely used to justify female subordination and to exclude human rights abuses at home from public scrutiny". In addition, the exclusion of sexual and other violences against women from the human rights agenda stems from the failure to view the oppression of women as political. Bunch, thus rightly remarks, "female subordination runs so deep that it is still viewed as inevitable or natural". It is actually "politically construed reality maintained by patriarchal interest, ideology and institutions. The physical territory of this political struggle is women's bodies."

The United Nations Decade for Women (1975-85) was seen as a watershed in placing women's concerns on the international agenda and for facilitating women's co-operation. Women participated in the NGO Forums, etc. (like in the Beijing

World Conference, 1995) where women from different countries were "able to exchange strategies and develop ongoing working relationships" (Friedman). THe CEDAW was one of the most outstanding outcomes of the decade and has subsequently become the international standard for the protection and promotion of women's human rights. It sets out the duties that the States are required to promote in all areas of a woman's life, living and livelihood. The signatories to this "human rights charter" are required to "take all the necessary legislative, judicial, administrative or other appropriate measures to guarantee women the exercise and enjoyment of human rights and fundamental freedoms on the basis of equality with men" (Stamatopoulou, 1995). The bad faith of the framers of CEDAW - supposed to be the most comprehensive document for women's human rights - is shamelessly expressed in the provision that the signatory countries are allowed to make "reservations." (Similar thing is happening in India with regard to the "Women's Seat Reservation in the Legislative Bodies Bill." It is acceptable to the existing Parliamentarians, viz: men, only if women accept "men dictated reservation" within reservation). There are countries like Thailand who have demanded so many reservations that the "noble" rights have remained noble only on paper...Why should we be so shocked? Have not our Constitution, after 48 long years, fulfilled any of the promises and obligations? Have not the noble ideas in beautiful words remained merely decorative ?

Thailand acceded to the Convention in 1985 with reservations concerning seven Articles, viz.: Art. 7 Elimination of Discrimination in Political and Public Life.

Art. 9 Equal Citizenship Rights

Art. 10 Elimination of Discrimination in Education

Art. 11 ....Employment

Art. 15 Full Legal Capacity

Art. 16 Elimination of Discrimination in Marriage and the Family:

The usefulness of CEDAW or any such document, with regard to which the signatories are allowed to have reservations, is definitely in doubt. But, at the same time, the prolonged discussions and deliberations definitely make violations a little more difficult. The victims can possibly see a light at the end of a long, dark tunnel. Before the UDHR and before the "democratic, socialist, secular" Constitution of India it was the dead end or the pit of a very deep well....the fate of women, refugees and the indigenous people was like that of the Sikh women jumping into a well to avoid communal violence during the "Partition" frenzy! (Reference to Govind Nihalini's powerful film on the heart-rending story "Tamas" by Bhisham Sahni)." Human rights instruments and mechanisms provide avenues for challenging the systematic abuse of women, and governments can be made to take gender-based violations more seriously by being held accountable for the implementation of laws against them..." (Bunch, 1995).

Mayer (1995) identifies two important positions taken with regard to human rights that have an important bearing on women's human rights issues, viz.: the universalist and cultural relativist positions. The former position holds that "all members of the human family share the SAME inalienable rights." The cultural relativist position, on the other hand, demands the universal acceptance of "different traditions" and "cross-cultural standards." The danger in this position, as Rao argues, is in the probability of placing community rights above, or holier than, individual human rights. Abuses justified by this position is most blatantly in case of women's human rights. All the gender-exploitative religious laws are accepted and protected by the Indian governments (whichever political party is in power) with the "humane" intention of protecting the rights of a minority community....as if the women of that "oppressed" community are not oppressed by the patriarchs in that community itself! "Power relations may appear so secure and well-established that both subordinate and dominant groups" tend to be "unaware of their oppressive implications",...or are "incapable of imagining alternative ways of BEING and DOING" (Kabeer, 1994).

Nadia Youssef and Bina Aggarwal (1994 & 1995) and the latest Report of the International Food Policy Research Institute turned our attention to the "important but problematic aspects of the human rights agenda relating to women's rights to socio-economic development". Youssef points out that in rural Africa it is women's access to productive resources, viz: land, credit, cattle and technical knowledge, rather than income, that provides the relevant measures of social status...Women's access to land has diminished as its value as a marketable commodity has increased. Even the Land Reform Laws (by the so-called democratic governments) have discriminated against women. Needless to remind that such "law-based" discriminations are as blatant in our country and against the letter and spirit of CEDAW. Aggarwal draws our attention to the obvious links between the ownership of arable land (as the most important type of property) and gender empowerment or equality...A woman's social and economic status goes up in that proportion. Better job opportunities can merely be complements...not a substitute to land and property rights.

The IFPRI Report, titled "Women: the Key to Food Security", confirms the views above; it found that women still experience countless barriers to achieving their full potential as producers and providers of food. The greatest barrier is the absence/denial of this significant recognition. They do everything in the field except the actual act of ploughing because that is prohibited for them by religious dictum. Recently a woman was tied to the plough, dragged along like a plough and beaten up mercilessly because she dared plough her husband's field. She had to defy religion cum patriarchy because her husband was a drunkard, he was not ploughing the field and her children were starving. As a mother she had to opt for human rights as opposed to her religious duties....A woman always is the food-provider for her family even if she is not allowed to earn or have access to any source of income by her own right.

Women also are the best..and perhaps, the only—protectors of the environment not only as food providers, but also because (as mothers) they are much more concerned about the "future" of their future generation. Thus, no development can be sustainable unless Nature and women are allowed complete freedom—unless environment is conserved and women have major roles in the formulations of policies and implementations of plannings related to development. Extension and research programmes rarely acknowledge or take into account women's indigenous knowledge regarding environment and agriculture. The afore-mentioned Report observes that achieving gender equity, particularly in the countryside, will have an important bearing on the ability of the Third World countries to meet their future food needs and sustainable development. "The kinds of actions to be taken on behalf of women touch at the cornerstones of agrarian reform laws, family laws, rural employment strategy and a deeply embedded patriarchal mentality. Hence, it is imperative that women find mechanisms for addressing such issues as a whole, through self-reliant, participatory collective initiatives, in which these issues are addressed as fundamental to women's human rights" (Youssef, 1995).

As a result of globalization of capital and capitalism and the consequent capitalism-oriented development, women and other have nots (like the tribals in India) are getting more and more deprived and therefore, marginalised. As an inevitable consequence, landlessness (caused by usurption of land for "developmental" purposes) and poverty (caused by loss of natural resources and the work and livelihood related to that), have forced increasing number of women into casual labour or work in the low-paid unorganized sector, where the work and living conditions are shamelessly violative of all human rights, including the laws of the land. Men only are preferred in the "organized" and industrial sectors; women get less paid for the same work. On the contrary, most of the time women have to work longer on the pretext that women are "physically weak, not skilled and therefore, less productive". And, when it comes to promotion, women are hardly considered.

On the other hand, women (and children) are invariably

preferred (irrespective of any society-polity in the Third World) in all labour-intensive jobs. The arguments offered are that they have greater dexterity, speed and endurance. More "exploitative" than this is the argument that women and children are disciplined, docile, not inclined to industrial action and quiet about accepting low wages. More often than not pregnant women are retrenched; even if retained, they get no maternity benefits (they have to work extra later to make up for the "loss of industrial man-hour" during the birth of the child and a few days after that). A majority of the industries make it a point to appoint not more than 14 women workers because otherwise they will have to open a creche for their children.

In almost all the underdeveloped economies the twin brothers, capitalism and patriarchy, have a good hold. Thus violations of human rights are double with regard to women (and children, particularly girl children). The men of the deprived-marginalised sections, however exploited, do not obviously, become the victims of this kind of (viz: patriarchal) oppression. Woman in the unorganized sector not only work 16 hours on an average (survey conducted, by ILO, of the South Asian economies) for a meagre income to support her family (the major burden of which rests on her even in the developed economies), but also in her household, viz: to cook, clean, wash and take care of the children and the old. The magnitude of the problems facing women workers is indicated by the fact that despite their overwhelming responsibility for household and the reproduction of the labour force, they are not classified as economically active population.

The measurement standard is (i) anti-Nature, (ii) pro-capitalist and (iii) patriarchy-guided. Production, national income or contribution to economy is calculated purely by money; that is why, most of women's work (even if it is providing food, health and other needs to the male/"productive" labour force) is considered unproductive and is not calculated in the national income. That is why again, women are not allowed/encouraged in the sectors where minimum wages are enforceable by law.

Domestic work (in a way the most productive because in its absence the entire labour force will get extinct) is unpaid and therefore, not regarded as an economic activity. "The day is still far off when working women will everywhere be equal partners with men in the efforts to achieve economic and social progress" (ILO). The latest ILO survey shows that women constituted more than one-third of the worldwide workforce. The great majority of them live in the developing countries (though their economic contribution is seldom acknowledged) and about two-thirds of them are in the agricultural sector. Despite this, their access to or control over land is minimal, especially in South Asian and sub-Saharan African countries.

It is worthwhile, in this context, to have a look into the chronology of the major developments relating to the women's human rights issues.

1948 UN Universal Declaration of Human Rights.

1966 International Covenant on Civil & Political Rights

1966 ....Economic, Social & Cultural Rights

1975 First World Conference of Women (on Women), held in Mexico City....the beginning of the UN Decade for Women.

1979 Convention on the Elimination of all forms of Discrimination against Women (popularly known as CEDAW)....the most important and the most referred to human rights documents on and for women.

1980 Second World Conference of Women, held in Copenhagen.

1985 Third World Conference of Women, held in Nairobi (Kenya)....the end of Decade for Women.

1993 UN Conference on Human Rights, Vienna....the most important document on human rights after 1948.

1994 International Conference on Population and Development, Cairo. Population is the field where women "naturally" have the maximum contribution and the biggest role to play; yet, majority of the participants/decision-makers in this conference were men!

1995 Fourth World Conference of Women, Beijing. The definition of "family" and a statement on "lesbianism" were the new wheels added to the Women's Movement.

1998 UNIFEM (a UN Body committed specially to women's cause) world-wide campaign against gender-based violence.

Such statements, conferences, declarations and documents, too many in number and happening every other year, are clear enough proofs of the "bad faith" on the part of the UN member states, most of which had been signatories but never cared to implement. If UNDHR of 1948 could generate any seriousness in the minds of the framers and the signatories, so many declarations and statements every now and then would not have been necessary. Ironically, "human rights" were formulated and endorsed by those members who were on the top of the list of the violators! They had to appear noble (to appear not power-hungry is the surest way of having full control over affairs), but had also to create loopholes so that noble words remain words only and cannot get translated into action.

Let me conclude by making my readers aware of the key contents of the most important human rights document for women, viz: CEDAW.

Art. 1 Definition of Discrimination : "any distinction, exclusion or restriction made on the basis of sex, which has the purpose or effect of denying equal exercise of human rights and fundamental freedoms in all fields of human endeavour."

Art. 2 Policy measures to be undertaken to eliminate

	discrimination
Art. 3	Guarantees basic human rights and fundamentals freedoms on an equal basis with men
Art. 4	Temporary special measures to achieve equality
Art. 5	Against sex roles and stereotyping
Art. 6	Against prostitution
Art. 7	Promotion of political and public life.
Art. 8	Facilitating participation at the international level
Art. 9	Nationality
Art. 10	Equal rights in education
Art. 11	....employment
Art. 12	Health care and family planning
Art. 13	Economic & social benefits and freedoms
Art. 14	The Rights and position of the rural women as opposed to urban
Art. 15	Equality before law
Art. 16	Women-friendly marriage and family laws
Art. 17-22	Procedures of the functioning of the CEDAW
Art. 23-30	The actual Administration of the Convention

The following are a few excerpts, referring to WOMEN'S human rights, from the Vienna Declaration and Programme of Action of 1993.

> "Recognizing and affirming that all human rights derive from the dignity and worth inherent in the human person, and that the human person is the central subject of human rights and fundamental freedoms.

Re-affirming their commitment to the purposes and principles contained in the Charter of the United Nations and the Universal Declaration on Human Rights..." Why did it become necessary to "Re-affirm" their commitments after long 45 years? Should not the inequalities and oppressions have disappeared on their own-even without such an exclusive body of statements and commitments? Is not equality or human rights an inseparable and automatic process with more and more nations freeing themselves of the bondage of colonialism, and more and more polities becoming democratic? Human rights is an integral part of democratic theory, belief, structure and practice; one cannot stand or survive without the other. Yet, human rights have continued to remain the privileges or the rights of a few men...not to speak of women at all!

The Vienna Declaration "recalls the Preamble to the Charter of the United Nations, in particular the determination to reaffirm faith in fundamental human rights....and in the equal rights of men and **WOMEN** and of nations large and small."

The group was "deeply concerned by various forms of discriminations and violence, to which women continued to be exposed all over the world" It also "recognized that the activities of the United Nations in the field of human rights should be rationalized and enhanced...to further the objectives of universal respect for the observance of international human rights standards".

The excerpts above are from the Preamble to the Vienna Declaration. The following are from Part II of this document.

"The World Conference on Human Rights reaffirms the sole commitment of all States to fulfil their obligations to promote universal respect for, and observance and protection of all human rights and fundamental freedoms...Democracy, development and respect for human rights and fundamental freedoms are interdependent and mutually re-inforcing..The World Conference..reaffirms the right to development... and the human person is the central subject of development". But in reality, particularly under a capitalist structure and system, the human persons become the ingredients...like fodders in the canon Natural human rights or the rights to conserve Nature get completely eroded in the process and Human Rights Conferences and Charters thus, become necessary...a futile attempt to cover up the misdeeds and anti-human rights programmes.

The human rights of women and the girl children are an inalienable, integral and indivisible part of universal human rights. The full and equal participation of women in the political, civil, economic, social and cultural life at the national, regional and international levels, and the eradication of all forms of discrimination on the grounds of sex are priority objectives of the international community," because "gender based violence and all forms of sexual harassment and exploitation, including those resulting from cultural prejudices and international trafficking are incompatible with the dignity and worth of the human person, and" therefore, "must be eliminated. This can be achieved by legal measures and through national action and international co-operation"...But the framers of this Body of Rights are the leaders of the violators; these are the political powers who constantly dig the soil from under the foundation of international co-operation". This, i.e. gender based violence and discrimination, is the primary reason why the need for special human rights charter for women was so anxiously felt. Ironically but, there has been a rise, in geometrical proportions, in all kinds of inhumanity against women and girl children ever since the UNDHR and CEDAW were declared and ratified (in various countries). When Capitalism holds the spectre of imperialism all over the world, how can any space be left for socialism, egalitarianism and human rights? More the repressions, more the "cover up" by noble ideas..just as religion, which is supposed to be the epitome of humanitarianism, is actually the birth-place and perpetrator of all kinds of inhuman divisions between man & man and man & woman. In Part III, the World Conference coming out with the Vienna Declaration, "recognizes the importance of enjoyment by women of the highest standard of physical and mental health throughout their life-span. In the context of the three World Conferences on Women and the Convention on the Elimination of all forms of Discrimination against Women, a woman's right to accessible and adequate health care and the widest range of family planning services, as well as equal access to education at all levels" is recognized. Interestingly, and disturbingly enough for women, "family planning services" are recommended for women, but not family planning "choices," which means full reproductive choices and complete, uninterferred control over her reproductive system! Even the Cairo Conference on Population overlooks the vital factor that it is the woman's body which is the sole "owner" of the reproductive system and therefore, women and women only should be sole decision makers...The erring governments lately, are paying more attention to the Nobel Laureate Amartya Sen than they ever paid to women screaming loud and hoarse.

This Conference had also "urged the governments and the regional and international organizations to facilitate the access of women in decision making posts and their greater participation in the decision making process"...But, when, if ever at all, will the parliaments and other decision taking bodies in the various democracies of the world represent fifty percent of the population proportionately? Right to decision making is the mother of all other basic human rights. Till that is acquired and exercised, all other rights will remain piece-meal and inconsequential. Once that happens (at present and even for years to come "that happening" will be only in utopia), the discourse on rights will be meaningless or totally unnecessary, because people will enjoy rights automatically--- like a birth right. In other words, that can be true classless society or Marx's Communism!

The Declaration concludes with the hope that "human rights issues will play an urgent part in the deliberations of the Fourth World Conference on Women" (held in Beijing in 1995). "Challenging the prevalent concept of, and reinterpreting the movement for human rights from a feminist perspective is not merely a matter of semantics; it is about the lives and deaths of individual women everywhere, everyday" (Charlotte Bunch, 1995).

References

1. C. Bunch, "Transforming Human Rights from a Feminist Perspective."
2. E. Friedman, "Women's Human Rights: the Emergence of a Movement".
3. A.E. Mayer, "Cultural Particularism as a Bar to Women's Rights: Reflections on the Middle Eastern Experience."
4. A. Rao. "The Politics of Gender and Culture in International Human Rights Discourse."
5. E. Stamatopoulou, "Women's Rights and the United Nations."
6. J. Peter & A. Wolper, "Introduction."
7. N.H. Youssef, "Women's Access to Productive Resources: the Need for Legal Instruments to Protect Women's Development Rights."

   All these essays, above, are from the book "Women's Rights, Human Rights: International Feminist Perspectives", edited by J. Peters & A. Wolper. Routledge, New York, 1995.
8. India's Country Paper on Women, prepared by the Govt. of India, for the Fourth World Conference on Women at Beijing, 1995.
9. Thailand's Report on the Status of Women and Platform for Action, 1994.
10. IFPRI (1995), "Women, the Key to Food Security."
11. K. Tomasevski, "Women and Human Rights", Zed Books, London, 1993.
12. B. Aggarwal, "Gender and Command over Poverty: A Critical Gap in Economic Analysis and Policy in South Asia," in "World Development", vol. 22, no. 10.
13. Human Rights Watch Global Report on Women's Human Rights. New York of 1993 & 1995.

4

Offences Against Women

Dr. Mamta Rao

The subordination of women to men was one of the supreme principles of government, Confucius. *Woman may be said to be an inferior man,* Aristotle. The German Philosopher Nietzsche says, *when you got to meet a woman take your whip along*. The Hindu sage Manu condemned women to eternal bondage whereas the followers of Prophet Mohammad placed the fair sex behind the purdah. Under the common law, women were treated as chattels. All that is written above can be succinctly put in the words of Manifesto of the Woman's Rights Convention, *the history of mankind is a history of repeated injuries and usurpation on the part of man towards women, having in direct object the establishment of a tyranny over her.*

In the chequered history of mankind one finds that different and disparate cultures, however distant they may be in time and space, have at least one thing in common and that is the contempt for women. This unequal status of women being offensive to human dignity and also violative of human rights has emerged today as a fundamental crisis in human development the world over. Human rights are derived from the dignity and worth inherent in the human person. These human rights and fundamental freedoms have been reiterated by the Universal

Declaration of Human Rights. Democracy, development, respect for human rights and fundamental freedom are inter dependant and have mutual reinforcement. The human rights for women including girl child are therefore inalienable, integral and indivisible part of Universal Human Rights. The full development of personality, fundamental freedom and equal participation by women in political, social, economic and cultural scenario are concomitants for national development, social and family stability and growth - culturally, socially and economically. All forms of discrimination on grounds of gender, are thus violative of fundamental freedom and human rights.

Gender injustice taking the shape of crimes against women has escalated all over the world and India is no exception to this. Despite the fact that the Indian mythology placed women on a very high pedastal, deterioration in this glorious status suffered a socio-cultural setback resulting in loss of their freedom and decline in their personality. Despite the social reform movement in the 19th century arousing considerable awakening, constitutional and legal provisions aimed at preventing discrimination, positive judicial trends, welfare schemes and activism of voluntary sector, women continue to suffer from increasing tide of violence both in and outside homes. According to the data compiled by the National Commission for Women, *a rape is committed every 54 minutes, a dowry death every 92 minutes molestation every 26 minutes and an act of cruelty every 33 minutes.*

Realising this inequality, the United Nations passed various instruments with a focus on women's emancipation, maintaining and enhancing the dignity of women. Some of the important instrument are Article 29 (1) of the Universal Declaration of Human Rights 1948 which speaks of the duties of individual essential for the free and full development of personality of every individual, Declaration on the Elimination of Discrimination against Women 1967, The Declaration of Mexico on Equality of Women and Peace 1975, Convention on the Elimination of All forms of Discrimination against Women

1979, Convention on the Suppression of Traffic in Persons and of the Prostitution of others 1949, Convention on the Political Rights of Women 1952, Convention concerning Equal Remuneration for Men and Women Workers for Work of Equal Value 1951, Convention concerning Discrimination in respect of Employment and Occupation 1958. The meet of the women in China was the recent focus on the violation of dignity of women. India being a signatory of the Conventions and Declaration of United Nations incorporated various provisions relating to equality and dignity of women.

The Preamble of the Indian Constitution gives equality of status and opportunity. Article 14 provides for equality in general and Article 15 (18) prohibits discrimination on special grounds of, *inter alia*, sex, Art 15(3) embodies the exception which permits the state to make special provisions for women. The 73rd and 74th Amendment in the Indian Constitution provides for reservation of seats of women in election to panchayats and municipalities. Article 23 prohibits trafficking in human beings. Dasi system has been held to be trafficking by the Supreme Court. Similarly Article 39 (a), (b), (c) and Article 42 and 44 of the Constitution provides provisions for the benefit of women. Article 44 gains importance in achieving the goals of gender justice. Article 15-A (e) in the chapter on fundamental duties makes it obligatory, *inter alia*, to renounce the practices derogatory to the dignity of women.

However the dynamic philosophy of the Constitution has been distilled by stagnant, changing and oppressive parallel regime of laws. Let us now discuss various types of crimes and violence against women which is linked to their disadvantageous position in the society and amounts to violation of human dignity and human rights. The violence can be categorised into sexual and domestic violence. Sexual Violence is the most brutal form of expression against not only the person of a women but against the entire society. This form of violence can be studied in different heads which are elaborated.

Rape

Rape is a humiliating and the most shocking of the crimes against human conscience and morality. This crime occupies a significant place in the penal status of every country. The laws relating to sexual offences do not have adequate provisions for the protection of female victims.

Section 375 to 376 (D) of Indian Penal Code deal with the issue of rape. Section 375 defines the statutory offence of rape. It denotes the sexual intercourse with a woman first, against her will, secondly without her consent; thirdly with her consent obtained by putting her in fear of death or hurt; fourthly with her consent when man knows that he is not her husband and if consent is given under her misconception of his identity as her husband; fifthly with her consent when at the time of giving such consent she is under the influence of unsoundness of mind or administration of some substance to make her give consent; sixthly with or without consent when she is under of sixteen years age. Thus it could be seen that it is a comprehensive definition by any standards.

The Explanation of Section 375 provides that mere penetration is sufficient to constitute the sexual intercourse necessary to the offence of rape. Therefore it is not necessary that there must be complete and total penetration.

The fact that in every rape trial consent beyond all reasonable doubts is difficult to prove was highlighted in the famous Mathura Trial (Tukaram V. State of Maharashtra AIR 1979 SC 185) which triggered the campaign for change in rape laws. Along with this case on the recommendations of, the 84th report of Law Commission on rape and allied offences, certain amendments were introduced and section 376 A to 376 D were introduced in the Indian Penal Code. These changes include protection of victim during investigation, change in the definition to remove the element of consent, addition of custodial rape as a crime and increase in the punishment of custodial, gang rape and rape of a pregnant women.

In order to give teeth to the provisions of rape, Cr. P.C.

and Evidence Act were also modified by the Amendment Act of 1983. When these amendments were introduced it was feared that more stringent punishment would result in fewer convictions but the judgments proved otherwise.

The Amendments have not decreased the crime in any way. The devastating, dehumanizing and brutal crime continues. However there is need to compensate the victim. In this scenario, the Supreme Court judgment in Delhi Domestic Working Women's forum V. Union of India (1995 (1) SCC 14) suggesting the formulation of a scheme for awarding compensation to rape victims at the time of convicting a person found guilty of rape is appreciable. The court suggested the setting up of a Criminal Injuries Compensation Board under Art 38 (1) of the Constitution. It was also held that the trial of rape case *in camera* should be the rule and an open trial an exception.

The Supreme Court's direction in Bodhisattwa Goutham V. Subhra Chakraborty to the guilty person to pay interim compensation to the prosecutors during pendency of criminal case is also important.

Law remains but the number of victims (including children) increases destroying the very soul of the helpless female. The concept of marital rape does not exist in our country. There is no time limit for the trial. It is a sad reflection on the attitude of indifference of the society towards violation of human dignity. Contrary to the popular belief rape is almost never perpetrated for sexual gratification. It is an act of violence that happens to be expressed through sexual means.

Indecent Representation

Derogatory depiction of women whether in print or electronic media is rampant. In the existing statutes Sec. 292, 293 and 294 of IPC deal with obscenity. However, the concept of obscenity was based on the 19th century notion which considered anything concerning sex as dirty and obscene. Under these sections, the definition of obscenity was vague and the interpretation depended on the individual judges. The test was whether the tendency of the matter charged as obscene was to deprave and corrupt those whose minds are open to such immoral influences and into whose hands such a publication may fall. This basically is a question of fact. As over the years the concept of obscenity has changed from depiction of sex *per se* to sex with crime or violence or sexually humiliating situation, there was thus a need for special enactment against indecent representation which was passed known as the Indecent Representation of Women (Prohibition) Act 1986. This Act prohibits indecent representation of women through advertisements or in publications, writings, paintings, figures or in any other manner. Sec. 509 of IPC also deals with intention to insulting the modesty of any women and prescribing punishment for the same. If a man intending to outrage the modesty of a woman exposes his person indirectly to a woman or uses obscene words intending that she should hear them or exhibits to her obscene drawing, he commits this offence.

Interpreting indecent representation, the Supreme Court in State of Kerala V. Hamsu, ((1998) 3 Crimes 161) held the accused to be guilty of indecent representation where he beckons the prosecutrix by winking his, eyes in public and caught hold of her hand.

Similarly in Rupan Deol Bajaj V. K.P.S. Gill, (AIR 1996 SC 309) slapping senior lady officer on her posterior in the presence of elite gathering was held to be outraging the modesty of the lady officer.

Domestic Violence

With increase in the number of cases relating to violence against women especially in matrimonial homes, a new terminology was coined that is domestic violence. This term distinguishes it from external violence. As this type of violence increased day to day there were pressures and protests against it. Since the police in a majority of cases refused to register cases, there was a demand for a special act under which the offenders could be punished. Generally complaints can be registered only after an offence has been committed but in a situation of domestic violence a women needs protection even before the crime is committed as she apprehends danger to her life from the assaulter on whom she is dependent and the threat is constant.

To meet this challenge of increasing domestic violence, the Criminal Acts were amended in 1983 and 1986 to create special categories of offences dealing with cruelty to wives, dowry harassments and dowry death. The first amendment introduced a new section cruelty to wives under 498-A of IPC. Although it aimed to deal with dowry harassment and suicide it was wide enough to cover the incidents of domestic violence also because the word dowry as such is not mentioned. It includes physical as well as mental violence or cruelty. The section is an effective deterrent to violent husbands if the judiciary and police interpret and enforce it in the right spirit. Denial of food, insistence on perverse sexual conduct etc. were held to be examples of domestic violence for registering cases under IPC. Further the law of Evidence was also amended to provide presumption in law against husband, his relatives if a married woman commits suicide within seven years of her marriage.

In Ramanarayan Gupta V. Ramaswami Gupta (AIR 1988 SC 2766) the Supreme Court made an important observation that domestic crimes are committed in a fit of fury due to sexual jealousy. Women are ill-treated, frequently beaten showing intense and extreme indignation to social feelings.

In Lalita Devi V. Radha Mohan it was held that legal cruelty is no confined to causing physical injury only, there may be cruelty, which may be covered under violence to the mind of another.

There cannot be greater mental cruelty than to compel a chaste to submit to the overtures of other persons for the desire of gain by prostituting the wife. (Krishna Ravi V. Radha Mohan.)

Dowry

Dakshina, originally a token having its origin in the

sublime sentiments of parents and relatives of a bride in a marriage gained all characteristics of a market transaction where women were killed, burned or thrown out of their house. With increase in cases of dowry deaths or bride burning or suicide it became a unique form of violence experienced by women in India.

To curb the evil of dowry both – giving and taking - Dowry Prohibition Act 1961 was passed. In this Act, dowry was defined as any property or valuable security given or agreed to be given directly or indirectly by one party to the marriage to other party. The act of giving and taking of dowry or abetting to take dowry became an offence with the punishment prescribed. The Amending Act of 1986 made the law more stringent and the period for filing complaint was removed and the court was given powers to act *suo motu* or on a complaint by a registered welfare organisation. By the amendment, a new section 304-B on dowry murder was introduced in IPC. The Indian Evidence Act was amended to shift the burden of proof to the husband and his family, where dowry is demanded and the bride dies within seven years of marriage, otherwise than under normal circumstances.

A new dimension was added to the concept of dowry by the Supreme Court in Shoba Rani V. Madhukar Reddi. It was held that the demands for dowry prohibited under the Act amounts to cruelty and the same entitles the wife to get a decree for dissolution of marriage. Convicting the husband in State of Punjab V. Iqbal Singh, the Supreme Court observed that the legislative intent behind incorporating Sec. 113 A of Indian Evidence Act and Sec. 304-B of IPC was to strengthen the hands to the prosecution in a crime generally committed within the privacy of residential homes.

Sati

Sati or self immolation by a widow on the pyre of the dead body of her husband is get another act which is violative of human dignity. It is manifestation of the barbaric attitude of man in violation of the human rights of a woman. The practice has the social and religious sanctions.

Incident of Sati of Roop Kanwar in Deorala Rajasthan caused furore amongst various sections of the society. This led to widespread protests demanding legislative protection in matters relating to the practice of Sati. The first legislation against the practice of Sati was promulgated in 1827. A plea was made to the Privy Council to repeal the same on the religious grounds. The argument was countered on the ground that no freedom of religion could go beyond the claims of humanity and justice.

No doubt, the abetment of Sati and Sati itself could be brought under the Indian Penal Code and punished, a need was felt for a separate law to deal with the offence.

The Roop Kanwar's incident added fuel to the fire and led to the promulgation of the Rajasthan Sati (Prevention Ordinance) 1987 and ultimately federal legislation, the Commission of Sati (Prevention) Act 1987 (Act No. 4 of 1988) providing for stringent punishment including death sentence for abetment of Sati was passed having application throughout the country. The Act stipulated punishment not just for practice of Sati but also its glorification. The important component of the Act was establishment of special courts for trying offences under the Act.

Prevention of malady lies in bringing about a change in the attitude of the people as no religion can preach to burn or bury a person alive. At the same time the law must be implemented effectively and the offender punished to prevent this barbaric act.

Female Foeticide

Girls are discriminated right from the beginning, even before they are born. India, unfortunately, is one of the countries where female foeticide is on the rise. This can be one of the most glaring example of violation of human rights and striking at the roots of the concept of dignity of women or elimination of discrimination. With the technological advances, the latest scientific techniques are used to abort female foetuses. The technique used is known as amniocentesis. What was intended to detect genetic or chromosomal disorders became a tool for those who wanted to get rid of a female foetus by determining the sex of the foetus.

The Parliament realising the consequences and implications of such pre-natal diagnostic techniques and its abuse passed the Pre-Natal Diagnostics Technique (Regulation and Prevention of Misuse) Act 1994 which came into effect only in 1996.

The Act provided for the regulation of pre-natal diagnostic technique and prevent its misuse. It seeks, *interalia*, to prohibit misuse of pre-natal diagnostic technique for determination of sex, prohibition of advertisements of such techniques for the determination of sex, permission to use such techniques only under certain conditions by registered institutions and prescribing punishment for violation of the provisions of the Act.

One more method of termination of pregnancy of the unwanted female foetus and illegitimate children was by unregistered medical practitioners and quacks. The provisions of Indian Penal Code were applied to punish persons responsible for miscarriage. However, inspite of these provisions, causing miscarriage continued and forced the Parliament in 1971 to pass an Act known as the Medical Termination of Pregnancy Act. This Act provided for termination of pregnancy in certain circumstances of risk to life of pregnant woman or unborn child by registered medical practitioners. Women thus obtained the right to safe, scientific and legal abortions. Inspite of the legislative control of the crime, female foeticide continues in contrast to jubilations on the birth of the male child.

Immoral Traffic

Prostitution is said to be the oldest among the professions in the world and is rampant throughout the world. The need for gratification of sexual urge impelled men and women of all ages in every country to exploit the other sex. Though in some countries it was regulated by law or regulations. The prostitution and the accompanying evil of traffic in human beings for the purpose of prostitution are incompatible with the basic human dignity and worth of human beings. As is said by the Supreme Court in Vishal Jeet V. Union of India ((1990) 3 SCC 318), *prostitution always remains as a running sore in the body of civilisation and destroys all moral values. The causes and evil effects of prostitution maligning the society are so notorious and frightful that none can gainsay it. This malignity is daily and hourly threatening the community at large slowly but steadily making its way onwards learning a back marked with broken hopes. Therefore, the necessity for appropriate and drastic action to eradicate this evil has become apparent.*

The State realising this bane and made efforts to abolish the pernicious system of 'flesh trade' in the larger interest of society. Putting spirit in Art. 23 of the Constitution which prohibits trafficking in human beings Suppression of Immoral Traffic in Women Act, which was later renamed as Immoral Traffic Prevention Act 1986 was passed. This Act realised the fact that prostitution is not confined to females and children only. The purpose of the enactment was to inhibit or abolish commercial traffic in women, men and children for the purpose of prostitution as an organised means of living. The aim was not to render prostitution *per se* a criminal offence or punish a woman merely because she is a prostitute. In Re Ratanmala, (AIR 1962 Madras 31 (33)) it was held that the Act was aimed at suppression of commercialised activity. What is punishable under the Act is sexual exploitation for commercial purpose so as to make a living thereon. However, the practice of prostitution in or in the vicinity of certain places such as places of public, religious, educational institution, hospitals etc. is made punishable. The Act deals with prostitution not merely as a social problem but a socio-economic problem therefore the provisions of the legislation are more preventive than punitive. Thus essentials, as per the law of prostitution are that a female must offer her body to indiscriminate intercourse with men, usually for hire.

It must be promiscuous intercourse for hire.

In *Gaurav Jain* V. *Union of India* (AIR 1997 SC 3021-A) a public interest litigation, the plight of women in the flesh trade and their progeny was highlighted. Directions were sought for rescue and rehabilitation of the children of these prostitutes. The Supreme Court issued directions for the prevention of induction of women in various forms of prostitution. It said that women should be viewed more as victims of adverse socio-economic circumstances rather than as offender in our society. Their rehabilitation in various welfare measures so as to provide them dignity of a person, means of livelihood and socio-economic empowerment, was directed.

In *Vishal Jeet* V. *Union of India* (1998 (3) Crimes 161) the Supreme Court suggested certain remedial measures. All governments (central and state) should be directed to eradicate child prostitution without giving room for any complaint of remissness or culpable indifference. Setting up a separate advisory committee consisting, *inter alia*, sociologist, criminologist, women's representatives for suggesting measures to be taken for eradicating specially child prostitution and social welfare programmes to be implemented for care, protection treatment, development and rehabilitation of young victims namely, children and girls. Provide adequate and rehabilitative houses manned by well qualified trained social workers, psychiatrists and doctors.

In the country presently, a debate is going on regarding licensing of prostitution. It is demanded by a section of the society that license be given to sex workers so that various health and safety measures can be imposed.

It is sincerely hoped that the Parliament will make suitable changes in the existing law so as to make it more effective for the purpose of eradicating prostitution a scar on the society.

Sexual Harassment at the work place

With the increase in the number of working women a new arena has opened in which the violation of human rights and the dignity of women is challenged, that is, sexual harassment at work place. Each such incident results in the violation of fundamental right of gender equality and right to life and liberty. It is a clear violation of rights under Articles 14, 15 and 21 of the Constitution. One of the logical consequence of such an incident is also the violation of victims' fundamental rights under article 19(1) (g) to practice any profession or to carry out any occupation, trade or business. The right depends on the availability of 'safe' working environment. Right to life means right to life with dignity. The primary responsibility for ensuring such safety and dignity through suitable legislation and the creation of a mechanism for its enforcement is of the legislature and the executive. When however the domestic law in the field is absent, there is a need to formulate effective measures and find an alternative mechanism to fill the legislative vacuum.

In *Vishaka* V. *State of Rajasthan* ((1997) 6 SCC 241), a writ petition was filed as a class action by certain social activists and NGOs with the aim of assisting in finding suitable methods for realisation of the true concept of gender equality and to prevent sexual harassment of working women in all work places through judicial process. The immediate cause for the filing of the writ petition was an incident of alleged brutal gang rape of a social worker in a village of Rajasthan.

Taking note of the fact that the present civil and penal laws in India do not adequately provide for specific protection of women from sexual harassment in work places and that enactment of such legislation will take considerable time, the Supreme Court held it necessary and expedient for employees in work places as well as other responsible persons or institutions, to observe certain guidelines to ensure the prevention of sexual harassment of women.

Incest

Incestuous relationship can be defined as sexual intercourse between two persons who are related closely or are within the prohibited degree of relationship. This prohibited degree of relationship includes full blood, half blood and uterine blood relationship and those by adoption. Although all personal laws prohibit marriage within the prohibited degree, the offence of incest is being committed rampantly within the four walls. Once initiated the incestuous activity continues unabated. This is more so because of the nature of the crime. Being closely related, the victims are forced to continue for fear or social ostracism. Incestuous offences are more heinous and action lies under the Indian Penal Code for rape. However, such crimes are rarely reported. The most common examples of such crimes are father—daughter or brother-sister relationship.

Paedophilia

The target here are children. Sexually perverted persons in such cases prefer sexual activity with children. Such an activity may be homo sexual or hetero sexual. It includes seducing, teasing and caressing children. Exhibition and Voyeurism are also varieties of this perverse sexual activities in which direct physical control may be secondary, the pleasure being almost exclusively due to visual contact that is seeing and showing of.

Police and Enforcement of Women's Rights

The role of police is very crucial in presenting crime against women. Police are still governed by the Police Act of 1861 and archaic pre-independence Police Manual. Too much emphasis is laid on the physical training and the sensitization aspect is totally neglected. The result is that sometimes the protectors of the society or the guardians often become the perpetrators of the crime. Be it Maya Tyagi's case or cases in Bihar, Kerala or Assam, large scale molestation by the police have been reported. The reason behind these can be seen from two point of view-first the ordinary policeman is ill equipped to deal with the difficult and sensitive cases of crime and secondly, the social background from which the policemen are drawn is itself found to be wanting in its behavioural attitude towards female sex. Thus there is no gainsaying that the police force needs fundamental changes in concept, attitude, training and above all motivation. There are also examples of individual initiatives like creation of special cells in Delhi to deal with crimes against women. The legal requirements also sometimes are a stumbling block for the enforcement machinery. Be it rape or dowry death gathering evidences are difficult. The professional frustration creeps in and a stage comes when such crimes take a back seat *vis-a-vis* more mundane enquiries. But even this does not absolve the negligence shown in lodging FIR, protecting the victims from harassment and taking complaints of domestic violence seriously. It would also be helpful if the victims are provided basic information relating to the offence and the help which could be available. Constant rapport between NGOs and police will also be effective.

National Commission for Women

The United Nations Commission on the Status of Women in its 25th report had recommended to all member states the establishment of National Commission or a similar body with a mandate to review, estimate and recommend measures and priorities to ensure equality between men and women and the full integration of women in all spheres of national life.

Acting on this resolution and on the demands of several women organisations, the Government of India set up a Committee in 1971 known as the Committee on the Status of Women to evaluate the changes that had taken place in the status of women as a result of the constitutional, legal and administrative measures adopted since independence and to examine the impact of the complex process of social change on various sections of women, and suggests measures to enable women to play their full and proper role in building up the nation. In order to ensure the implementation of various measures, the committee recommended the constitution at the center and in the states of a commission. It is indeed surprising to note that the government took sixteen years to give effect to the recommendation of the committee for a setting up a National Commission.

The Commission has been entrusted toinvestigate and examine all matters relating to safeguards provided for women under the Constitution and other laws, presentation to the central government annually and at other times reports upon the working of those safeguards. Making recommendations in such reports for the effective implementation of safeguards for improving the conditions of women by the union or any state; reviewing of the existing provisions of the Constitution and other laws affecting women and recommending amendments so as to suggest remedial legislative measures to meet any lacunae, inadequacies or shortcomings in such legislations. Taking up the cases of violations of constitutional provisions or other laws with the authorities; looking into complaints and taking suo-moto notice of matters relating to deprivation of women's rights, non implementation of laws meant to provide protection to women and also to achieve the objective of equality and development, non compliance of policy decisions, guidelines or instructions aimed at instigating hardships, ensuring welfare and providing relief to women and taking up issue arising out of such matters with authorities; calling for special studies or investigations into specific problems or situations arising out of discrimination and atrocities against women and identifying the constraints so as to recommend strategies for their removal. Undertaking promotional research; participating and advising on the planning process of socio-economic development of women; evaluating the progress of the development of women under Union and State; inspecting jails, remand homes, women's institutions or other places of custody of women; funding litigation involving issues affecting a large body of women and making periodical reports to the government.

Legal Aid

With reference to dignity of women it is very important that some legal assistance is given to women in need who want to have redress of their rights through court of law but their financial position does not permit them. In this context it is necessary to study the concept of legal aid. The Legal Services Authorities Act is one of the most important pieces of social legislation that parliament adopted in the 40th anniversary year of Indian Independence. The government both at the centre and in the states instituted expert committees on legal aid to make recommendation for evolving proper schemes and policies for legal services, delivery to the women and poor among them, the report of the expert committee on legal aid titled "Processual Justice to the People" submitted to the Union Government in May 1973 provided the foundational guidelines for later development of approaches, strategies and programmes in the matter of legal aid. In 1977 through the Constitution (Forty-second Amendment Act) Parliament inserted Article 39-A as a Directive principles of state policy which reads, "Equal justice and free legal aid. The state shall secure that the operation of the legal system promotes justice, on the basis of equal opportunity, and shall, in particular, provide free legal aid, by suitable legislature or schemes or in any other way, to ensure that opportunities for securing justice are not denied to any citizen by reason of economic or other disabilities."

The Supreme Court did not lag behind in actualizing the above Directive Principles. Through a series of judicial decisions the Supreme Court amplified the nature and scope of legal aid to the poor and finally interpreted it a fundamental right which the state is constitutionally obliged to provide for, to every indigent accused in criminal proceedings in *Sukh Das vs. Arunachal Pradesh.* Further, the court evolved the strategy of public interest litigation and allowed third parties to seek grievances on behalf of different classes of the poor. The Supreme Court and the High Courts even set aside technical rules of procedure, allowed invoking the judicial process through letters and telegrams, resorted to the "Commission system" for gathering facts and evidence on mattes of public interest and issued directions in the nature of affirmative action dispensing meaningful social justice to the poor and the needy. This silent revolution in the judicial process brought about the activist judges, public spirited lawyers, journalists, teachers and social workers to a new poverty jurisprudence which, those associated with the movement expected, would be given legislative approval through the Act.

Recommendations

After studying a variety of crimes violating the dignity of woman, which is an integral part of human rights, lets now try to answer the question, why the crimes against woman increase day by day? Why do the atrocities on women continue despite the fact that many laws have been enacted and sea changes have been introduced in the Indian Penal Code, Criminal Procedure Code and Indian Evidence Act. The number of changes brought about are shift in the burden of proof, enhancement in the punishment and a wide discretion given to the courts.

First and foremost reason is that mere passing of laws cannot check the increase in violence against women. It has to be backed by sensitization of the implementing machinery and the society as a whole. Certain recommendations to prevent crimes against women are given below :-

1. Establishment of special courts to deal cases of crime against women.
2. Setting up a time limit for the disposal of cases against women. Protracted criminal trials are an impediment in securing justice.
3. A new evidence code put together by the United Nations which says that prior sexual conduct or the victim shall not be admitted as evidence, should be strictly followed in India also.
4. Attempts should be made to prevent delay in investigations of crimes like rape, dowry deaths etc.

5. Capital punishment be awarded to persons committing the offence of rape. Marital rape should also be recognised.

6. Compensatory Board be established on the lines suggested by the Supreme Court for the victims of rape.

7. Gender sensitization to ensure equality and removing discriminatory practices should be brought about in society.

8. Demand of dowry should be a ground for obtaining divorce. A person convicted of an offence under Dowry Prohibition Act should face dismissal from service. To curb the practice of dowry deaths there is an urgent need to reinforce the punitive and preventive measures.

9. Legal literacy be given to women to make them aware of their rights.

10. In case of offences of incest and paedophilia punishment should be capital and the potential abusers and victims should not be left alone.

11. The police should avoid seeking conciliation between assailants and victims.

12. Law relating to sexual harassment of women at work place should be enacted.

13. Mandatory Crime (women) Cell should function in every police station and powers to given to DGP (Crime/women) to take *suo motu* cases for investigation. There is a need and scope for active and direct involvement of women police in investigation specially trained to deal with the offences relating to the women.

14. Attempts be made to find out ways and means to rescue girls from the clutches of person forcing immoral trafficking.

15. National Commission for Women be given more powers than just be a recommendatory body. Its branches should be established at every district so that violation of human rights of women can be reported.

16. Legal aid should be made available to women in distress.

17. Women NGOs should be involved in all decisions taken affecting women.

As is evidence, there has been a spate of legislations to protect her human rights and dignity. What is needed is that instead of amendments the existing laws should be enforced strictly last but not the least, it is only by a co-ordinate effort of sociologists, philosophers, administrators, jurists and police that crimes against women can be controlled.

References

1. Emancipation of Women - S. Lalitha, the Academy Law Review, Vol. 13:2, 1989.
2. A Saga of Victimology Sans Penology - Article by Justice V.R. Krishna Iyer from the book, Crimes against Women.
3. Constitution of India - V.N.Shukla.
4. Problem and Concerns of Indian Women - B.K.Pal.
5. Constitution V. Personal Law Article by Rani Jethmalani. LEX ET JURIS 21 June, 1986.
6. Women and the Law - G.B.Reddy.
7. Sexual Abuse of the girl child - Dr. Ashok Bhiman.
8. Protecting Women Against Violence - Flavia Agnes, EPW, April 1992.
9. Prostitution Laws - Ideological Dimensions and Enforcement Practices - Jean D'Cunha, EPW, April 1992.
10. Fighting Female Foeticide - A long way to go - Ravinder R.P., The Lawyers Collective, Aug. 1991.
11. Sati as a Religious Rite - Vasudha Dalmia Luderitz, EPW Jan. 1992.
12. 30 JILI, 1989.
13. 31 JILI, 1989.
14. 34 JILI, 1992.
15. CILQ, Vol. IX. 1996.

5

Victims of Rape and their Right to Live with Human Dignity and to be Compensated : Legislative and Judicial Responses in India

K.I. Vibhute

I. Introductory Remarks

Women in India, in spite of a prohibitive and severe punitive approach of criminal law and untiring efforts of a host of Women Organisations and the National Commission for Women (NCW), constituted under the National Commission for Women Act, 1990, to liberate them from the hitherto unjust social, political and economic subjugation and suppression, are being sexually exploited, abused and assaulted.

During the recent years, unfortunately, crimes against women are on increase. Amongst all the crimes against woman, rape[1] is the most heinous and inhuman act of sexual aggression and violence against a hapless woman. It not only amounts to a brutal attack on integrity and dignity of a woman but also unjustifiably disregards her legitimate control over her body. Invariably it shatters the foundations of the lives of the rape victims. It also impairs their capacity for personal relationships and alters their behaviour and values. "Raping a woman", according to Mr. L.K. Advani, the Union Home Minister, "is a much more heinous crime than murder, (because) rape reduces a woman to a state of living corpse."

However, in nineties, the inadequacy of the criminal law to protect women who have been victims of rape or assaults on their modesty was highlighted and severely criticised.[2] The Government of India, ultimately, on March 27, 1980 had to approach the Law Commission of India with a request to suggest, on top most priority basis, substantive as well as procedural reforms in law. In less than a month, on April 25, 1980, the Law Commission submitted its comprehensive Report[3] to the Union Law Minister. Subsequently, in 1983 the Parliament passed the Criminal Law (Amendment) Act, 1983 to give effect to majority of the proposals of the Law Commission.[4]

The Criminal Law (Amendment) Act of 1983, which came into effect in December 1983, *inter alia,* increased punishment for rape. It provides for mandatory minimum sentence of seven years imprisonment. It may be extended to a term of ten years or for life. However, it is permissible for a Court, for 'adequate and special reasons', to impose on a rape convict a lighter sentence of imprisonment for a term lesser than seven years.

However, a comparative glance, though painful and disgusting, at the pre and post-1983 Criminal Law Amendment Act (reported) incidence of rape in India[5] loquently demonstrates that the post-1983 criminal law has either desisted rapists or proved effective in combating rapes.

Mr. L.K. Advani and a few members of Parliament, in the recent past, probably, recalling the unsatisfactory performance of the post-1983 criminal law system and realising the unimaginable trauma of degradation and humiliation of victims of rape and of their (rape victims') immeasurable agony over acquittal of *de facto* rapists or allowing them to go with comparatively lighter punishments, have suggested that rapist be sentenced to death.

However, harsh punishments to perpetrators of rape (as revealed by the post-1983 statistical scenario) or sending them to gallows alone, though they, to some extent, might console the victims of rape, their relatives and women's groups, would hardly arrest the dangerously increasing incidence of rapes. It is a matter of common experience that efficacy of deterrent punishment, *inter alia*, is based on full proof investigation; speedy disposal and certainty of punishment. In India administration of criminal justice unfortunately is bridled with faulty, inadvertent or advertent, investigation of rape cases; undue delay in disposal of rape cases, and poor conviction rates.[6] Therefore, the suggested death penalty, like the prevailing mandatory seven years imprisonment and the permissible life imprisonment for rapists, in the present submission, would have a minimal impact.

Surprisingly, criminal and penal policy in vogue (as well as proposed) exhibits its insensitivity to the plight of rape victims and to their social, emotional as well as psychological rehabilitation. It also overlooks the pressing need to restore their untold trauma and humiliation experienced during the coercive sexual encounter. The Supreme Court of India aptly highlights such a pathetic plight of victims of rape in administration of criminal justice. Rape, according to it, does indeed a series of problems for the criminal justice system. "There are cries for harshest penalties", it laments, "but often times such cries eclipse the real plight of the victim."[7]

The Apex Court, highlighting defects of the existing criminal law system *vis-a-vis* victims of rape and indicating a set of broad parameters in assisting victims of rape, *inter alia*, directed the NCW to devise, in consultation with the Union Government, a scheme for the payment of compensation to rape victims.[8]

Against this backdrop, the present paper endeavours to highlight and evaluate the legislative scheme and judicial response to the right of victims of rape to live with dignity and to be compensated, by state or rapist or by both, for unlawful sexual attack and violence against them.

II. Compensating Victims of Crime: Legislative Policy

In India there is neither a comprehensive legislation nor a statutory scheme providing for compensation by state or offender to victims of crime. The state generally makes to the innocent victims of violence and major accidents, *ex-gratia* payment, which is not only *ad hoc* and discretionary, but also inadequate.[9]

Indian criminal law system does not provide for institutionalised payment of compensation to the victim of a crime for any 'loss' or 'injury'- physical, mental, or psychological-caused to him by the offender. Interestingly, the Law Commissioner felt it 'unwise' to create a legal right in favour of the victim to join in the criminal proceedings as a third party to avoid mixing up of civil and criminal proceedings, a confusion of issues and prolongation of the trial.[10] Similarly, it could not see any 'great advantage' in providing for 'duty to make amend for the harm caused' or 'payment of compensation to the victim of the offence' as an additional punishment. It favoured payment of compensation out of fine imposed on the offender.[11]

However, section 357 of the Criminal Procedure Code, 1973 (CrPC), *inter alia*, empowers a criminal court, *in its discretion*, to award compensation to any person for any 'loss' or 'injury' caused by an offence in those cases where 'fine' does or does not form part of the sentence imposed. And section 421, CrPC, empowers the criminal court passing a sentence of fine, *in its discretion*, to recover this amount by attachment and sale of any movable property of the offender and/or as arrears of land revenue from his movable or immovable property or both. However, it is not empowered to adopt either of the methods when the offender has undergone the whole of the imprisonment awarded in default of payment of the fine except for *special reasons* to be recorded in writing or where it has made an order for payment of *expenses or compensation out of the fine imposed under section 357, CrPC.*[12] In other words, undergoing of imprisonment in default of payment of fine does not operate as a *discharge* or *satisfaction* of the order of payment of fine if the court, for *special reasons* to be recorded, considers it necessary to recover the fine, and when the offender is ordered to pay *expenses or compensation out of the fine* imposed under section 357, CrPC. By virtue of section 431, CrPC, section 421, CrPC, along with its proviso, is equally applicable for recovery of a specified amount, which does not form part of the sentence ordered as compensation, under section 357(3) CrPC.

It is, thus, evident that the legislative response to compensating victims of crime is not impressive. The legislative scheme of award and payment of compensation to victims of crime neither mandates courts to compensate the victims (including rape victims) nor creates any legal right to be compensated in favour of victims of crime. It entirely leaves it to the sweet will of a criminal court to compensate victims of crime and to initiate and move legal machinery to recover the fine, out of which compensation is ordered, or the specified amount of compensation from the offender to pay it to the victims of the offence.

III. Compensating Victims of Crime: Judicial Response

It is also worth noting that courts in India have hardly invoked their statutory (discretionary) powers to compensate victims of crime. The Law Commission of India had not only admitted the fact that courts in India are 'not particularly liberal' in utilising these provisions,[13] but also observed: "it is regrettable that our courts do not exercise their statutory powers under this section as freely and liberally as could be desired."[14] A survey of the available empirical studies,[15] though scanty, also reveals very rare use of the legal provisions in awarding compensation and inadequacy of the compensation awarded. The Supreme

Court of India, when called upon to decide legality and propriety of compensation awarded under section 357, CrPC, by the Punjab and Haryana High Court; carried the same impression and appealed to all courts in India to exercise their powers liberally to meet the ends of justice in a better way. Referring to, and commenting on, sub-section 3 of section 357, the court observed :

> It is important provision but *Courts have seldom invoked it.* Perhaps due to ignorance of the object of it. It empowers the Court to award compensation to victims while passing judgment of conviction. In addition to conviction, the court may order the accused to pay some amount by way of compensation to victim who has suffered by action of accused. It may be noted that this power of courts to award compensation is not ancillary to other sentences but it is in addition thereto. *This power was intended to do something to reassure the victim that he or she is not forgotten in the criminal justice system.* It is a measure of responding appropriately to crime as well as reconciling the victim with the offender. It is, to some extent, a constructive approach to crimes.[16]

The court also failed to see any reason for the courts not directing compensation if the accused is in a position to pay it to the entitled injured persons. It, however, cautioned the courts not to award 'unduly excessive' compensation[17] and to first calculate the amount to be awarded and then impose a fine higher than the compensation.[18] The Apex Court also asserted that the requirement of social justice demands that heavy fine should be imposed in lieu of reduction of sentence to compensate the victims of crime.[19]

IV. Right to Live with Human Dignity VIS-A-VIS Victims of Rape : Constitutional Paradigm and Judicial Perspective

The Preamble of the Constitution of India assures, among other things, 'dignity of the individual'. And article 21 of the Constitution guarantees the right to life and personal liberty to individuals and mandates the State not to, except according to procedure established by law, deprive a person of his right. It reads:"No person shall be deprived of his life or personal liberty except according to procedure established by law."

The Supreme Court of India, through its inimitable judicial activism, added to the fundamental right to life and personal liberty a variety of positive dimensions and significant humanitarian contours basically to enhance the dignity and quality of the guaranteed right to life and to make 'life' something more than 'mere animal existence.' It, as early as in 1981, speaking through Bhagwati, J., delving into proper meaning and content of the fundamental right to life and stressing the need to interpret it in a broad and expansive spirit with a view to enhancing the dignity of an individual observed:

> ...[T]he right to life enshrined in Article 21 cannot be restricted to mere animal existence. It means something much more than just physical survival.... Every limb or faculty through which life is enjoyed is thus protected by Article 21.... [A]ny act which damages or injures or interfere with the use of, any limb or faculty of a person, either permanently or even temporarily, would be within the inhibition of Article 21.... [T]he right to life includes the right to live with human dignity and all that goes along with it,... Every act which offends against or impairs human dignity would constitute deprivation pro tanto of this right to live.[20]

On more occasions than one it, believing that human dignity is the basic factor amongst the human rights jurisprudence reflected in the Constitution of India and without it all human rights are meaningless, has also echoed and reasserted that right to life and personal liberty guaranteed under article 21 not only assures every one the right to live with human dignity but also includes all those aspects of life that make a life meaningful, complete and worth living.[21] According to it, the right to live with human dignity is the fundamental right of every citizen and the State is under the constitutional duty to provide at least minimum conditions ensuring human dignity.[22]

Against this backdrop, it is evident that article 21 guarantees a rape victim, who has been subjected to a non-consensual sexual encounter and a sexual violence, the right to live with dignity. Therefore, an unlawful intruder to her right to privacy and sanctity of her womanhood not only gives a serious blow to her supreme honour but also offends her self-esteem and interferes with the use of her body.

Recently, on December 15th, 1995 the Apex Court, in consonance with its hitherto widest possible humanitarian and humanised approach to article 21; its unquestionable stand that right to life is something more than a mere animal existence and it includes the right to live with human dignity, probably for the first time, has recognised that a non-consensual sexual assault on a woman goes against the hitherto judicially articulated and acknowledged basic tenets of article 21 and violates her right to live with dignity. Expressing its displeasure over the fact that the rape laws in vogue in India do not exhibit respect to, and recognition of, honour and the right to live with dignity of a woman, it observed:

Rape is thus not only a crime against the person of a woman (victim), it is a crime against the entire society. Rape is, therefore, the most hated crime. *It is a crime against basic human rights and is also violative of the victim's most cherished of the Fundamental Rights, namely, the Right to Life contained in Article 21*. To many feminists and psychiatrists, rape is less a sexual offence than an act of aggression aimed at degrading and humiliating women.[23]

It is pertinent to note that the Supreme Court of India, exercising its powers under Article 32 of the Constitution of India,[24] which enables a person, as a matter of right, to move the Supreme Court for the enforcement of his fundamental rights and mandates the Supreme Court to issue an appropriate direction, order or writ, for the enforcement of the fundamental rights guaranteed in Part III of the Constitution, and according a paramount constitutional significance to article 21, has forged a new tool and has devised a strategy unknown prior to 1983 to Public Law in India, by awarding compensation for violation of the right to life and personal liberty.[25] It, by liberalising the doctrine of *locus standi*, also allows a public spirited individual or organisation to move it for the enforcement of a Fundamental Right of a person or a class of persons who on account of his/their poverty, disability or social or economically disadvantaged position is/are unable to seek relief from the Supreme Court.

In *Delhi Domestic Working Women's Forum v. Union of India & Ors,*[26] (hereinafter referred to as the DDWWF), a public interest litigation espousing the pathetic plight of four domestic servants who were raped in a moving train, the Apex Court, on October 19th, 1994, highlighting ordeals of victims of rape and defects in the present criminal law system *vis-a-vis* victims of rape, outlined a set of broad parameters to assist them.[27] Relying heavily upon article 38(1) of the Constitution,[28] which directs the State, *inter alia* to strive to promote social order assuring socio-eco-political justice, and drawing inspiration from the Criminal Justice Act, 1991 of the United Kingdom, dealing with an institutionalised payment of compensation to victims of crime including rape, stressed the need to set up a Criminal Injuries Compensation Board (CICB) to compensate victims of rape. It also directed the NCW to formulate such a scheme within six months from the date of judgment (i.e. October 19th, 1994) and the Union of India to examine it and to take necessary steps for its implementation. The Apex Court also emphasised that courts in India should award compensation to rape victims on conviction of the offender and also by the proposed CICB even if the offender is acquitted.

However, NCW, for reasons best known to it, has not yet shown any positive response to the judicial direction.

Nevertheless, the Supreme Court of India, on December 15th, 1995, in *Bodhisattwa Gautam v. Subha Chakraborty*,[29] (hereinafter referred to as the *BOGA*), understandably, in the absence of a comprehensive compensation scheme, relying on the DDWWF and exercising its inherent powers (presumably under 142 of the Constitution of India) to do complete justice, *suo motu* gave effect to the right of a rape victim to claim compensation from the offender for violation of her constitutional right to live with human dignity. It, accordingly, directed Bodhisattwa Gautam to pay to Subhra Chakraborty a sum of Rs. 1000 every month as interim compensation during the pendency of the criminal trial and also to pay arrears of compensation at the same rate from the inception of the complaint filed by the victim.

However, it is very interesting to note that facts of the *BOGA* case, as outlined in the reported decision, disclose that the petitioner was *not at all charged for rape.* He was charged under ss. 312 (causing miscarriage); 493 (cohabiting with the girl deceitfully inducing a belief of lawful marriage); 496 (fraudulent marriage ceremony); 420 (cheating), and 498-A (subjecting his wife to cruelty) of the Indian Penal Code. It is, therefore, difficult to appreciate the judicial propriety in delving into rape laws and awarding interim compensation with arrears in the absence of an appropriate compensation scheme to assist victims of rape and to wipe out tears of unfortunate victims.

A commentator, doubting the judicial propriety of the BOGA case, rightly opined that the instant case, in the absence of qualitative discussion and argumentation, does hardly command a desired effect, acceptability and respectability.[30]

It is equally pertinent to note that recently the Gujarat High Court in *Mukeshbhai Nanubhai Patel v. State of Gujarat*,[31] (hereinafter referred to as the MUNA), a 1997 case identical to the *BOGA*, refused to rely upon the *BOGA* case as a precedent even though article 141 of the Constitution mandates it to follow the 'law declared by the Supreme Court of India.' Accordingly, it, on March 5th, 1997, quashed an order of one of its subordinate courts directing the accused of rape (petitioner) to pay Rs. 700 per month to the prosecutrix (alleged victim of rape) as interim compensation. Justifying its refusal to follow the *BOGA* principle the High Court observed:

> It may be noticed that it [BOGA] was not a case of rape, but of offences relating to marriage under Section 312, 493, 496, 498-A, causing miscarriage, cheating etc. but the Court *incidentally* considered the plight of the victim of rape and laid down parameters---. It may further be noticed that the *direction for maintenance does not form part of the said parameters.* Thus, for awarding interim maintenance to victim of rape, the positive suggestion of the Court is for setting up of a Criminal Injuries Compensation Board. The Court also directed the Government to prepare a scheme within a period of six months. The directions were given by the Apex Court as back as on 15.12.1995. It is unfortunate that the State Government has not yet prepared the scheme. Thus, *unless such a scheme is prepared and a Board is constituted, there is no provision under the Code of Criminal Procedure for awarding interim maintenance against the accused during the trial.*[32]

Probably referring to the provisions of article 141 of the Constitution, it observed:

> In the peculiar facts of Bodhisattwa's case, the Apex Court, in exercise of powers under Article 142 of the Constitution of India gave direction for interim maintenance. The Supreme Court in its plenary power under Article 142 of the Constitution of India can make any decree or order as may be found by it to be necessary for doing complete justice in any case or matter pending before it. Thus, when the Supreme Court in exercise of power under Article 142, pass an order that cannot be relied upon as precedent, unless the Apex Court so directs.[33]

A careful reading of the judicial opinions and deliberations on the right to live with dignity of victims of rape and their right to be compensated reflected in the *DDWWF*, the *BOGA* and the *MUNA* does not reveal any articulated judicial law making. These cases, on the contrary, unfortunately, confuse the issues and exhibit judicial inconsistency and contradictions. The *DDWWF*, in the light of article 38(1) of the Constitution, pleads for a CICB and directs the NCW to prepare, in consultation with the Central Government, within six months from the date of its judgment (19.10.94) a compensatory scheme to compensate victims of rape. Neither the Government nor the NCW, for reasons best known to them, have shown any positive response to the court's directive as yet. Both of them have preferred to exhibit their contemptuous silence and inaction. Similarly, the Apex Court, like in other numerous PIL, directives, demonstrates its judicial, rather hapless, tolerance to the executive apathy and insensitivity to its Directives and Orders.[34] It, in the *BOGA*, on the other hand, in its over judicial enthusiasm and activism read in the *DDWWF* the jurisdiction and power of a court trying an offense of rape to award, in the absence of either CICB or a Compensatory Scheme, compensation as well as an interim compensation. It, therefore, awarded an interim compensation (along with arrears) during pendency of a criminal trial, even though the accused was not charged for committing rape. The Gujarat High Court in the *MUNA* case, in the absence of convincing judicial reasoning in the *BOGA*, refused to read the right of a rape victim to be compensated and quashed an order of a lower court awarding an interim compensation.

Surprisingly, recently in August 1997 the Apex Court missed a unique opportunity to clarify and refine the judicial articulation of the right of a rape victim to live with dignity and to be compensated. In *Vishaka & Others v. State of Rajasthan*,[35] (hereinafter referred to as the *Vishaka*), the Court, *inter alia*, was called upon by certain social activists and NGOs to enforce the fundamental right to life and personal liberty of a working woman, who was an alleged victim of a brutal gang rape and of wilful delay in investigation and prosecution of the suspected rapists. The petitioners, among others, urged the Supreme Court, by exercising its jurisdiction under article 32 of the Constitution, 'to direct' the Union of India to appoint, in consultation with women's groups and individuals as well as lawyers, a Committee headed by the NCW 'to .prepare and submit guidelines for the prevention of sexual harassment and abuse of women' to it (the Union of India). The petitioners also prayed for an appropriate writ, order or direction against the State of Rajasthan directing it to pay rupees 10 lakhs to the alleged victim of gang rape.[36]

Curiously enough, the Apex Court on August 13th, 1997, speaking through Verma, the then Chief Justice of India, admitting that the immediate cause for the filing of (this) writ petition was an incident of alleged brutal gang rape of a social worker in a village of Rajasthan and reiterating that 'right to life means life with dignity', brushed aside the issue of the payment of compensation to the alleged victim of gang rape. It simply observed that *'that incident (alleged brutal gang rape) is the subject-matter of a separate criminal action and no further mention of it, by us is necessary.'*[37] It has not paid any attention to either the *DDWWF* and the *BOGA* or to the therein judicially recognised the right of a rape victim to be compensated for violation of her fundamental right to live with dignity.

Nevertheless, it, contrary to the petitioner's pray for setting up a Committee headed by the NCW to prepare and submit guidelines on sexual harassment and abuse of women, took upon itself not only the task of preparing a comprehensive set of 'guidelines and norms' with a view to protecting women from sexual harassment and to making their fundamental rights meaningful but also, unlike its hitherto judicial law making process, directed that these guidelines be treated as 'the law declared by the Supreme Court under article 141 of the Constitution'.[38] The Court read into, and placed heavy reliance on, the relevant International Conventions, Resolutions and norms to construe the fundamental rights of a woman guaranteed under articles 14, 15, 19(1)(g) and 21 of the Constitution and also to assume, in the absence of a domestic law, the legislative power 'to fill the legislative vacuum.' It felt (and rightly so) that relevant international Conventions not inconsistent with the fundamental rights and in harmony with their spirit can be used to read the constitutional guarantees and to enlarge their (fundamental rights) meaning and content.

Surprisingly, the Supreme Court in the *Vishaka*, for no convincing reasons, in the absence of a compensation scheme and the proposed CICB, has neither pursued the same line of judicial reasoning nor peeped into the Charter of United Nations and the International Bill of Human Rights [comprising the Universal Declaration of Human Rights (UDHR); the International Covenant on Economic, Social and Cultural Rights (ICESCR); the International Covenant on Civil and Political Rights (ICCPR), and the Optional Protocol to the International Covenant on Civil and Political Rights (OPICCP)] to also prepare a set of guidelines and norm and to devise an appropriate mechanism for the payment of compensation to 'fill the legislative vacuum' in the field of the payment of compensation to victims of rape. For devising an institutionalised compensatory mechanism to wipe out tears from the eyes of rape victims, the Apex Court could have also relied upon the Protection of Human Rights Act, 1993, which acknowledging that the human rights embodied in the ICCPR and the ICESCR are substantially protected in the Constitution of India, strives for better protection of human rights in India.

The central theme and concern of the International Bill of Human Rights and the Protection of Human Rights Act, in ultimate analysis, is the right to live with human dignity. The Charter of United Nations not only exhibits reaffirmed faith of the international community in fundamental human rights and human dignity but it also obliges every State to promote universal respect for, and observance of, human rights. And the UDHR, the ICCPR and the ICESCR, among other things, recognise that inherent dignity is the foundation of freedom and justice. The Protection of Human Rights Act, 1993 also defines the term 'human rights' to mean the rights relating to life, liberty, equality and dignity of the individual guaranteed by the Constitution or embodied in the ICCPR and the ICESCR and enforceable by Court of India.[39]

It is, thus, difficult to comprehend the judicial deliberations on, and the inconsistent judicial approaches to, the right to live with dignity of a victim of rape and her right to be compensated for infringement of her fundamental right exhibited in the *DDWWF* (1994), the *BOGA* (1995) and the *Vishaka* (1997). In the *DDWWF* the Court, directed the NCW, against its will, to frame an appropriate scheme, of course in consultation with the Central Government, to compensate victims of rape. While the same court in the BOGA, rejecting a Special Leave Petition, on its own, awarded interim compensation (along with arrears) to the rape victim, even though the petitioner, at no stage of his trial, was charged for rape. And the Court in the *Vishaka* felt it unnecessary to deal with the alleged brutal gang rape and the rape victim's right to be compensated for 'the incident' was 'the subject-matter of a separate criminal action,' even though the incident of rape, as admitted by the court itself, was 'the immediate cause for filing the writ petition' and the petitioners' prayed for an appropriate direction for the payment of compensation to the rape victim.

Further, the deliberations and judicial activism reflected in these cases unfortunately have either culminated in making the right to live with dignity of victims of rape more meaningful or theorising their right to be compensated by the rapist(s) or the State. These judicial pronouncements have also failed to render any justice to the victims of rape who or on whose behalf the compensation was sought in the respective cases. Hence, the right to live with dignity and to be compensated of a rape victim, despite the judicial sensitivity to victims of rape and their plight and acclaimed judicial articulation of the right to live guaranteed in article 21, is governed by the pre-*DDWWF* legislative framework.

V. Concluding Remarks

The Legislature, Judiciary, Government, and NGOs from other jurisdiction have been showing their immense sensitivity and concerted efforts to recompensate victims of rape and to wipe out their tears. The practice of requiring an offender (and/or the State) to pay his victim for the harm he caused has been at the heart of criminal jurisprudence of overseas nations.[40]

However, administration of penal justice is vague in India, which makes every possible effort to 'reform' and 'treat' offenders for their effective and meaningful resocialisation and reassimilation in the social mainstream from which they deviated, does not display equal concern to victims of rape and their right to live with human dignity. The fragmentary compensatory legislative scheme outlined in the Criminal Procedure Code, 1973 becomes more ineffective when courts in India, exercising their judicial discretion, show their unconvincing reluctance to invoke those legislative provisions to compensate victims of rape.

Recently, the Supreme Court of India in the *DDWWF*, probably realising the legislative and judicial apathy to victims of rape, not only read in article 21 of the Constitution of India the right of a rape victim to live with human dignity and to seek compensation for the deprivation of her dignity but also directed the NCW, in consultation with the Central Government, to formulate a compensatory scheme for victims of rape on the lines of British Criminal Injuries Compensation Scheme to enable victims of rape in India to seek compensation from the offender and the State. But unfortunately both, the NCW and the Central Government, have yet to inject the directive and noble sentiments of the Apex Court in our criminal justice system. Curiously, the Supreme Court also, for the arguments advanced in preceding paras, missed a unique opportunity in the *Vishaka* to fill in the legislative vacuum in the area of compensating victims of rape. Once again it has become evident that merely judicial directives, howsoever acclaimed and laudable they might be, are hardly capable to render justice in the absence of equally responsive executive response to these judicial directives. The *DDWWF* and the *Vishaka*, therefore, did either ameliorate the immeasurable plight of the victims of sexual violence (mentioned in these judicial pronouncements) or upheld their right to live with human dignity in true sense of the hitherto judicial articulation and spirit of article 21. They also hardly create any inroads in the legislative and judicial apathy and insensitivity to the right of victims of rape to live with human dignity.

Undoubtedly, it is a high time for the Legislature and the NCW to be sensitive to victims of rape and to act upon the directive of the Supreme Court of India. Such a move is imperative not only to make our criminal justice system at par with that of other civilised states but also to make sure that rape victims in India are treated with respect and are allowed to live with human dignity in consonance with the constitutional guarantee and mandate. A suitable legislation, therefore, be enacted at the earliest to provide for compensation to the victims of rape defining primarily the criteria for eligibility for seeking compensation from the offender and/or the state; mode of assessment of compensation and the composition, powers and responsibilities of the proposed CICB. The emerging human rights jurisprudence at home and abroad requires all public authorities to act not merely compatible with the global perception of the right to live with human dignity but also resort to all the possible means and strategies to strengthen and ensure the fundamental right to life and liberty of a rape victim.

References

1. Rape, as perceived under the Indian Penal Code, 1860 (IPC), in essence, involves a coercive non-consensual (as well as consensual in a set of specified circumstances) sexual intercourse with a woman. [See sec. 375, IPC.] A perpetrator is also subjected to severe punitive sanctions. [See sec. 376, IPC.]

2. For example see, An Open Letter to the Chief Justice of India, (1979) 4 SCC 17. Also see, Vasudha Dhagamwar, *Law, Power and Justice: The Protection of Personal Rights in the Indian Penal Code* (1992).

3. Law Commission of India, *Eighty-fourth Report on Rape and*

Allied Offences (1980).

4. The Criminal Law (Amendment) Act of 1983, among others, increased punishment for rape; distinguished gang rape and custodial rape and laid down stiffer penalties; distinguished rape on a pregnant woman and reversed the burden of proof in case of gang rape, custodial rape, rape on a pregnant woman.

5. For example, a number of rape cases reported in *Crime in India* (published by National Crime Records Bureau, Ministry of Home Affairs, Government of India) during the period of 1977-83 (seven years prior to the 1983 Criminal Law Amendment Act) and during the period of 1984-90 (seven years after the 1983 criminal Law Amendment Act came into force) reveals a disturbing trend in incidence of rapes in India. Rape cases reported during 1977-83 were: 4,058 (1977); 4558 (1978); 4,300 (1979) 5,023 (1980); 5,409 (1981); 5,427 (1982); and 6,019 (1983). Cases of rape reported during 1984-90, on the other hand, were: 6,740 (1984), 7,289 (1985); 7,952 (1986); 8,559 (1987), 9,099 (1988); 9,752 (1989) and 10,068 (1990).

   Recently, quoting the Union Home Ministry, it was reported that 3832 women were raped in the country during January-April 1998. [See, *Times of India*, Mumbai, August 04, 1998 p.8]. The latest *Crime in India* indicates that incidence of rape cases during 1996 over 1995 reported an increase of 7.9. [vide, *Times of India*, Mumbai, September 19, 1998 p.7.]

6. Recent revelation came from the Home Ministry in Parliament reveals that in 1995 out of 1,69,721 persons accused of rapes and molestation's only 33,315 persons were convicted by the trial courts. And against 1,95,436 persons arrested for the same offences in 1996, only 32,362 of them were convicted. [See *Times of India*, Mumbai, August 04, 1998 p.8].

7. *Delhi Domestic Working Women's Forum v. Union of India & Ors*, (1995) 1 SCC 14 (18).

8. See Ibid., pp. 19-21.

9. For details see K.I. Vibhute, Compensating Victims of Crimes in India: An Appraisal, 32 *Journal of the Indian Law Institute*

68 (1990).

10. Law Commission of India, *Forty-second Report: Indian Penal Code* 52 (1971).

11. *Id.* at 53. However, Justice R.L. Narasimham, one of the members of the Commission, in his separate note, strongly pleaded for direct reparation from the offender by imposing a duty on him to amend the harm caused. (*id.* at 381-82).

12. Sec. 421(1)(a) r.w.cl. (3).

13. Law Commission of India, *Forty-first Report: The Code of Criminal Procedure*, vol. 1, p.356 (1969).

14. *Supra* n. 11 at 52.

15. See, S.G. Pradhan, Compensation for the Victims of Crimes of Violence, 5 *Police Science Congress* 70 (1966); S.G. Pradhan, Compensation for Victims of Crime, 12 *Indian Police Journal* 36 (1965); V. Tuli, Compensation of Victims of Crimes, 3 *Police Research and Development* 1 (1979). Also see, Rajan, *Victimology in India: An Introductory Study* 70-72 (1981); Bureau, Police Research and Development, New Delhi, and Research and Documentation Centre, Bomaby, *A Monograph on Compensation to Victims of Crime* (1978).

16. *Hari Kishan & State of Haryana v. Sukhbir Singh*, AIR 1988 SC 2127 at 2137. Emphasis added.

17. *Sarwan Singh v. Punjab*, AIR 1978 SC 1525.

18. *Palaniappa Gounder v. Tamil Nadu*, AIR 1977 SC 1323.

19. See *P.P. Sah v. Bihar*, AIR 1977 SC 704; *N.B. Pant v. State,* AIR 1977 SC 892; *Guruswami v. Tamil Nadu*, AIR 1979 SC 1177; *Hari Kishan & State of Haryana v. Sukhbir Singh, supra* n.16; *Palaniappa Gounder, ibid; Sarwan Singh, supra* n. 17.

20. *Francis Coralie Mullin v. Administrator, Union Territory of Delhi,* AIR 1981 SC 746 at pp. 752-753.

21. See *PUDR v. Union of India*, AIR 1982 SC 1473; *Bandhua Mukti Morcha* v. *Union of India*, AIR 1984 SC 802, *Olga Tellis v. Bomaby Municipal Corporation,* AIR 1986 SC 180; *Suk Das v. Union Territory of Arunachal Pradesh,* AIR 1986 SC 991; *Centre for Legal Research v. State of Kerala*, AIR

1986 SC 1322; *State of Himachal Pradesh v. Umed Ram*, AIR 1986 SC 847; *Delhi Transport Corpn. v. DTC Mazdoor Congress,* AIR 1991 SC 101; *Unni Krishanan v. State of Andhra Pradesh,* (1993) 1 SCC 645 and *Vishakha v. State of Rajasthan, AIR* 1997 SC 3011.

22. *Vikram Deo Singh v. State of Bihar,* AIR 1988 SC 1782.

23. *Bodhisattwa Gautam v. Subhra Chakraborty,* (1996) 1 SCC 490 at 500.

24. 32. *Remedies for enforcement of rights conferred by this Part-* (1) The right to move the Supreme Court by appropriate proceedings for the enforcement of the rights conferred by this Part is guaranteed.

    (2) The Supreme Court shall have power to issue directions or orders or writs, including writs in the nature of *habeas corpus, mandamus,* prohibition, *quo warranto* and *certiorari*, whichever may be appropriate, for the enforcement of any of the rights conferred by this Part.---

    Article 226, *inter alia* also empowers the High Court of a State to issue an appropriate direction, order or writ against 'any person, authority or government' for the enforcement of the fundamental rights.

25. See *Rudal Sah v. State of Bihar,* AIR 1983 SC 1086; *Sebastian M. Hongray v. Union of India,* AIR 1984 SC 904; *Bhim Singh v. State of J&K*, AIR 1986 SC 494; *Saheli v. Commissioner of Police*, AIR 1990 SC 513; *Nilabati Behera v. State of Orissa,* AIR 1993 SC 1960. Also see, K.I. Vibhute, Compensatory Jurisdiction of the Supreme Court of India - A Critiquè, 21 *Journal of Constitutional and Parliamentary Studies* 136 (1987).

26. *Supra* n. 7.

27. *Ibid*. pp.19-20.

28. Art. 38(1): The State shall strive to promote the welfare of the people by securing and protecting as effectively as it may a social order in which justice, social, economic and political, shall inform all institutions of the national life.---

29. (1996) 1 SCC 490 (503).

30. See, K.N. Chandrasekharan Pillai. A Comment on Bodhisattwa Gautam v. Subhra Chakraborty, 20 *Academy Law Review* 205 (1996).

31. 1998 Cri.L.J. 194.

32. *Ibid.*, at pp.195-196. Italics supplied.

33. *Ibid.* at 196.

34. See generally, S.K. Agrawala, *Public Interest Litigation in India: A Critique* (1985).

35. AIR 1997 SC 3011.

36. For excerpts of the Writ Petition, see *Kali's Yug*, August 1998, pp. 10-15.

37. See *supra* n. 35 at p.3012. Emphasis supplied.

38. See K.I. Vibhute, Law Declared by the Supreme Court of India: Some Reflections on its Meaning an Scope, 9 *Journal of the Bar Council of India* 52 (1982).

39. See sec. 2(1) (d) and (f).

40. Generally, see K.I. Vibhute, Victimology: An International Perspective, 14 *Cochin University Law Review* 145 (1990).

6

How Far Personal Laws Have Hampered Dispensation of Justice to Women

Ms. Parul Modi

1. Gender Justice

Dispensation of Justice to women world over is an age-old problem dating back to the origin of the human society on this planet. Human Society has always remained male dominated and mainly patriarchal in social character even after man began to progress in organising his social order. The natural consequence of this state of things was the domination of the males over females in almost all social dealings.

Recently the question of gender Justice has assumed importance in our country on account of a sort of politicals agitation for the implementation of about half a century old Constitutional directive of Article-44 which directs the State "to endeavour to secure for the citizens a uniform civil code throughout the territory of India". It cannot be denied that we have not "endeavoured" even to undertake a serious debate" to secure uniform Civil Code" for all our citizens for fear of touching the sensibilities of status quoists of the defenders of gender injustice which almost every personal law, usage and custom prevailing in our Country has implicated on our society singe ages. Our vote catching politics has prevented us from giving serious thought to the necessity of reforming our age old and worm out social inequalities and reprehensible male mentality of treating our womanhood as no better than a part of our proprietory rights. And the tragedy is that all this is done in the name of "protecting" our so called "religious" practices and "culture". It is time now to shed this hypocracy and face the realities of the situation.

2. Gender Justice De Hors Article - 44

At the outset, it is necessary to clarify that dispensation of justice to our womanhood has not much to do directly with the implementation of Article-44. It is undoubtedly true that the implementation of Article-44 would have surely brought about substantial dispensation of Justice to women, but even without Article-44, our Constitution has sufficient vital provisions in the form of Articles-13, 14 and 15 to prevent inequality or unequal treatment purely on the ground of sex and thus to eliminate gender in justice from all personal laws and customs prevailing in the Country. Even if the Constitutional progressive directive of Article-44 was not there on the Statute book we could have eliminated gender injustice by invoking the equality clauses of Articles-13, 14 and 15 of our Constitution, and this happens to be the main purpose of my key vote address today.

3. Constitutional Provisions for Justice

Let us, therefore, straight away to go to these wholesome provisions of our Constitution.

Article-13 (1) says that all laws in force in India immediately before the commencement of the Constitution shall be void to the extent to which they are inconsistent with the Fundamental Rights conferred by Part-III of the constitution clause-(3) (a) of this Article says that the word "law" used above includes "Custom or Usage" having the force of law. This Article may be read along with Article-372 which provides that all 'laws" in force in India immediately before the commencement of the Constitution shall continue in force till altered or repealed, but such a continuation *is subject to other provisions of the Constitution*. These "other provisions" are contained in Articles-13, 14 and 15. So, personal laws and custom which are "laws" administered by Courts immediately before the commencement of the Constitution are subject to Articles-13, 14 and 15 and can continue only, if they are not inconsistent with our Fundamental Rights described in Part-III.

In order to know whether some of our personal laws are consistent with our Fundamental Rights of equality and want of discrimination purely on the ground of sex. We shall have to go to Article-14 and 15. Article-14 says that the State shall not deny to *any person* equality before law or equal protection of the laws.

So, when the Courts in India administer and execute those clauses of personal law which deny our females equality and protection which is equal to their males, we are infringing the mandate of Article-14.

Article-15 goes a step further and provides that the State shall not discriminate against any Citizen on the grounds *only of* religion race, caste, sex, place of birth or any of them.

So whenever we find that our female citizens are discriminated against in the matters of personal laws such as marriage, divorce, inheritance and succession, adoption, guardianship and certain other proprietry rights simply because of their sex or gender we are infringing the mandate of Article-15.

The above discussion would make it clear that the question of gender justice under our personal laws can be easily resolved, if we are so inclined, without even touching the salutory mandate of Article-44. Implementation of Article-44 is bound to take some time due to the resistance of obscurantists, religious bigots and political manoeuvres, of power thirsty politicians. If we are really serious in our efforts to bring dispensation of justice to our mothers and sisters, the easiest course is to give a legal challenge to the obnoxious provisions of our personal laws which create gender injustice under articles-13, 14 and 15 in the Courts of law.

4. Review of Personal Laws

Let us now shortly review how far our personal laws have hampered dispensation of justice to women. The history of this aspect is rather long and tedious and, therefore, we shall skip over some details and touch only broad aspects of every personal law to show how they have hampered dispensation of justice to our women.

5. Hindu Law

5.1. Concept of Equality

Let us first take up the position of females under Hindu Law. Hindu Law like every other personal law evidences two trends - One trend which is based on the doctrine of equality, is represented by Vedic thinkers who were intellectual leaders of the Society. The other trend is represented by those who ruled and worked the Social order and who thereby acquired some vested interests to safeguard their hold on the society. The former emphasised ideological content of human existence, while the later came to emphasise material aspects of life and consequently degenerated in ideological approach. Rigveda says:

> "No one is superior or inferior. All are brothers. All should strive for the interest of all and should progress collectively."[1]

Atharva Veda says :

> "All have equal rights in food and water. The yoke of life is placed equally on the shoulders of all.
>
> All should live to-gether with harmony supporting each other like spokes of a wheel connecting rim and hub."[2]

This concept of equality which was part of "Dharma" (law) degenerated in the hands of a caste ridden society with all the perversities of superiority and inferiority complexes. Though no sacrament or ceremony was considered complete without the presence of ones wife, and though God was worshipped in form of the Divine Mother, the social position of average women in general in later Hindu Society gradually degenerated and reached its ebb during about 700 Years of Muslim rule.

5.2. Matrimonial Relationship

Inseparability of matrimonial relationship was the firm foundation of original strict Hindu law because marriage was, and is, still considered a "Sanskara" - a sacrament which was at the root of family life and the consequent development of national culture and ethos. Marriage under Hindu Law is never considered a mere contractual Social arrangement for satisfying carnal and material desires of worldly existence. It was considered a bondage of souls who were supposed to endeavour jointly in search of "Dharma, Artha and Kama." The bridegroom is at the time of marriage ceremony, asked by the father or a guardian of the bride:

> "You shall not transgress her in the attainment of Dharma, Artha and Kama."

The bridegroom is expected to promise :

> "I shall not transgress."[3]

The Seventh step which the bride takes in the essential marriage ceremony asks the bride to be her husband's "Sakha" i.e. a friend (Sakha Saptapadi Bhava).

Thus the concept of marriage in Hindu Law is the concept of Unity of two souls by a permanency of relationship is an endeavour to achieve Dharma, Artha and Kama for both.

5.3. Remarriage when Allowed

Though inseparability of marriage bond has treated as

fundamental, remarriage by husband and also by wife was permitted under certain conditions.

Manu permits second marriage by a husband in following conditions only—

He says:

> "A wife not found child bearing may be superseded in the eighth year. She, whose all children dies, in the tenth year, she who bears only daughters, at the eleventh year, She who is quarrelsome—without delay."[4]

Though these conditions do not prescribe unfettered freedom to a husband to take a second, they do disclose a bias in favour of males as the wife was considered responsible for not bearing any child or bearing only female child.

According to Vasistha, Narada and Manu even a wife could take second husband under certain circumstances e.g. when her husband is lost, dead, has become a religious ascetic or is found impotent and other such circumstances.[5]

However, gradually even this limited latitude to females to remarry was gradually tightened by social customs and usages.

Vasistha permitted an abducted woman to be given in marriage to another man. To the modern mind, the concept of permanence of matrimonial bond and liberty both the husband and wife to remarry under certain circumstances would appear contradictory, but that was not so in the society which was both polygamous and polyandrous.

Most of these old concepts of permanency of marriage and liberty to remarry when the other spouse has not taken divorce have been abolished now after drastic amendments made in 1976 to the Hindu Marriage Act providing for voluntary divorce. Now monogamy in the rule and basis of a valid Hindu marriage and matrimonial rights of a Hindu female are put at par with her husband.

5.4. Inroads on Hindu Personal Laws in Favour of Females

Hindu reformers and thinkers have been able to counteract Hindu orthodoxy with the result that the whole social complexion of Hindu Society has become more responsive to modern needs and gender justice. There have been many legislative inroads on some of the most important fundamentals of Hindu law, but we may take note here of only those which have been made in favour of females :-

(1) Hindu Widows Remarriage Act, 1856 under which marriage of Hindu widow in certain cases was declared legal.

(2) Hindu Law of Inheritance (Amendment) Act, 1928 under which son's daughter, daughter's daughter, sister and sister's son were given inheritance rights. However, this Act stands now repealed by more comprehensive and liberal Hindu Succession Act, 1956.

(3) Child Marriage Retraint Act, 1929 put restriction on marriage of children – including female children below the prescribed age.

(4) Hindu Woman's Right to Property Act, 1937 which is now repealed by Hindu Succession Act, 1956.

(5) Hindu Married Women's Right to Separate Residence and Maintenance Act, 1944 – now replaced by Hindu Adoption and Maintenance Act, 1956.

The legislative dents made on strict Hindu Law by these and other legislations did not mitigate the gender injustice to Hindu females. They were merely patch-work legislations which had no comprehensive outlook of "Samatwa" (equality) which was the basic concept of ancient Indian culture. Substantial progress is, however, made after the Constitution came into force as will be clear from the following enactments introduced by Parliament :-

(1) Special Marriage Act, 1954 providing for marriage by registration.

(2) Hindu Marriage Act, 1956 as amended by the Act of 1976 providing for divorce by consent.

(3) Hindu Succession Act, 1956 which took a great stride by converting the limited estate of a woman into an absolute one and providing equal share of daughters along with sons in the property of their father, provided he has died intestate.

(4) Hindu Minority and Guardianship Act, 1956.

(5) Hindu Adoption and Maintenance Act, 1956.

It is apparent that under earlier personal laws of Hindus a woman occupied a very dependent financial position in the family and her rights to hold and dispose of property were very limited. This was the natural consequence of the principle of "Patria potestas", which though long ceased to be recognised, had its lingering shadows on the social structure of Indian Society as a whole.

However, as observed in the introductory note on Hindu Marriage Act in Mulla's `Principles of Hindu Law' Hindu was at no time in its long history static, but was impiric and progressive. It was only after the reduction of India Law by the British and because of their policy of non-interference in matters of personal law that it ceased to grow with the times. Its principal characteristics of elasticity and assimilation were ignored and the degree of rigidity that was given to it was such that legislation alone could cope with the felt necessities of the times."[6]

The enactments to which were introduced in an attempt to reform Hindu Law were substantially progressive and took great steps forward in improving the Status of females in matrimonial matters and inheritance.

5.5. Gender Justice in Hindu Matrimony

Special Marriage Act, 1954 allowed all Communities to get their marriage registered under that Act which is modelled on the modern notions of monogamy, divorce and desertions. Hindus could avail of its provisions freely but that was no more necessary as soon the Hindu Marriage Act came into force, on 18th May, 1955 and amended in 1976. This resulted in violent break with the past giving proper response to the fast changing social concepts of the modern age.

Following Clauses are worth notable in context of the principle of gender equality :-

(1) A broad connotation of the word "Hindu" has been accepted ignoring divisions of caste, creed and religion by including even those like Jains and Buddhists who do not subscribe to some very basic tenets of Vedic religion. Clause (c) of Section – 2(1) lays down that it is to be presumed until contrary proved, that any person who is not a Muslim, Christian, Parsee or Jew by religion is governed by this Act. This widens the scope of choice, interaction and integrity in the social order.

(2) Principles of monogamy is firmly established.

(3) Bigamy is rendered punishable.

(4) Reliefs by way of Divorce, judicial separation, declaration of nullity are equally available by males and females.

(5) Provision is made for alimony pendant lite, permanent alimony and maintenance.

Most of the fundamental notions regarding basic principles are based mainly on the English Act.

For making these reforms and for achieving a measure of gender equality in matrimonial matters, the reformers had to encounter some resistence from Hindu Orthodoxy, but "Hindu" Society has never discarded its fundamental capacity to be elastic and assimilative of new ideas.

5.6. Snag in Gender Equality - Remedy

However, we should take note of the snag in gender equality in matrimonial matters created by Sub-Section (2) of Section – 2 of the Hindu Marriage Act, 1955, which exempts members of a Scheduled Tribe from the provisions of the Act. The result is that male members of a Scheduled Tribe continue obnoxious and unmoral practice of polygamy under the cover of their custom and usage.

In my opinion, all that Sub-Section (2) of Section-2 of the Act does is not to apply the provisions of the Act to members of Scheduled Tribe unless Central Government otherwise directs, but this position does not obliterate the equality clauses enshrined in Articles-13, 14 and 15 of the Constitution, under which such an unequal treatment purely on the ground of sex can be challenged as unconstitutional even if it has the sanction of custom or usage.

5.7. Hindu Succession and Gender Equality

Hindu Succession Act of 1956 is a great step forward in bringing up the Status of females on the question of succession to intestate property of "Hindu".

The principle reform that was called for in matters of succession was equable distribution between male and female heirs and the enlargement of the "limited estate" rights of Hindu women in family property into full ownership rights.

The scheme of the Act applies to the estate of a "Hindu" dyeing intestate. Sections – 8 to 13 lay down general rules of succession to males which are based on the principle of gender equality recognising equals rights of females along with males, without distinction.

Sections-15 and 16 have separate rules for succession to the property of female intestate, recognising even the parents of the female and the heirs of her mother.

5.8. Discrimination Still Persists: Its Remedy

Inspite of all these attempts of gender equality on the question of succession, the concept of Hindu Co-parcenery still persists with the result that the reforms have not been able to provide gender equality of the females in the property which is governed by Mitakshara Co-parcenery property with the result that, except for the provisions of Section-6, (to which reference will be presently made) the superior male position in co-parcenery property still persists. A female of a coparcenery has no status to demand partition as she has no share in her personal capacity.

However, Section-6 of the Act makes a big dent even in this position as is it confers right on certain preferential heirs to claim partition upon the death of co-parcener through whom they are claiming, some of such preferential heirs are female relatives of Class-I including daughter, predeceased daughter's son and predeceased son's daughter.

Retention of gender inequality in ancestral coparcenery property is the result of continued recognition of the doctrine of survivorship in joint family scheme. The best solution would have been to abolish the system by proper legislation. But if this is not done and if this offends the doctrine of Equality, as if apparently does, it can also be challenged in Court by invoking Articles -13, 14, 15 of the Constitution.

5.9. Hindu Adoption

Under the law prevailing before Hindu Adoption and Maintenance Act, 1956 was passed, only a male Hindu had a right to adopt a son. Wife could adopt a son to her husband but she could do so on express consent of her husband. In some parts of the Country she did not require such consent. But a wife could never adopt a son to *herself*, because all adoptions were mean for husband. Only a male (son) could be adopted lot a daughter. Such were the inequitable provisions previously.

Now all these inequalities are removed by the present

Act. Rights of women are put on equal footing with those of males in this branch of law. Act now provides for the adoption of girls and a woman can adopt for herself also.

In almost all respects the Act is observing the equality principles and is considered to be a good piece of legislation for a "uniform code" for all communities on the subject. Maharasthtra Legislature has recently passed a uniform legislation on this subject.

5.10. Maintenance under Hindu Law

Before Hindu Married Women's Right to Separate Residence and Maintenance Act, 1946, a wife had no right to separate residence or maintenance unless she satisfied the Court that her husband had refused or neglected to maintain her or was guilty of misconduct. The Act of 1946 liberalised the law in favour of wife but not to the required extent. Now the Act of 1956 entitles the wife to live separately from her husband and claim maintenance if he has deserted or neglected her, is cruel or suffering from leprosy, has another wife or a concubine, has ceased to be a Hindu by conversion etc. This act also provides for the maintenance of a daughter in law in certain circumstances and also of other dependent relatives as enumerated in Section-21. The heir who inherits the property of the deceased who is bound to maintain is also legally obliged to maintain out of the estate inherited by him.

Thus even the law of maintenance is made equitable and drawn on modern concepts.

5.11. Hindu Guardianship

Hindu Minority and Guardianship Act, 1956 does not codify the entire law of guardianship but is only supplementing the provisions of Guardian and Wards Act, 1890, and is principally intended to crystallize the persons who are entitled to act as natural and testamentary guardians. However, the provisions of the Act have a male bias in as much as the father is considered the natural guardian of legitimate children and after him, the mother. In case of illegitimate children reverse is the position. But the custody of children under five years of age is ordinarily to be kept with mother.

5.12. Thus the Hindu Code is amended by the above referred enactments has substantially progressed towards securing gender justice and equality and whatever unjust provisions are found and noted above can be removed by invoking the provisions of Article-13, 14 and 15 of the Constitution.

6. Muslim Personal Law

6.1. Degeneration of Equality Doctrine

Muslim rule in India actually started after the defeat of Prithviraj Chauhan by Mohamad Ghori in the year 1192 A.D. and ended with the end of Moghul dynasty in 1858 with Bahadur Shah II. It thus lasted for more than 750 years in most of the parts of our country. These Rulers were required to rule in conformity with the tenets of Quran as interpreted by their Ulemas (Theologians) as most of them were illiterate or semi-literate in their own scriptures. Kingship in Muslims of India was mainly dependent on comparative strength of power among the members of royal family and circle, as there was no scriptural guidance in form of a rule for peaceful succession. Under Muslim Law non-Muslims were treated as secondary citizens who were not considered in law as equal to Muslims and were called "Zimmis". Their evidence was inadmissible as against Muslims; they had to pay additional tax called "Jizya" and even other normal taxes were to be paid at double the rates than what a Muslim would pay. If they did so and accepted the suzerainty of the Muslim ruler they had a right of protection of their personal laws.[7]

This position was cased when the Ruler, as a good administrator, understood the importance of the good will of his subjects. Moghal Emperor Akbar was a ruler of great understanding and wisdom and his liberal policies started a process of social and cultural integration of Hindus and Muslims—much to the chargin and annoyance of Muslim fundamentalists of the day. He carried the following reforms of liberalisation :-

(1) Repealed discriminate law of citizenship and brought unanimous system of justice for all.

(2) Abolished Hindu Pilgrim Tax and "Jizya".

(3) Permitted Hindus and Christians to build temples and churches.

(4) Permitted forcibly converted persons to Islam to return back to their original faith.

(5) Repealed the law which imposed death sentence for criticising Islam or the conduct of the Prophet.

(6) Prohibited Sati by compulsion.

(7) Modified Muslim personal law by providing that a Muslim can take only one wife unless she is barren.

(8) Prohibited marriage between cousins and of a boy below 16 years and girl below 14 years.[8]

Thus in many respects Akbar was more progressive than even the modern Muslim States of the world. But this liberal and reformist process was gradually reversed by his successors. This process of reversal was complete after Aurangazeb snatched the Delhi throne by treachously killing his brothers and imprisoning `his' father. The process of gender justice and equality, for which a liberal and reformist attitude is a must, thus ran only for a few years during the long Muslim reign of more than the quarter of a millennium in India. The psychological impact on Hindu Society was to conserve more by frightening its caste system and making their social customs and usages more rigid. Though Hindu Society was male dominated and a woman was financially more dependent on males the Hindus had developed a culture which gave her a divine status of the Universal Mother and no sacrament was perfect without the presence of wife. She had free intellectual discourses in the assembly of the learned and never valid her face to show respect to the males. With the impact of long rule of Muslim Orthodoxy this position in the status of women's was greatly changed in the reverse gear.

Even after the advant of the British Rule the position remained the same upto the time of reformists like Raja Ram Mohan Roy and Lord Bentik since the British Rulers were more interested in non-integration of the two main communities of India to keep their imperialist hold tight, they intentionally preserved and encouraged the personal laws of all communities. So, except for some social reforms like abolition of Sati, some liberal interpretations of Dharma Shastra by Courts and some property right reforms through legislation in thirties, nothing comprehensive was done even during the British Rule before the advent of political freedom, for doing gender justice.

6.2. Resistance to Reforms in Muslim Personal Law

No law of the land whether personal or otherwise can afford to remain static and must change according to the social needs, local environment and national ethos at a given point of time. Social Laws are meant to serve the day to day material and moral requirements of the people whom they govern and have little to do with religious practices which are mainly concerned with metaphysics and spiritual upliftment. It is gross pollution of metaphysics and religious philosophy to mix them with things which are purely temporal and secular. Muslim theologians of India have missed this line of thinking and have preferred to adhere to their fanatic and dogmatic belief that their own understanding and interpretation of Quranic verses is the last word of "Allah" (God) which cannot be changed at any time, under any circumstances and at all places even though their accepted interpretation is found to be per se absured, illogical and even anti-social. The result is that the Muslim personal law which was originally evolved in a foreign country like Arabia in different set of social and political circumstances, and which came to be interpreted by different schools of Islam differently could not be reformed to suit the changed social conditions of Muslim Society in India. Muslim clergy and Politicians joined hands in maintaining their orthodox hold on those large segments of Indian Muslim population who has remained ignorant, illiterate or semi-literate but highly religious.

It cannot be disputed that strict Muslim personal law is highly detrimental to gender justice and is completely male dominated. 750 years of Muslim rule and subsequent British Rule which was interested in encouraging separatist tendencies of personal law did not result in any improvement in the legal position of Muslim women in India, even though other Muslim Countries of the world like Egypt, Algeria, Turky, Pakistan, Malayasia, Indonesia and even some middle East Arab Countries reformed their personal law and tried to mitigate sex inequality.

6.3. Reformist Movement

There are, however, strong reformist trends emerging from Muslim intellectuals of both the sexes. But they have to work against great odds which are at times aggressive, intolerant and even violent. It is our national duty to encourage these trends because we cannot afford to allow our crores of mothers and sisters to remain in ignomy and crude male domination. Social revolutions the world over have never been made without tears and blood shed by the resistance of vested interests. The role played by Muslim Law Board in Shah Bano Case and on the question of triple talak is, to put plainly and frankly, not only anti-social but also anti-national and shows that vested interests can never be contained without strong resistance and sacrifice.

6.4. Orthodox Criminal Jurisprudence Superceded

Law of Evidence of Orthodox Muslim personal law was highly irrational and punishment prescribed for offences very cruel and full of unjust treatment of females. Some of the rules of evidence were as under :-

(1) No capital sentence could be inflicted on a Muslim on evidence of a non-Muslim.

(2) Evidence of one Muslim was considered equivalent to two non-Muslims.

(3) Evidence of *two women* was considered equivalent to that of *one man*.

(4) Evidence must be direct, not circumstantial. So in cases of rape offences *eye witnesses* were necessary.

(5) For proving theft evidence of two men or one man and two women was necessary.

(6) Evidence of women was inadmissible to prove charge of murder in all cases of Kisa (i.e. retaliation for cutting limb for limb or committing murder for murder by private victims) and Hadd (i.e. punishment for offences like Apostacy, Adultery, intoxication, theft, Robbery etc.)[9]

Death sentence was required to be executed be heirs of the deceased.

Warren Hastings critised this system as "barbarous"[10] and undertook reforms by invoking powers of East Indian Company under different charters. He prepared a scheme for judicial administration on 15th August, 1972, and restored the Status of Hindu and Muslim personal laws. Gradually the utility of justice, equity and good conscience as practiced in English Courts came to be incorporated, Muslim Criminal Law began to be modified. Under Regulation VI of 1832 Fatwa of Muslim Officers were dispensed with and finally in the year 1860 Indian Penal Code was enacted. This, together with Indian Evidence Act, 1872 and Criminal Procedure Code, 1973 completely superseded the personal law of Indian Muslims in administration of criminal justice. The obnoxious system of denegration of female status in criminal jurisprudence was given a death blow but orthodoxy could not raise its head and suffered the same as it was done by the strong hand of a foreign imperial power.

6.5. Civil Laws other than Personal Laws also made Uniform

For administrative facilities, the British brought uniformity in all other civil laws except the personal laws of marriage, divorce and succession. The obvious reason was that the process of social integration which was started by far sighted national instinct of Akbar the great did not suit imperialist aims of the British Rulers who saw their security in India only by keeping the Indian people divided.

Even after the British left the persons in power could not bring reforms in Muslim Personal Laws for fear of alienating their Vote banks.

6.6. Objectional Features

Without going into details of Muslim Personal Laws which have, and are still hampering dispensation of justice to women we shall touch only some broad features touching the questions of monogamy, divorce and rights of inheritance and succession of a Muslim women. These questions are emphasised mainly because enlightened Muslim intellectuals also agree that there is good scope of reforms in these subjects.

6.6.1. So far as Muslim marriage is concerned it is based on the principle of relationship by contract which in theory can be taken as a proper procedure for safe guarding dispensation of justice to women.

6.6.2. However, on the most vital question of *maintenance of a divorced wife*, the passage of Muslim women (Protection of Rights on Divorce) ACt, 1986 pursuant to the Supreme Court judgment in Shah Bano Case is the most disgraceful Act of insulting Muslim womanhood of India and requires to be successfully challenged in Courts under Article-13, 14 and 15 of the Constitution.

6.6.3. *Polygamy* enabling a Muslim male to marry maximum four wives is another out dated and obnoxious feature of Muslim personal Law. When the original idea was mooted out in Arabia by the Prophet, who was secular as well as religious head of his followers, there was very good reason for such liberty given to males as it was necessary to give protection to war widows and destitude females. But the scholars agree that this was merely an enabling provision to solve the then prevailing social conditions and was not intended to create on inviolable male right to marry four times. In fact, the scholars also agree that taking of a second wife was mainly frowned upon and made conditional on various circumstances.

Polygamy, where ever practiced, is anti-social immoral and repressive of human values. It is based on the notion that a woman is an object of satisfying male carnal desires. Of repeated argument of some status quoists that this disease is more prevalent amongst Hindus than among the Muslims in simply puerile because even if the date relied upon is accepted, an unjust act committed by one community would not justify another national community to resort to similar unjust act. There cannot be national competition in anti-social practices.

It is interesting to know that no Muslim or Hindu male would at present agree to the system of polyandry where a wife can take more than one husband.

Thus the very concept of polygamy is obnoxious to fair sense and equity and can be successfully challenged under Articles-13, 14 and 15 as discriminatory purely on the ground of sex.

6.6.4. Divorce

Whether it is triple or otherwise, instantaneous or

periodical, it is totally inequitable and unjust if it gives unilateral right only to one spouse. It is true that Dissolution of Muslim Marriage Act, 1939 enables a Muslim Woman to demand separation and divorce under certain limited circumstances, but so long as the male partner enjoys unilateral right to act on his own whines without equal and corresponding right to female partner the doctrine of equality enshrined in Articles-13, 14 and 15 is infringed and constitutional safe-guards are destroyed.

Tendency of some Muslim reformists to follow modifications on this subject adopted by Countries like Pakistan, Egypt and Turkey will not help in solving the problem so long as the fundamental requirements of Articles-13, 14 and 15 are not satisfied.

6.6.5. *Inheritance and Succession* is the subject where the Muslim Personal Law scrores over other personal laws in as much as it visulises equitable distribution of the estate of the deceased amongst all near and distant relatives which include females. On this subject a Hindu Woman has suffered much under all Hindu Law but now the position of Hindu women is greatly improved as already discussed above.

One thing which, however, requires to be emphasised in this connection is complexity of the laws of Succession in Shias and Sunnis and the still persisting bias in favour of male heirs who take double the shares than females in certain cases.

Such inconguancies can be settled by a proper legislation, but if it is not so done a recourse can be taken under Articles-13,14 and 15 as in other cases.

6.6.6. Wrong Invocation of Articles - 25 and 26

These two articles of our Constitution are generally called in aid by fundamentalists to resist reforms in personal law on the ground that their personal law represents their religious practice and hence the same cannot be changed or even modified.

Simple answer to this argument is that Social practices, conventions, usages and customs can never be treated as "religious" and even if one is inclined to treat them as "religious"; Articles-25 and 26 do not create absolute rights as they are specifically made subject to (1) other provisions of Part-III which includes Articles-13, 14 and 15, (2) Public Order and (3) Morality. Infringement of equality Clause only on the ground of sex results not only in breach of Articles-13, 14 and 15 but in both immoral and against public order.

7. Other Public Laws

Other personal laws relate to other two religious minorities namely Christians and Parsees.

Christians are governed by Christian Marriage Act, 1972, Special Marriage Act, 1954 and Divorce Act, 1869 so far as their matrimonial rights are concerned and succession Act, 1925 so far as their intestate inheritance and succession is concerned. All these enactments are based on the principles of justice, equity and good conscious and do not discriminate against women.

The same can be said about even Parsi Personal Law which is governed by Parsi Marriage And Divorce Act, 1936 and Succession Act of 1925.

8. Conclusion

Question of gender justice is not a communal question or a question touching any particular religion. It is a Social question having humanist contents. Political democracy is never complete without social democracy and the human society which keeps fifty percent of its population under social servitity can never hope to prosper. No social progress on this planet would have been possible if the fundamentalists and status quoists were not effectively challenged by social reformers. I, therefore, firmly believe that it is now the task of Indian reformists to openly accept the challenge of obscurantist elements of our society in defence of gender justice.

References

1. Rigveda Samhita, Swadhyay Mandate (1957) - S.D. Satwalkar P.321.
2. History of Dharmashastra Vol.II, Part-I, P.19-48.
3. Hindu Sanskara - Dr. Raj Bali -Motilal Banarasidas, P.215.
4. Manu Smruti 1 X 81.
5. Dharmakosha—Laxman Shastri.
6. 15th Ed. p.902 of Mulla–Principles of Hindu Law.
7. Legal and Constitutional History of India. Vol. II P. 7 by Rama Jois.
8. Ibid. P.8.
9. Ibid. P.15.
10. Ibid. P.13.

7

Muslim Girl Child Domestics in the Child Rights Perspective

Nadeem Mohsin

Introduction

The rights of the child and especially those of the girl child have assumed special significance in the agenda of the International Human Rights Commission. In developing countries, working children who are denied the right to survival, protection and development languish in the quagmire of apathy and neglect. In India, the problems of working children have assumed alarming proportions in recent years. The girl child workers are the worst sufferers. They have not only to bear the brunt of gender disparity in a patriarchal society, but also have to protect themselves from various forms of physical insecurity, specially in work situations. Although they are entitled to all societal resources, this entitlement is frequently denied. Discrimination generally begins at birth and has a cumulative effect on inequality, producing despair and powerlessness. It is important for the girl child to internalise the concept and experience of equity in order to avoid the tolerance and perpetuation of gender disparity as an adult. At present the girl child in India is denied the very acquisition of an identity. Even parents do not visibly support her rights to dignity, health and education.

Girl children belonging to families living in poverty get marginalised from a tender age. The vocational responsibility of a girl child starts early at the age of three years when she has to assist her mother in domestic chores, carry fuel and fodder, gather grains, feed poultry and cattle and look after her young siblings.

While poverty constitutes a major source of deprivation of all children of the weaker sections in a developing country like India, greater vulnerability of the girl child derives from traditional Indian cultural ethos. The strangle hold of his non-egalitarian gender-discriminatory ethos continues to exercise its baneful influence on most castes, classes and communities though in varying ways and degrees.

Girl child workers are found to be engaged in hazardous occupations like the match industry in Sivakasi, the pottery industry in Khurja, the brassware industry in Moradabad, etc. They are also found to be engaged in non-hazardous occupations like stitching of inflatable balls in the sports goods industries in Jalandhar and Meerut, in hosiery and garments industries in various parts of the country, in construction industries, in garbage collection, rag picking work, etc. However, all these occupations are, by and large, visible, providing scope for the governments, NGOs and other social groups to formulate policies and programmes for such child workers. A number of research studies have also been conducted to assess their socio-economic situations.

Perhaps the most invisible form of girl child labour is girl child domestics. Although it is very difficult to estimate the number of the 'invisible' or 'no where' category of girl child workers, their number in the metropolis and in the bigger cities is extremely high. Girl child domestics may suffer from the worst forms of exploitation. Being in the 'no where' category, they are not covered under any programme of intervention. They have never been a subject of concern for the government, NGOs, trade unions or activist groups. Even researchers tend to shy away from this area of study.

The situation of Muslim girl child domestics is even more complex and has to be understood in the perspective of the socio-economic condition of Muslims in this country. The opportunities provided to Muslims in core areas of health and education have never been at par with their population. In most of the states in the country, Muslims represent the lot of economically and socially depressed masses. Their job profile reflects a pattern of inadequate representation in white collar and other office jobs. The level of literacy among Muslims is primarily low for reasons of discrimination and among girls it is lower because of the stigma attached to girls' socialization. The doctrine of Muslim females being within the confines of the house has created a situation of acute economic distress.

Although adhering to the practice of the purdah system is a matter of grace for the Muslim woman, abstaining from education has its negative fall-outs. The concept of modern Islamic education is based on the fundamental principles of logic and reasoning and on the premise of struggle for existence. The rigidity of individuals, which is not a part of Islamic teachings, has to be prohibitive.

Muslim girls need to be given proper education. Unfortunately the scenario that presently exists and the facilities provided by the government are not in consonance with the community's needs.

The present study of the socio-economic status of Muslim girl child domestics in east Delhi is an outcome of a series of interaction the author had with some of the elder Muslim women who send their girl children to work. These women are migrants from the East, mostly West Bengal and Bangladesh and have settled in ghettoes in east Delhi to work as domestic servants to eke out a living. The slum in which they have settled are in the neighbourhood of multi-storied apartments owned mostly by the middle class city dwellers. Around the neighbourhood of Vasundhara Enclave, a conglomeration of nearly fifty apartments, each one having an average of hundred flats, are scanty settlement of migrant families, living in conditions of extreme deprivation, congestion and filth. The houses here are temporary thatched ones and established on land belonging mostly to the Municipal Corporation of Delhi (MCD).

It is here where the domestic workers, both women and girl live and provide services as maid servants to the apartment dwellers. The husbands of these maid servants have a very flexible job pattern. They work as labourers, rickshaw-pullers, garbage collectors, etc., and even remain iddle for a major part of the year. Majority of them are dependent on incomes earned by women and girl children.

Incidentally, majority of families settled in these slums belong to the muslim community. Among such families, most of the physically abled women are domestic workers who work in the apartments on a part time basis. Their daughters also work on a part time basis.

This study is based on field investigations conducted on 200 girl child workers, aged 7-16 years. The study indicates that majority of these girl child domestics are literate upto the primary level and work because of economic necessity. Several of them get married at a tender age of 15-16 years and attain motherhood even before 18 years of age. The fall-out of this composite life structure manifests in several ways. It revolves in a vicious circle of deprivation.

The girl child domestics need to be given a clear cut life perspective based on Islamic principles. They need to be given education in a way to enable them understand the purpose of life and how it could be made meaningful. This study also makes an attempt to provide insights into some of these issues.

Findings

Status of Girl Child Domestics

Status (N=200)	No.	%
Part-time	157	78.50
Live-in	43	21.50

As mentioned earlier, part-time girl child domestics are those who work for 1-2 hours everyday and get a monthly salary ranging between Rs. 300 and Rs. 500. On the contrary, live-in girl child domestics are those who stay in the employers' house and may go on an annual leave for a week or so. As is evident from the table, majority of girl child domestics are part-time workers.

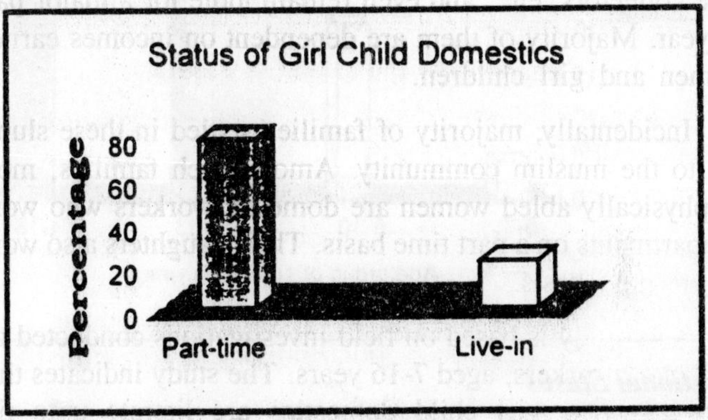

Age Profile

Age Group of Children (N=200)	No.	%
5-7	9	4.50
8-10	42	21.00
11-13	68	34.00
14-16	81	40.50

The table shows that 55 percent of the girl child domestics are in the age group of 8-13 years. This is the most vulnerable age group of children being brought into the work force. Even at an early age children are made to work, but generally within the family, attending to domestic chores, looking after younger siblings, etc. By the time children attain the age of fourteen, they are considered full time workers and are expected to make monetary contribution to the family kitty. This is the general scenario in poverty stricken families, especially in the cities.

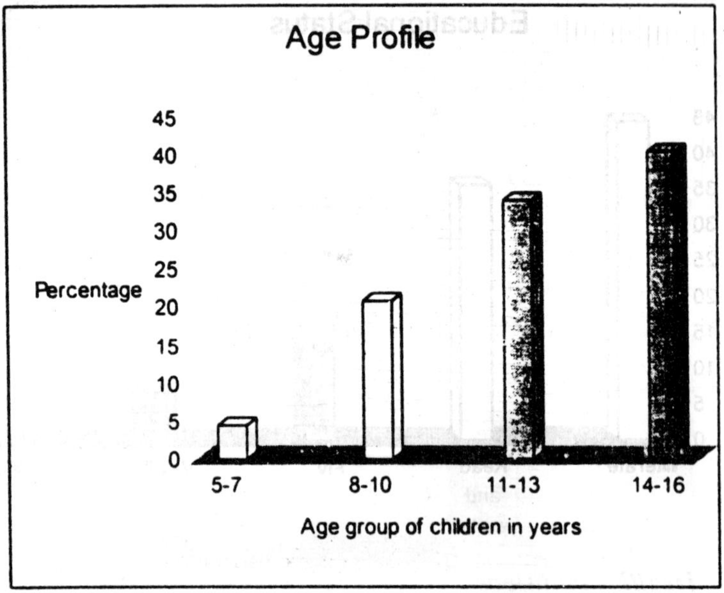

Educational Status

Educational level (N=200)	No.	%
Illiterate	89	44.50
Read and write	71	35.50
I-IV	25	12.50
V-VIII	14	7.00
IX-X	01	0.50

Nearly 45 percent of the girl child domestics are illiterate, that is, they can neither read nor write. A little ever one third of them are barely able to read Urdu and Hindi and are able to write their names in either of the languages.

Nearly 20 percent of the girl child domestics have studied in schools between class I & VIII. Only one girl was in a position to reach upto class IX before she had to give up studies for economic reasons. Although most of the girls want to pursue studies, schooling is a far cry.

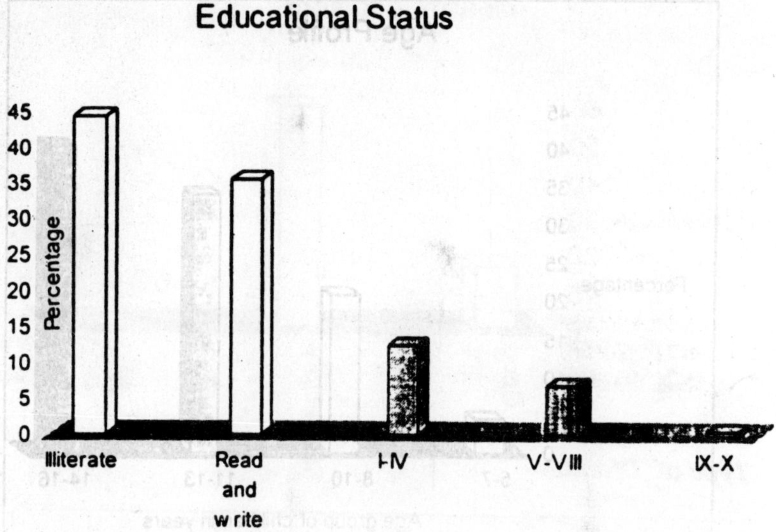

Health Conditions

Health Conditions (N=200)	No.	%
Good	33	16.50
Satisfactory	119	59.50
Poor	48	24.00

The health conditions of 59.50 percent of the girl child domestics appeared to be satisfactory. The health conditions of these children were not measured in terms of their height and weight and other indicators like eyesight, blood pressure, etc. It was based on the general physical appearance and the overall fitness condition. Girl child domestics with poor health were those who appeared thin or skinny and generally lethargic in terms of physical activity and mental alertness. Those who had good health conditions had never suffered from any sickness/ disease during the previous one year.

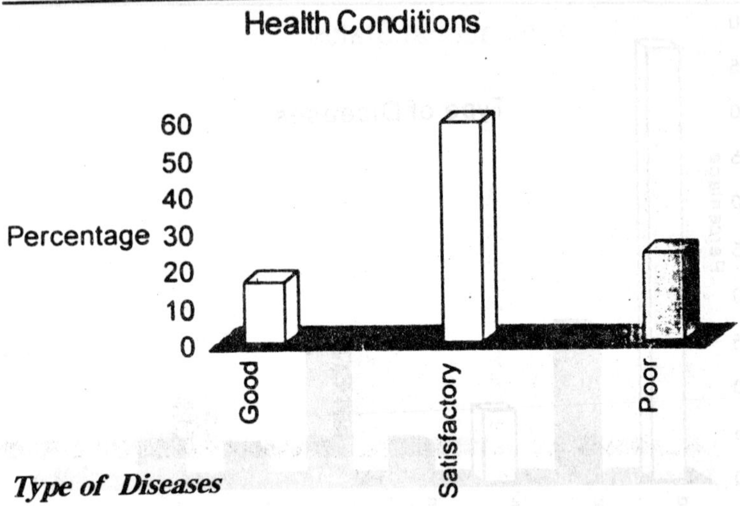

Type of Diseases

Type of Diseases (N=167)	No.	%
Fever/Cold	79	47.30
Diarrhoea	28	16.76
Gastric problem	13	7.78
ENT infection	07	4.20
Skin infection	24	14.37
Jaundice	06	3.59
Mumps	08	4.79
Others	02	1.21

The table depicts the major diseases girl child domestics have encountered during the last one year. The table shows that fever/cold is the major sickness or disease which has affected 47.30 percent of the girl child domestics. This is followed by skin infections affecting 14.37 percent of the children. These ailments are common because of the hectic life style as also because of their exposure to the vagaries of nature which makes them susceptible to common ailments

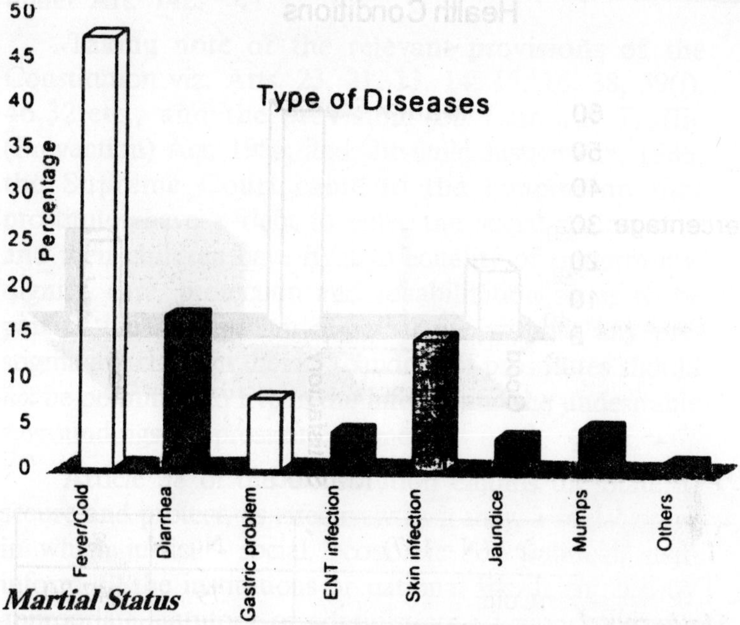

Martial Status

Age group	Total No. (N=149)	%	Total no. married (N=56)	%
11-13	68	34.00	05	7.35
14-16	81	40.50	51	62.96

34 percent of the girl child domestics are in the age group of 11-13 years of whom 7.35 percent are married. In the age group of 14-16 years, the percentage of girl child domestics is 40.50 percent, out of whom 62.96 percent are married. In the age group of 14-16 years, although girl children mature physically, they are mentally still in their formative years. Marriage at such an early age has both physical and mental fall-outs, which manifests in later years of life. It reduces the gradual transformation of childhood into womanhood and comes so abruptly that children are unable to cope up with this transformation both mentally and physically.

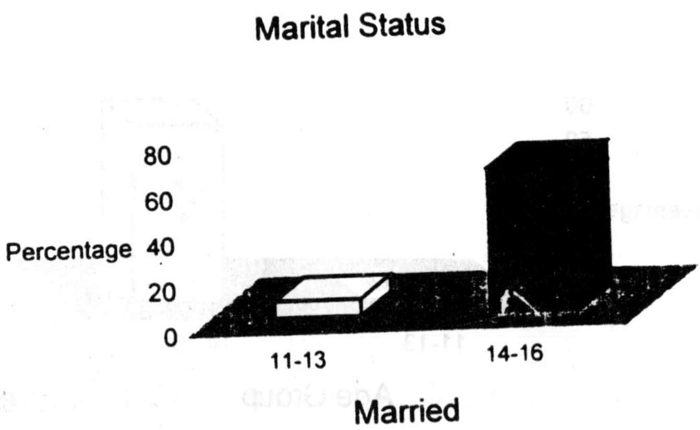

Motherhood

Age group	Motherhood	
(N=56)	No.	%
11-13	02	0.40
14-16	26	51.00

It is interesting to see that out of the five married girl child domestics in the age group of 11-13 years, two of them had attained motherhood. Similarly, in the age group of 14-16 years, 26 girl child domestics had attained motherhood out of 51 in that age group. Conception at a very early age has several ramifications, both physical and mental and may have serious negative impact on the behaviour patterns of such young women and the way they rear their child. It may also develop physical abhorrence towards males and such young women may completely lose the luster of physical attraction with the opposite sex even before attaining adulthood.

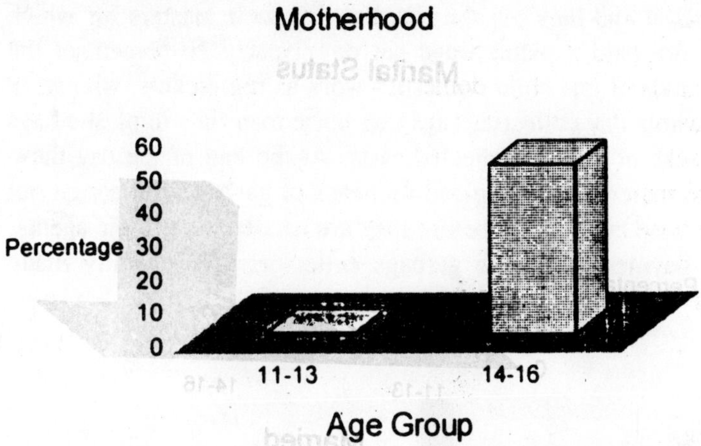

Husband's Occupation

Husband's Occupation (N=56)	Among those married	
	No.	%
Labourer	06	10.72
Rickshaw puller	28	50.00
Servant	02	3.58
Porter	06	10.72
Driver	01	1.78
Tailor	01	1.78
Rag-picker	11	19.64
Others	01	1.78
All categories	56	100.00

The husbands of 50 percent married girl child domestics

are rickshaw-pullers. Incidentally, none of them have their own rickshaw and they ply the rickshaw for their masters for which they are paid a paltry wage per day. Nearly 20 percent of the husbands of girı child domestics work as rag-pickers, who work the whole day collecting rags and waste materials in plastic bags or sacks or even in wheeled carts. At the end of the day these waste materials are dumped on heaps of garbage and sorted out item wise every week before they are handed over to the agents. The payments to these garbage collectors are generally made on a weekly basis.

Hasband's Occupation

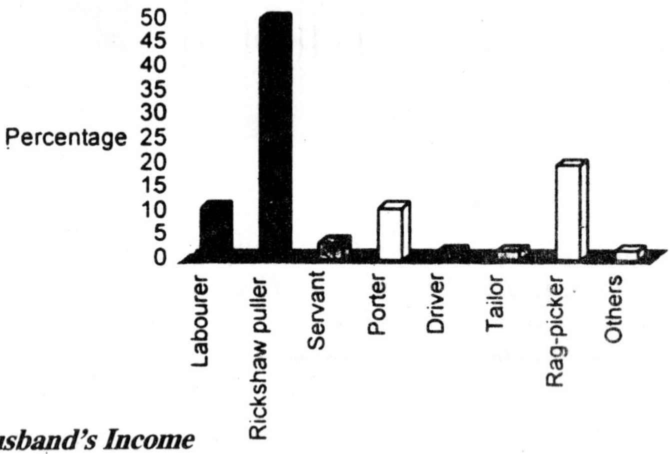

Husband's Income

Income Range (Rs. Per month)	No. of husbands (N=56)	%
Upto 500	01	1.78
501-1000	20	35.72
1001-1500	20	35.72
1501-2000	14	25.00
Above 2000	01	1.78

More than 70 percent of the husbands earned between

Rs. 500 and Rs. 1500 per month. Their monthly earnings could have been higher had they worked everyday, for many of them abstain from work for day's together, sitting idle at home.

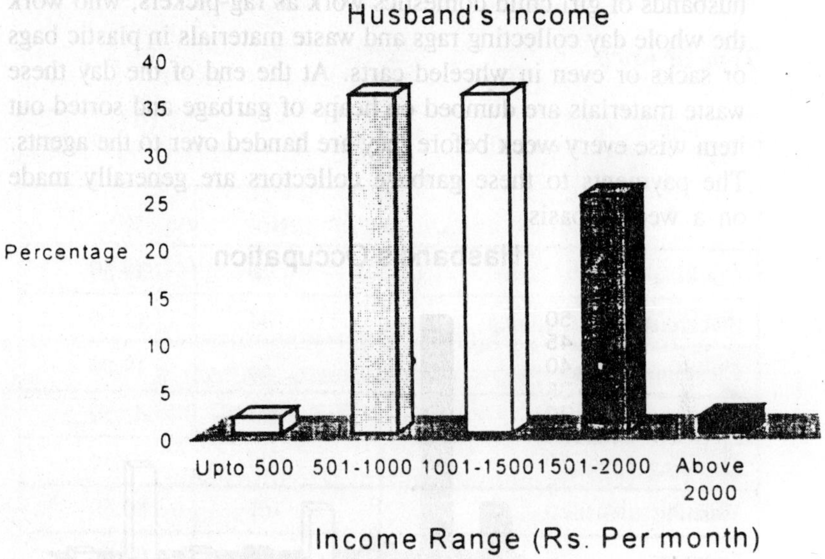

Employment of Girl Child Domestics

Reasons for going to work

Reasons for working (N=200)	Child	Domestics
	No.	%
Poverty	188	94.00
Ill treatment	42	21.00
Orphanage	08	4.00
Abandonment	08	4.00
Mother also working	24	12.00
Others	8	4.00

94 percent of the girl child domestic adduced poverty as one of the reasons for going out to work. This gets corroborated by the data on income and family size of girl child domestics.

21 percent of girl child domestics work because of the ill treatment meted out by the parents. These are mostly live-in girl child domestics who have left the house and are independent.

Type of work

Type of work (N=200)	No. of respondents reporting	
	No.	%
Cooking	79	39.50
Sweeping and Cleaning	184	92.00
Cleaning toilets	38	19.00
Washing clothes	83	41.50
Grinding spices	05	2.50
Washing utensils	161	80.50
Dusting	125	62.50
Taking care of children	45	22.50
Others	20	10.00

The table shows that most of the girl child domestics have to undertake more than one work. Majority of them have to do sweeping and cleaning work (92%), washing utensils (80.50%) followed by dusting the house (62.50%) and other work. Although none of the work is hazardous, it is definitely monotonous and becomes quite taxing especially during winter months. Live-in girl child domestics have to undertake practically each and every type of work. In several houses the entire cooking is done by them, in addition to the normal work they have to do like washing clothes and dusting the home, etc. There is no escape from this monotonous routine which continues day in and day out.

Hours of Work

Hours of Work (N=200)	No.	%
2 - 4	37	18.50
4 - 6	60	30.00
6 - 8	60	30.00
8 - 10	25	12.50
10 - 12	18	9.00

The table shows that 60 percent of the children work between 4 and 8 hours. Live-in child workers work on an average for 8-12 hours. The working hours of part time girl child domestics is about 2 hours in one house, but since they work in more than one house, their average working hour per day goes up, depending on the number of houses they work in. In fact, it is more difficult for part time workers to carry out the work, since every house has it own work requirement. Moreover, while there is scope for some relaxation for the live-in child domestics, part time domestics have hardly any time with them. Their work starts in an absolutely mechanical manner and the moment the work is completed, the girl child domestics shift to the next house.

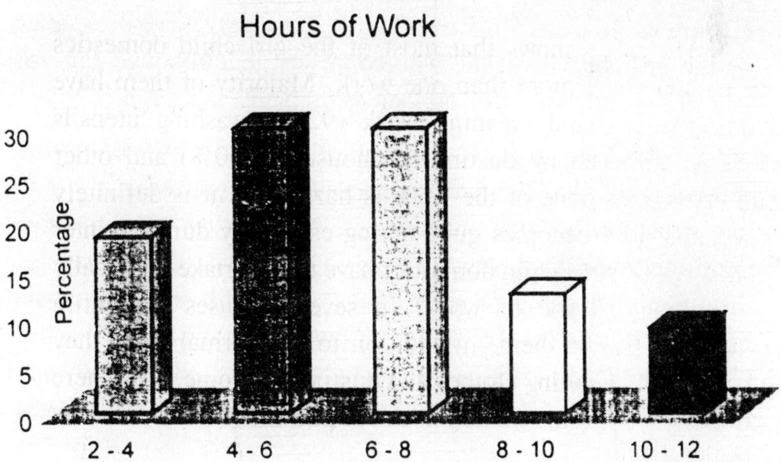

Income

Monthly income in Rs. (N=200)	No.	%
Nil	04	2.00
Upto 100	07	3.50
100 - 200	29	14.50
200 - 300	55	27.50
300 - 400	32	16.00
400 - 500	16	8.00
More than 500	44	22.00
Not fixed	13	6.50

The table shows that 2 percent of girl child domestics do not receive salary. They are live-in girl child domestics. Employers generally pay low salaries to live-in girl child domestics on the plea that they take care of these children in all respects, giving them clothes and gifts from time to time. In an informal discussion with an employer keeping a live-in girl child domestic it was revealed that the girl child was treated by him in the same fashion as he treated his own child. This was, however, denied by the girl child domestic who confessed that although she was not ill treated, she was neither treated like a daughter.

The fact that 22 percent of the girl chiid domestics receive more than Rs. 500/- per month does not reveal the high pay structure, but that such girl child domestics work in more than one house to be able to earn that amount. On an average, the monthly income of a part time girl child domestic would be about Rs. 100 to Rs. 200 from one house and that for a live in girl child domestic, it would be about Rs. 300 to 400 per month. In case of 13 live-in girl child domestics, the income is not fixed

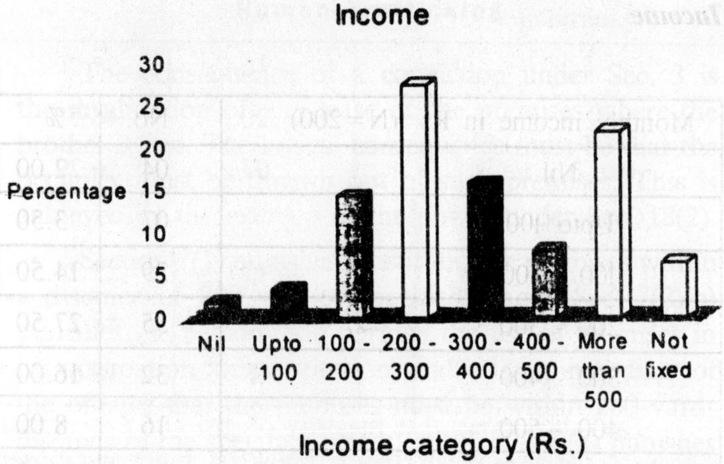

Basic Needs of Live-in Girl Child Domestics

Whether live-in girl child domestics are treated like family members or not can be ascertained by the extent to which the basic needs of such children are fulfilled and also by the provision of other facilities to such children. Parameters like time of taking meals, quality of food, time or place of sleeping and other benefits and recreation facilities are important indicators to assess the quality of life of girl child domestics.

Time of Taking Meals

Time (N=43)	Among those married	
	No.	%
Morning		
7-8	12	10.72
8-9	9	50.00
9-10	22	3.58
After 10 a.m.	Nil	0.00

Afternoon		
1-2	16	37.20
2-3	20	46.51
After 3 p.m.	07	16.29
Evening		
9-10	10	23.25
10-11	25	58.13
After 11 p.m.	08	18.62

The table shows that majority of girl child domestics are given all the three meals, that is, breakfast, lunch and dinner later than the normal time. The ideal time for taking food for children is 7 to 8 a.m. for breakfast, 1 to 2 p.m. for lunch and 9 to 10 p.m. for dinner.

46.51 percent of the girl child domestics have no fixed time for meals. Generally, they get food after everyone else in the house has finished eating. At times, when there are guests in the house, the meal timings get disturbed, as a result of which girl child domestics also suffer.

65.21 percent of live-in girl child domestics never get milk, 20.93 percent get milk some times and only the rest get milk regularly. As far as non-vegetarian food items are concerned, most of the girl child domestics get non-vegetarian items whenever it is cooked in the house.

Time for Going to Bed

Time for going to bed (N=200)	No.	%
10 p.m.	22	51.16
Between 10 & 11 p.m.	11	25.58
Between 11 & 12 p.m.	Nil	0.00
After 12 p.m.	Nil	0.00
No fixed time	10	23.26

The table shows that 51.16 percent of the live-in girl child domestics go to bed at 10 p.m., 25.58 percent between 10 and 11 p.m. and 23.26 percent of girl child domestics have not fixed time to go to bed.

Most of the live-in girl child domestics have fixed place to sleep. They generally sleep in the children's room and are given quilt, pillow etc. The only difference between girl child domestics and employers' children is that while the latter sleep on comfortable beds, the former have to use floors to sleep.

Minor differences in the life style of girl child domestics and the children of employers may have a lot of psychological impact on the former. With the mind set of despair and negativism, girl child domestics may not mature into normal adults who have a lust for life and the urge for having a successful future.

Benefits and Recreation

Types of benefits (N=43)	No.	%
Oil, soap, etc.	43	100.00
Quilt, pillow, etc.	43	100.00
New clothes	43	100.00
Old/worn out clothes	43	100.00
Money given while going home	43	100.00
Schooling	Nil	0.00
Medicine	43	100.00

Oil and soap are given to all live-in girl child domestics regularly. They are also given pillows and quilts for sleeping. All of them get new clothes once-a-year. Of course, these clothes are not of the same quality which employers get for their own children. Girl child domestics are given old clothes normally rejected after use by the members of employers' family, mostly children.

Girl child domestics are also given some money while they go home. The amount varies from child to child. Generally the home visits are once-a-year and takes place during Id-ul-fitre. Some of the girl child domestics who are without family go to their relatives place or even stay with the employers family.

None of the girl child domestics are sent to school. Some of them are taught basic alphabets and numbers by the female member of the house or the son/daughter of employers. While the latter go to school, girl child domestics slog for hours together at home and prepare meals for employers' children when they come back from school.

Live-in girl child domestics have access to television and other home entertainment like toys and games, etc. In most cases, they are not allowed to operate TV independently or even play with games and toys in the absence of employers' children. In fact, they are so hard pressed with work that they hardly have time to enjoy these facilities. Many a times they are made to accompany family members of the employers when they go out of the house for shopping/recreation or to a restaurant.

Child Abuse

The practice of child abuse is very common among working children. The abuse may be in the form of physical abuse, as is the case in most of the unorganised sectors like mechanic shops, tea stalls, restaurants, etc. or verbal abuse as in the case of agriculture, construction work, domestic service or even in organised sector employment like children working in factories, etc.

India has ratified the UN Convention on the Rights of the Child and is legally bound to provide protection to children from all forms of exploitation and abuse. At the national level too, a number of laws have been enacted to protect the interests of children. The Constitution also lays down provisions vide its articles number 24, 39(E) and (F), etc. to protect children from working and from any type of exploitation. However, in spite of all these provisions and legislation, children undergo the worst forms of exploitation and abuse. The girl child is even more affected because of her physical vulnerability and her tendency to give in under situations of economic distress and in a typical male dominated psychological set-up.

While it is possible to check the practice of child abuse in formal sector employment or even in the unorganised sector where child labour exists in a visible form, it is difficult to prohibit such a practice in the context of domestic work, where child labour exists in an invisible form. The extent of abuse in case of child domestics, especially girl child domestics is extremely difficult to gauge, for the simple reason that girl child domestics feel inhibited in revealing the extent of abuse which they have to undergo from employers. While verbal abuse temporarily disturbs the mental set-up of the girl child domestic, physical abuse, which may be in the form of sexual advances may even threaten the physical security of girl child domestics and may even put them in state of mental disequilibrium.

In case of this study, on the question of abuse, 17.5 percent of girl child domestics revealed that they were subjected to abuse of one kind or the other.

Child Abuse (N=200)	No.	%
Yes	35	17.50
No	165	82.50

Out of 17.50 percent of girl child domestics who admitted at they were abused by their employers, 5.7 percent also admitted that they were subjected to physical abuse.

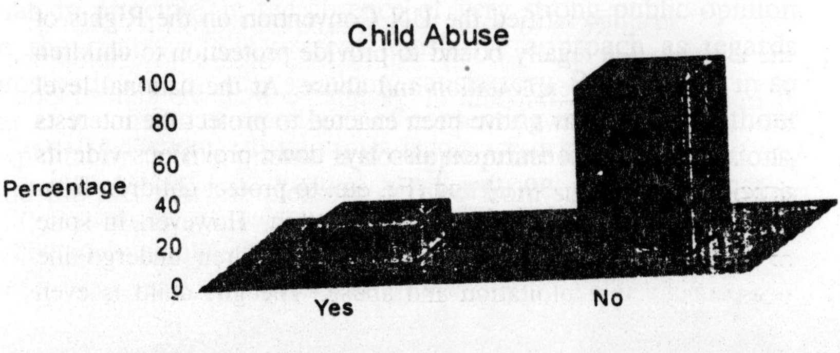

Awareness On Child Rights

The declaration of the Rights of Child was adopted by the UN General Assembly in 1959. The declaration has been the guiding framework for children's rights. In the thirteenth year of the declaration, the UN General Assembly held a Convention known as the UN Convention on the Rights of Child. This Convention came into force as an international law on 2nd Sept. 1990.

The Convention consists of 54 articles, a set of international standards and measures that intends to promote and protect the well being of children in society. The Convention provides the legal basis for initiating action to ensure the rights of children in society. The draft of the Convention was prepared by the UN Commission on Human Rights.

The Rights of the Child have broadly being discussed under four heads; the rights to Survival, Protection, Development and Participation.

The Right to survival ensures the right to life, the highest attainable standard of health, nutrition and adequate standards of living.

The right to protection guarantees freedom from all forms of exploitation, abuse, inhuman or degrading treatment and neglect.

The Right to Development incorporates the right to education, support for early childhood and care, social security and right to leisure and recreations.

The Right to Participation calls for respect for the views of the child, freedom of expression, access to appropriate information and freedom of thought, conscience and religion.

The first major global action for the implementation of the Convention was the World Summit on Children held on September 30, 1990. The Summit adopted the declaration on the survival, protection and development of children along with a plan of action for implementing the Declaration. The Convention on the Rights of Child and the Summit constitute an ambitious and focused agenda for the well being of children to be achieved by the year 2000. All governments having ratified the Convention were urged to prepare their own plan of action.

The Government of India ratified the Convention on 2nd Dec. 1992. India is also a signatory to the World Declaration on the survival, protection and development of children. A National Plan of Action for children was formulated by the Ministry of Human Resource Development, Government of India in which the priority areas where health, nutrition, education, water, sanitation and environment.

As far as the Plan of Action related to education is concerned, the following actions were envisaged :

- Universal Enrolment of all children including girls, using both full time formal schools and part-time non-formal arrangements.
- Reduction of drop out rate between class 1 to 5 and 1 to 8 from the existing 45 and 60 percent to 20 and 40 percent respectively.
- Achievements of minimum levels of learning for all children at the primary level and introduction of this concept at the upper primary stage.
- Reduction in gender disparities by emphasis on girl's education and special measures for children belonging to the scheduled castes and the scheduled tribes group.
- Universalisation of effective access to schooling.
- Expansion of early childhood development activities including appropriate low cost family and community based interventions.

The measures to be taken up for the girl child included:

- Removal of gender bias
- Improvement in the status of the girl child
- Universalisation of primary education among girls including health and nutrition education

- Upgradation of home-based skills
- Promotion of decision making ability among girls

A lot of discussion and debate has taken place in the last one decade on the issue of child rights in general and the rights of the girl child in particular. However, the girl child scenario in India is one of extreme disgust and deprivation.

Girl child domestics are not aware of their rights. They tend to revolve in a vicious circle of poverty, are extremely fatalistic in their attitude towards life and feel that education is a distant dream for them.

Conclusions

The Muslim migrant families settled in East Delhi are in a state of distress and deprivation. They are an invisible group, deprived of all basic amenities of life. They live in slums which do not provide basic infrastructure facilities like proper housing, drainage, health and sanitation facilities, schooling for the children and even adequate water and electricity.

They live in houses which lack proper lighting and ventilation. The houses often cannot bear the onslaught of climatic variations and create problems for the inmates, especially during the rainy season. The living conditions are such that the health of children get badly affected, since they are exposed to the chill of winter, the scorching heat of summer and the filth of rains.

The families are mostly illiterate. Although most of them realise the importance of education, they feel they cannot send their children to school because schools are expensive and do not meet the time requirements of children who generally go out to work. Although some of the boys go to schools, girls invariably are not sent to school. Girls look after younger siblings at home or work as domestic workers.

Among the adults, both men and women go out to work. While most of the men work as garbage collectors, rickshaw pullers, labourers, etc. women generally work as maid servants in apartment flats on a part time basis, working in 3-4 flats at a time, earning between Rs. 250 and Rs. 400 from each flat. The average family income of about 80 percent of the families range from Rs. 1000 to Rs. 3000 per month.

All in all, the income from work is not sufficient enough to meet the bare monthly expenses. It is for this reason that children are sent to work. Majority of the girl child domestics are part time workers while some are live-in girl child domestics.

Girl child domestics are in the age group of 5-16 years. They are mostly illiterate or can barely read or write. Child marriage is a common phenomenon among these families. Nearly 70 percent get married before attaining the age of 16 years, out of whom several attain motherhood. Marriage at a formative year of life and motherhood have their physical and mental fall-out. Early marriage may result in diseases and motherhood at an early age may bring in mental irritants. In any case, transformation from childhood to adulthood, skipping the vulnerable phase of adolescence, may have its own ramifications on the physical conditions of the mother, and more so on her mindset.

Girl child domestics work for long hours under conditions of stress. Most of them have to over work themselves owing to paucity of time. The work they have to undertake is extremely mechanical and does not provide scope for innovation. This system, over a period of time, brings in stagnation among girl child domestics. In the process, they lose their mental capacities and may even become dull after attaining a certain age.

It is difficult to ascertain how girl child domestics compare themselves with children of employers. Like any normal child, they must be encountering moments of trauma and disgust. The price of deprivation they have to pay definitely manifests in their behaviour patterns and attitude towards life in general.

The findings of the study clearly indicate that Muslim girl child domestics are languishing in the quagmire of indifference and neglect. In the formative years of life, when children are supposed to spend time in fun and leisure, these unfortunate girl child domestics have to slog for long hours for meeting their bare subsistence needs.

These children live in conditions of abject poverty. They have to work because work is a necessity for them. Their parents are poor and illiterate as a result of which they do not attach too much importance to education. Girl children domestics have either never been to schools or have dropped out because of economic reasons. Many of them are extremely intelligent, but their intelligence cannot be put to proper use for no fault of theirs. By the time they reach adulthood, they attain a state of mental stagnation. Their personality gets isolated and they are unable to relate themselves to society at large. This is the price they have to pay for being born and brought up in a state of poverty.

Recommendations

On the basis of the findings of the study, the following recommendations may be useful for bringing Muslim girl child domestics into the mainstream of socio-economic life.

1. Muslim migrant families who have settled in India need to be given treatment at part with Indian citizens in all walks of life.

2. They should be given minority status, with reservation in education and employment.

3. They should be provided residential facilities in organised community settlements with basic amenities of water and drainage, schools and hospitals and other basic infrastructures like banks, ration shops, libraries, etc.

4. There should be a provision of community schools for children of Muslim migrant families. These schools should be affiliated to the Central Board of Secondary Education managed by NGOs, preferably those who have the credibility and the wherewith all to provide their valuable services to the minority community.

5. Since education is the major concern for the upliftment of children, Muslim organisations in the West and the Middle East should provide financial support for the effective functioning of such schools through organisations of repute.
6. The entire control and management of funds should be the sole responsibility of such institutions.
7. Monitoring and evaluation of activities and inputs provided in such community schools should be undertaken regularly by such institutions.
8. The course content in such schools should be in tune with modern Islamic education and should be based on the concept of joyful learning.
9. The course materials should be based on the concept of minimum levels of learning and should incorporate children's skills and competence.
10. Experts preparing course materials should be drawn from schools well versed with modern Islamic education and needs of the community.
11. Islamic education should be neatly amalgamated into the general course content leading to the school certificate examination.
12. Since children belong to the deprived community, vocational training should be an inbuilt component of the course content.
13. Vocational courses should be designed not only to meet the interests and needs of children, but also be based on the marketing prospects of these courses.
14. Children should be encouraged to set-up their own vocations after completion of vocational training.
15. Feasible project proposals should be prepared for starting such vocations in consultation with experts.
16. Initial financial support should be provided as fixed and working capital partly in the form of loans and partly as subsidy.

17. Meritorious students should be given scholarships in the form of monthly stipends to enable them to feel motivated and perform better. These scholarships should be given through recognised institutions.

18. Muslim migrant families should be supported through community based income generating programmes.

19. Income generating programmes should be implemented through the formation of self-help groups and cooperative credit institutions.

20. Muslim women should be encouraged to participate in meaningful income generation activities like embroidery, tailoring, knitting, etc.

21. Awareness generation and sensitization workshops should be organised every quarterly for the vulnerable groups to create empowerment among them, so that they help themselves to get mainstreamed into socio-economic life.

22. School level education should be made compulsory for all Muslim children in the community and particular emphasis should be given to girls education.

23. Marriage of girls below the age of eighteen years should be strictly prohibited.

24. There should be a complete ban on girls' employment in all services till the completion of high school.

25. A coordination committee should be constituted to monitor the programme activities envisaged for the community.

References

1. Ansari, I.A. *Cultural Sources of Deprivation of the Girl Child in India*; paper presented at the Conference on Human Rights and Dalits, organised by the Indian Social Institute, New Delhi; October, 1999.

2. Ahmed, I. *The Education of Muslim Girl Child : A Human Rights Perspective*; paper presented at the Conference on Human Rights and Dalits, organised by the Indian Social Institute, New Delhi; October, 1999.

3. Saxena, N.C. *Public Employment and Educational Backwardness among Muslims in India; Man and Life,* Vol. 4 No. 4, 1983.

4. *The Times of India*, New Delhi, December 28, 1990.

5. *Report of Survey on the Educational Status of Muslim Women in the States of Bihar and Rajasthan*; Hamdard Education Society, New Delhi.

6. Kazim, S., et. al. *Towards Gender Equality;* Commonwealth Publications, New Delhi, 1994.

7. Kazim S., *Media Campaign on the Girl Child*; paper accepted for presentation at the International Conference 'Children At Risk', Trondheim, Norway, 1992.

8. Mohsin Nadeem, *Child Labour : Status Issues and Options*; document prepared for the India Canada Cooperation Office, Canadian High Commission, New Delhi 1995.

9. Mohsin Nadeem, *Street and Working Children in South Asia*, paper prepared for the Independent Commission on Population and Quality of Life, UNESCO, Paris, 1994.

10. Mohsin Nadeem, *Child Rights and Abuses* : Strategies to Remove Child Labour Practices; Canadian International Development Agency, New Delhi, 1992.

8

Minorities and Human Rights

P.D. Mathew, S. J.

The Human Rights of Minorities

Fifty years ago, representing unanimous voice of the global human fraternity, the United Nations had proclaimed a Universal Declaration of Human Rights. It was adopted by the UN General Assembly on 10th of December, 1948. This Declaration set out for the nations the goal of establishing and promoting a just social order in which every person could freely enjoy all basic human rights irrespective of numerical strength, caste, creed, race, sex, place of birth, colour, language, political opinion or status. The first article of the Declaration stated:

> "All human beings are born free and equal in dignity and rights."

Thus the Nations unanimously agreed to wholly outlaw the out-moded concept of hegemony of one national group over any other only because of its numerical strength in the matter of equal enjoyment of the civil rights and liberties.

Later on 28th November, 1981, the UN proclaimed a specific Declaration on the Elimination of All Forms of Intolerance and Discrimination Based on Religion or Belief. It stated that:

> "Discrimination between human beings on the ground of

> religion or belief constitutes an affront to human dignity and a disavowal of the principles of the Chapter of the United Nations."

While upholding the basic principle of human dignity and equality this Declaration warns that:

> "No one shall be subject to discrimination by any state, institution, group of persons or person on the grounds of religion or other beliefs."

It further suggests that:

> "All States shall take effective measures to prevent and eliminate discrimination on the grounds of religion or belief in the recognition, exercise and enjoyment of human rights and fundamental freedom in all fields of civil, economic, political, social and cultural life."

Not satisfied with the above declarations on the absolute equality of mankind in the matter of human rights and the prohibition of any religion-based discrimination and to clarify and specify the principles of rights in a more outright and straight forward way, the United Nations came out with a third Declaration on 18 December, 1992 on the Rights of Minorities, issuing a mandate to the nations. This Declaration stated:

> "States shall protect the existence of the national or ethnic, cultural, religious and linguistic identity of minorities within their respective territories and shall encourage conditons for promotion of that identity."

For carrying out this mandate, the 1992 Declaration asked all the nations to take measures "to ensure that person belonging to minorities may exercise fully and effectively all their human rights and fundamental freedoms without any discrimination and in full equality before the law." (Article 4)

So as it stands, today" minority rights" are enjoying a social status along with the human rights in .general. Though in the beginning the United Nations did not offer very clear cut mandate for the protection of minorites, it created an instrument in the very beginning of its own inception in 1947, a Sub-Commission on Prevention of Discrimination and Protection of Minorities to look after the needs of minorities.

Though its three Declarations issued one after the other within 45 years, the United Nations made it absolutely clear that Rights of Minorities constitute an internationally accepted, legally recognized, logically sound, jurisprudently tenable and morally justified social norm. So violation of the Rights of Minorities is a violation of internationally accepted legal, jurisprudential, moral and social Code of the modern world.

Our country which has been always multi-religious, multi-linguistic, multi-cultural and multi-racial in nature had no objection to accept this reality right from the time of country's Independence. This is the reason our Constitution has accepted fully the principles of unity in 'diversity' or 'pluralism in togetherness.'

The Rights of the Minorities in India

Our Constitution has already taken care much of what the United Nations Declaration, on the Right of Persons Belonging to National, or Ethnic, Religious and Linguistic Minorities, spelled out in detail. They are incorporated in Part III of the Constitution dealing with the fundamental rights of citizens. This part contains both the common rights and the specific rights of the Minorities in India. In the common rights the following fundamental rights and freedoms are covered:[1]

> **Article 14**: Provides the equality before the law. The Universal Declaration of Human Rights cover the same right in Article 7.
>
> **Article 15**: Prohibition of discrimination on the ground of religion, race, caste, sex or place of birth, which is dealt in Article 2 of the Universal Declaration

Article 16: Equality of opportunity in matters of public employment, which in the Universal Declaration is dealt in Article 23.

Article 19: Protection of certain rights regarding speech, expression etc., which in the Universal Declaraton is dealt in Article 19.

Article 20: Protection in respect of conviction for offences, which in the Universal Declaration is dealt in Article 10.

Article 21: Protection of life and personal liberty, which in the Universal Declaration is dealt in Article 3.

Article 22: Protection against arrest and detention in certain cases, which in the Universal Declaration is dealt in Article 11.

Article 23: Prohibition of traffic in human beings and forced labour; in the Universal Declaration all forms of slavery or servitude is prohibited in Article 4.

Article 24: Prohibition of employment of children in factories, etc. There is no equivalent Article of right in the Universal Declaration.

Article 25: Freedom of conscience and free profession, practice and propagation of religion; which in the Universal Declaration is dealt in Article 18.

Article 26: Freedom to manage religious affairs. There is no equivalent Article of right in the Universal Declaration.

Article 27: Freedom as to payment of taxes for promotion of any particular religion. There is no equivalent Article of right in the Universal Declaration.

Article 28: Freedom as to attendance at religious instruction or religious worship in certain educational institutions. There is no equivalent Article of right in the Universal Declaration.

On the other hand there are two different kinds of specific rights considered as fundamental rights of the minorities in India. The first such right is open to all the citizens, who form minorities in different parts of the country. Their rights against injustice and cultural rights are protected in Article 29, which states:

(1) "Any section of the citizens residing in the territory of India or any part thereof, having distinct language, script or culture of its own shall have the right to conserve the same.

(2) No citizen shall be denied admission into any educational institution maintained by the State or receiving aid out of state funds on grounds only of religion, race, caste, language or any of them."

The next comes the specific right given to linguistic and religious minorities in the area of education under Article 30. It States:

(1) "All minorities, whether based on religion or language, shall have the right to establish and administer educational institutions of their choice.

(2) The State shall not, in granting aid to educational institutions, discriminate against any educational institution on the ground that it is under the management of a minority, whether based on religion or language."

The Constitution of India is very clear in its preamble that the over all goal of India as a Sovereign Socialist Secular Democratic Republic is "to secure to all its citizens socio-economic and political justice, liberty of thought, expression, belief and worship, equality of status and opportunity and to promote among them all fraternity assuring the dignity of the individual and the unity and integrity of the Nation. These ideals of the Nation, especially with respect to minority can be achieved only by enforcing their constitutional rights.

Apart from the fundamental rights stated in Part III of the Constitution, there is another set of rights stated in Part IV, which are connected with social and economic rights of the people. These rights are known as "Directive Principles of State Policy." Which are not judicially enforceable like the fundamental rights but are "fundamental in the governance of the country. It is the duty of the government to apply these principles in making laws. (Article 36).

In Part IV-A the Constitution spells out the fundamental duties of the Indian citizens. This part focuses on the duty of all citizens in fulfilling the goal set in the preamble of our Constitution. It is also important from the point of view of the minority rights. The fundamental duty specified in clauses (e) & (f) of Article IV-A reads:

(e) "It shall be the duty of every citizen of India—to promote harmony and the spirit of common brotherhood amongst all the people of India transcending religion, linguistic and regional or sectional diversities; to renounce practices derogatory to the dignity of women;

(f) to value and preserve the rich heritage of our composite culture."

In the implementation of the above rights and freedoms, care needs to be taken that these should be protected in such a way that protecton for the minority rights should not take place at the cost of majority.

II

The National Commission for Minorities

It is very clear that the minorities do enjoy all the fundamental rights and freedoms, which have been offered to the citizens of our country in general as well as special rights, which our Constitution provides for them. But it seems there have always been doubts about the effective enforcement and implementation of these rights of minorities. Therefore there arose a need for a special body to look after this concern of the minorities and in response to this need in February 1978 the Government of India established an important body to be known as the "Minorities Commission".

Fourteen years after the inception of the Commission, Parliament enacted the National Commission for Minorities Act 1992, changing the name of the Commission to "National Commission for Minorities" (NCM) and giving it a statutory status. This Act was passed on 17 may 1992 and it came into effect exactly after one year on 17 May 1993. This Act gives the Commission six members and a chairman. The functions of the Commission are the following:

(a) evaluate the progress of the development of minorities under the Union and States;

(b) monitor the working of the safeguards provided in the Constitution and in laws enacted by Parliament and the State Legislatures;

(c) make recommendations for the effective implementation of safeguards for the protection of the interests of minorities by the Central Government or the State Governments:

(d) look into specific complaints regarding deprivation of rights and safeguards of the minorities and take up such matters with the appropriate authorities;

(e) cause studies to be undertaken into problems arising out of any discrimination against minorities and recommend measures for their removal;

(f) conduct studies, research and analysis on the issues relating to socio-economic and educational development of minorities;

(g) suggest appropriate measures in respect of any minority to be undertaken by the Central Goverment;

(h) make periodical or special reports to the Central Government on any matter pertaining to minorites and in particular difficulties confronted by them; and

(i) any other matter which may be referred to it by the Central Government".

In order to carry on its functions and the right use of its power, in order to protect the rights of the minorites in general and specially to evaluate the progress of the development of minorities and to look into specific complaints regarding deprivation of rights and safeguards of the minorities, the Commission in exercising the powers conferred by Section 8(2) of NCM Act 1992 has prepared and adopted a very comprehensive and clear "(Procedures & Process) Regulation 1997" on June 17, 1997.

A very clear procedure for looking into specific complaints has been spelt out in Regulation 7. The introductory section (1) of Regulation 7 reads as; "in terms of Section 9(1) (d) of the Act, specific complaints of deprivation of Minorities rights and safeguards can be lodged with the Commission by any individual, institution or organisation within its jurisdiction. These may be addressed to the Chairperson, a Member or the Secretary of the Commisson. No fee will be chargeable for entertaining and disposing off a complaint, unless otherwise directed."

III

Prevailing Situation of Attacks on the Identity of Minorities

A peculiarity of the minority situation[2] in India is the size of the minorities. Minorities elsewhere ar small in size, whereas in India they are multi-million strong, sometimes larger than the entire population of many countries of the world. Hence, the deprivation of a minority in India involves the deprivation of many millions of people. The practical experience of the minorities, especially since 1960, has been particularly bitter. Their general educational backwardness, poverty, low representation in political institutions and government service and recurrent riots testify to it.

The minorities in India have remained backward, since there has been no let up on the communal disturbances. From the Jabalpur riots in the early 1960s to this day the country has witnessed literally thousands of communal holocausts. In these communal riots mostly the properties of minorities were systematically destroyed.

Thus the practical epxerience of the minorities has been quite harrowing. The minorities are now facing the hostility of the 'Hindu revivalism', of an unprecedented, most virulent, ugly and intolerant kind. The provocative slogans against the minorities, often asking them to leave the country, defiling of thier places of worship at some places and the threats to carry on such acts elsewhere, open discriminaton of varying kinds, partisanship of the law and order machinery, unabashed playing of communal card by the politicians, be it on the Babri Masjid issue, TV coverage of their going to temples with fanfare, lighting up of lamps at official functions, or talking of establishing 'Rama Rajya', have all stocked the fire of communalism.

The majority community toady interprets "national mainstream" as "Hindu mainstream" and insists that all the minorities join it, submerging their identities in it.

The Hindu communalists today aim at erasing everything that helps preserve minority identities. The demands for the abolition of the Minority Commission, personal laws of the minorities, second language status of Urdu in U.P. and Bihar, etc., constitute part of this attempt. The minorities are asked by them either to join the "national mainstream" or be prepared to be relegated to the status of second-class citizens. Under the influence of Hindu revivalism, the masses are getting increasingly communalised. Communal violence and the attacks on the identity of the minorities are on the rise. The prevailing situation is extremely grim and hostile for the Indian minorities.

IV

Recent Violations of Human Rights of Minorities[3]

Ever since the BJP led government took over power at the Centre, there has been a steep rise in the attacks on Christians particulary in BJP-ruled states. The pattern of violence shows that the RSS, VHP, Bajrang Dal and Shiv Sena cadres are carrying out a well-chalked out plan to harass, intimidate and terrorise the minority Christian community in India who number around 23 million, forming barely 2.6 percent of the Indian population.

The highest number of attacks have taken place in Gujarat where the VHP has the most widespread network. In Gujarat, VHP activists have burnt copies of the Bible, demolished Churches, desecrated Christian cemeteries, brutally attacked prayer meetings and vandalised missionary institutions. Similar attacks have also taken place in Madhya Pradesh, Maharashtra, Uttar Pradesh, Rajasthan and Punjab in the last few months.

In the North-East and in Bihar, the RSS cadres have been carrying out a campaign against the Church for many years and have stepped this up further. The recent rape of nuns in Jhabua district of Madhya Pradesh is the most horrific instance of the atmosphere of hatred resulting in such atrocities. The subsequent justification by the VHP of the rape and other incidents of violence proves that far from being isolated cases, the violence is a manifestation of the Fascistic Hindutva Ideology that has become brazenly aggressive with the acquisition of State power. There have been 133 cases of incidence of violence against the Christian community in India in recent years and particularly during 1997-98.

A feeling of insecurity prevails among the minorities, because in many cases even the police and the administration have failed to take action against the Sangh Parivar activists. These activists have been taking advantage of the BJP rule in the state to harass minorities, feel many religious and social leaders of the minority communities, namely Muslims and Christians. These attacks have shaken the faith of minorities in the credentials of the BJP government in Gujarat. The incidence of the last three months prove that the administration lacks will to take action against the anti-social elements parading as Sangh Parivar activists.

After receiving a report[4] from a team appointed by the National Commission for Minorities in India, on the violation of human rights of Christians and Muslims in the State of

Gujarat by members of the BJP, RSS, Bajrang Dal and Vishwa Hindu Parishad, the Commission had taken a serious note of the deteriorating situation in various parts of the State on the communal front. The findings of the NCM team and the information received by the Commission from other authentic sources indicated violations of the Constitutional provisions relating to both fundamental rights and duties and commission of offences relating to religion under Section 295 to 298 of the Indian Penal Code 1860. The Commission observed that these events have seriously wounded the religious sentiments of the minorities and created feelings of fear, dismay an disillusionment with the nations secular and egalitarian traditions. Seeing the feelings of insecurity and receiving complaints continuously on deprivation of civil rights of the minorities the commission urged the concerned custodians of Constitutional authority in Gujarat to take effective steps to establish complete religious harmony in the State and to ensure that the fundamental rights are freely enjoyed and the fundamental duties diligently adhered to by all citizens living in various parts of the State.

V

Challenges Ahead: Suggestions to Protect and Promote the Rights of Minorities[5]

1. Religious harmony groups consisting of heads of various religious groups should be formed in every Districts and Taluks to promote harmony, mutual respect and love among all religious communities.

2. Every State Government must be persuaded to make legislation to pay adequate compensation to all riot victims irrespective of their religion, status or caste, sex or place of birth on the basis of the judgement delivered by the Delhi High Court in Harbhajan Kaur case (a victim of 1984 anti-Sikh riots).

3. Minorities of different states and union territories where there are no commissions must be brought within the jurisdiction of the NCM. National Commission for

Minorities Act must be amended to make it mandatory for all State Governments to establish statutory minorities commission.

4. Make all official and constitutional agencies function under the only sound policy of recognition of social diversity and disparity as a fact of our national life. This must be objectively studied and findings widely disseminated so that measures are taken by the governments, the NGOs and the communities for removal of disparities while allowing the groups, the freedom to retain their cultural diversities.

5. Government must be asked to direct the Census Commissioner to officially publish the data on socio-economic and educational status of each religious community collected during census 1951, 1961, 1971, 1981 and 1991. The next Census of 2001AD must clearly bring out the socio-economic and educational profile of all religious minorities in the country. It will also help the government to fulfill India's obligation to the international community under the UN which requires each member state to make the condition of the minorities known.

6. Every state government be urged to set up a separate department to address minorities' grievances.

7. An earnest effort needs to be launched to bring unity among the religious minorities in India. The alienation between the minority religious groups especially among Christians and Muslims is not only unfortunate but also unwarranted. This division among them is being used by the vested interests from the majority communities to attack them and weaken them. Their current alienation aggravates their vulnerability.

8. Proper electoral reforms should be introduced by the State and its custodians, both at the constitutional and political level, to ensure that all minorities of India get a proper and effective representation in the central and state legislatures, central and state governments and local self-governments.

9. Proper legal and administrative steps should be taken to evolve a system that will secure proper representation of all minorities in the proposed Prasar Bharti Corporation and in the existing state agencies like the Planning Commission, Press Council, Union Public Service Commission, State Public Service Comissions, Staff Selection Comission, Law Commission and State-owned newspapers and periodicals, etc.

10. Efforts must be made to increase the representation of minorities in the state police and other units of law and order machinery to at least 25 percent to avoid a repeat of Bombay tragedy caused by the communal riots of 1992-93.

11. The mass media, electronic and print, must endeavour to create a nation-wide awareness and consciousness regarding the fact that each of the minorities in this country is part and parcel of the vast Indian nation and is entitled to enjoy all privileges and benefits along with other Indians indiscriminately.

12. School and college text books must be thoroughly revised so as to eliminate matters which create ill-feelings against any particular minority community or all minorities in general. Concerted efforts must be made to include in the text books lessons of an absolute equality of all the communities of India including the minorities, so as to teach their readers respect and love for all the communities of India.

13. A proper machinery should be evolved by the state for the propagation, popularisation and proper implementation of all the fundamental rights and fundamental duties enshrined in the Constitution laying equal stress on both the rights and the duties and getting them translated into concrete action.

14. There are certain matters about which some communities are sentimentally concerned - e.g., the issue of personal law and family traditions of the minorities and the administration of schools run by the minorities. All these should be dealt with sympathetically and in consultation with the acclaimed spokesmen of these communities.

Conclusion

The Universal Declaration of Human Rights by the United Nations in 1948 upholds the human rights of minorities everywhere in the world. It is the unanimous voice of the global human fraternity. India is a signatory to this declaration and bound to implement its provisions.

Our country has incorporated most of these provisions in Part III and IV of the Constitution of India. But these provisions are not properly implemented by the successive governments. So a special body was established in 1978 by the Government of India to protect the rights of the minorities and to look after their interests. This body is now known as National Commission for Minorities. This Commission is expected to evaluate from time to time development of minorities and the implementation of the Constitutional and Statutory provisions related to the rights of the minorities, to look into their complaints and to take up relevant matters with the appropriate authorities.

Violations of human rights of minorities are increasing day by day especially in States ruled by Bharatiya Janata Party (BJP). The country has witnessed hundreds of communal riots in which thousands of persons belonging to minorities have lost their life and properties. Now they are facing the hostility of the Hindu revivalism of an unprecedented, most virulent, ugly and intolarent kind. The hate and violence recently lashed against the minorities, especially against Christians in Gujarat, Rajasthan, Maharashtra, Madhya Pradesh and UP are seen as an intrinsic part of the RSS-BJP-VHP's strategy to pave the way towards their "Hindu-Rashtra".

The present situation of attak on the minorities must be fought by the Government, members of minority groups and human rights activists with courage. There are many challenges ahead of us to protect and promote the rights of minorities. The time has come for all the patriotic persons to come together and work to eliminate the divisive forces that destroy this great country and to promote the values of justice, equality, liberty, fraternity and unity envisaged by the framers of our Constitution.

References

1. Massy, James Dr., "NCM's Role in Protection of the Human Rights of Minorities," *Legal News and Views,* Vol.12, No.5, May 1998, p. 30.

2. Tahir Mahmood (ed.), "Minorities and State at the Indian Law," Institute of Objective Studies, New Delhi: 1991, PP.22-26.

3. "Resolution on Attacks on the Christian Community," *Indian Currents*, 91-5 November, 1998, p.21.

4. "Violence on Christian and Muslims-Minority: Commission Indicts Gujarat State," *Legal News and Views*, Vol..12, No.11 November, 1998, p.23.

5. (No. 8-14) "Recommendations of the Seminar-Text and Comments," in "Minorities and State at the Indian Law," Tahir Mahmood (ed), Institute of Objective Studies, New Delhi: 1991, pp.170-171.

9

Rights of Dalits: A Human Rights Perspective

Mohd. Shadan Zeb Khan

"People only live full lives in the light of Human Rights".

In the contemporary India Dalits bear the anguished burden of a long and unbroken legacy of the deepest social degradation.[1] Although the word 'Dalit' literally means poor and oppressed persons, it has acquired a new cultural context to imply those who have been broken ground down by those above them in a deliberate and active way.[2] It constitutes a larger formation which includes members of scheduled castes and tribes, neo-Buddhists, the working people, the landless and poor peasants, women and all those who are being exploited politically, economically and in the name of religion.[3] It is this class which is also called as the fourth world.[4] From the pariah, an untouchable whose very shadow was considered polluting by orthodox caste Hindus, to the present day Dalit has been a long journey—troubled, contradictory and painful. For the different communities, juridically encapsulated within the bland and official categories like scheduled caste and tribes, receiving recognition as an equal citizen of a democratic republic far less the recovery of self-hood, is a project still waiting to be actualized.

Acts of brutality and terror continue to be part of the atrocities perpetuated on the Dalits and other lower classes, the more so the more they become conscious of their rights and begin to assert themselves. Entire communities are found to be in deep turmoil, facing constant humiliation and growing erosion of their identity and sense of being part of civil society, the nation and the state.[5] The widespread atrocities and all round discrimination against Harijans and the ruthless attempts to suppress them whenever they try to assert their rights pose the problem of denial of human rights to a substantial section of our population. Whether it is a struggle for wages or for land, their movement is brutally suppressed. The state which is supposed to create the necessary conditions to enable the weaker sections to exercise their right and protect them when they are attacked often behave in a manner which helps only the oppressor and exploiters. (Flourishing of forces like Ranbir Sena which is indulging in ethnic cleansing of Dalits in Bihar under the very nose of govt. can be cited as the recent example.). Thus millions of poor people in villages are faced with a helpless situation in which they are not allowed even to enjoy the rights guaranteed under law. Is this not tantamount to denial of basic human rights?[6]

In pursuance of the constitutional provisions for the Dalits, a number of measures have been undertaken by the Central and State Government since independence for their economic, educational and social upliftment. Such measures may be grouped into three categories: *protective, developmental and preferential*. The Abolition of Untouchability Act of 1955, later amended and renamed as Protection of Civil Rights Act (Nov. 1978) and prevention of atrocities against scheduled castes and scheduled tribes fall under protective measures. Programmes for their educational and economic development under the central and state governments, the special component plan, special assistance and formation of Scheduled Castes Development Corporation, fall under the second category. Reservations in education and employment and preference in various other areas, constitute the third type of measures.[7] But besides all these efforts we discover that there is no substantial improvement in the condition of Dalits. Everyday we find newspapers replete with reports of atrocities though untouchability as a rule has practically diminished to a considerable extent in many places. But Dalits are still lowly placed specially in the North India.[8] Atrocities they are subjected to are linked to their search for liberation. They are the result of their efforts to own land, are reaction for their refusal to let Dalit women be exploited by upper caste men or are the consequences of their resistance to age-old forms of exploitation.[9] The greater their search for a new humanity, the higher the number of atrocities against them. Thus atrocities are another form of interaction between the forces of status quo and the forces of change, and a reaction against the Dalit search for a new identity.[10] Thus the assertion of rights by members of scheduled caste, particularly their refusal to accept humiliation as a part of their being, is being retaliated against in many areas by other communities.[11]

In this search for a new identity Dalits and some of their messiahas have tested several methods. A critical survey of some of the well known perspectives reveal their weakness in ensuring a dignified life to Dalits.

1. **Gandhian Perspective**: This primarily involved renaming Dalits as Harijans alongside campaign to eradicate untouchability.[12] When Anti-untouchability League was converted into the Harijan Sevak Sangh, the emphasis clearly shifted from anti-untouchability to service and constructive programmes. The Sangh undertook several welfare activities for the untouchables. The main programmes were: (i) providing scholarships for education, (ii) maintaining hostels for untouchable students, (iii) maintaining separate schools for primary education of untouchable children, (iv) providing medical aid and running dispensaries, (v) digging new wells, installing tube wells and pumps for supply of water, (vi) organising industrial schools and cooperative societies for artisans and others.[13] Gandhiji also campaigned for reform in the Hinduism so that Dalits may also enjoy a respectable position within the ambit of Varna system. It also included reservation of seats for Dalits (Poona Pact). Today when the scope of reservation has been widened what we have achieved

is an equality of results more than an equality of opportunity the dalit challenge to the Gandhian perspective is a part of a new stirring of consciousness among the subjugated which rejects patronising and insist on their rightful share in the power structure of society.[14]

2. **Ambedkar's Perspective**: The Ambedkar's legacy which focussed essentially on the secular realms – resources, education, jobs and power achieved limited success.[15] Ambedkar came to believe, late in life, that the solution lay in conversion. But even conversion to religions which doctrinally disallow caste has not helped Dalits evade stigmatization, not just vis-a-vis Hindus but even within their new religious communities.[16] It has by now been established that in changing their religion only a miniscule minority of the low castes has achieved the objective of upward mobility. For example, in predominantly Christian villages, the Dalit colony is distinct and separate from the upper caste settlement. Their economic conditions are also deplorable. Data on educational mobility and occupational advancement of Protestants in Madras reveal that the Dalits lag far behind. In Andhra Pradesh, Kerala and Karnataka the Dalit's economic position, despite their conversion, has not improved. In Kerala the Dalit Christians are mainly landless labourers. There is no question of inter-dining or inter-marriage between the Dalits and the Syrian Christians.[17] According to Jose Konanaikil, those who changed their religion seem to have got some psychological satisfaction or spiritual fulfilment by doing so. For some it may also have contributed to the process of changing self-perception of one's identity and dignity. The writer stresses that in many cases, their situation seem to have become worse.[18] Even if some changes after conversion are visible, they are minor cultural changes viz. names, dress, eating habits, rituals, festivals and celebrations, etc.

3. **Caste Perspective**: This aims at upward mobility through the process of Sanskritization.[19] This includes (a) giving up certain social practices such as eating meat, (b) giving up traditional occupations, (c) migrating to towns and cities.[20] But

in any case the positive orientation for reference and imitation of upper caste values did not lead to any significant change in the status of the Dalits.

4. **Class Perspective**: Notwithstanding the denial of Marxists the fact remains that class perspective is reductionist in its nature and orientation. That is why communist movement in India has historically failed to win over Dalit Proletarian base of Indian society. The failure emanates from the fact that it does not address the questions of dignity. It has also failed to provide the kind of praxis that socially oppressed populations needed.[21] Some of the ultra-left parties also justify use of violence for the emancipation of Dalits. As is evident from the role of CPI (ML) in Bihar and PWG in Andhra Pradesh. This may only produce and reproduce the degenerated and brutalised system.[22] According to Rajni Kothari "As for the Naxal groups, after waging some heroic struggles in various micro and regional settings, most of them have shown signs of exhaustion and have sought entry into the legislative – electoral arena, mostly fielding upper and middle caste candidates. Even the more Maoist groups committed to 'annihilation of the class enemy' are riven by caste bickerings arising from domination by Brahman and Brahmanic individuals."[23] It should also be realised that the formerly socialist societies got into crisis because also of ignoring the concern for human rights – rights concerning justice, freedom and above all human life and its dignity.[24]

5. **Dalit Perspective (BSP-RPI Perspective)**: While accepting the prevalence of a caste order, it seeks to subvert the benefits accruing perpetually to the top rungs by uniting the lower rungs. It aims to conscientise the non-caste Hindus, subsumed within the Hindu social structure degradingly as backwards, scheduled castes or adivasis, into a conglomeration of the "sufferers," hence advocating also the need to come together. The mere numerical strength of these victims, per se is sought to be made use of to question the predominance of a miniscule minority like the Brahmins.[25] The category's prime focus is to point out the marginalisation of the majority by the

minority caste Hindu groups. The present condition is sought to be changed through electoral politics which would empower the victims to restructure their socio-economic order favouring Savarnas, as the Bahujans would reign.[26]

But the lack of enlightenment among the Dalits leads to the legitimisation of Dalit politics which has become self-limiting as it eludes the question of Dalit emancipation.[27] It also makes the Dalits, willing partners in supporting their political leaders who lack an ability to offer an alternative vision of politics. Moreover, exclusivist Dalit politics based on consolidating narrow caste loyalties to extract advantages and concessions from the state is also meeting increased resistance, both from within and without. At one plane is the retaliatory violence of the savarnas. At the other is the increasing difficulty of consolidating the Dalits, MBC and OBC blocks with specific caste and segments seeking individual routes and alliances. Since the dalits on their own rarely represent viable electoral strengths, more than winning seats, they or rather their parties, have been reduced to becoming spoilers. A series of opportunist alliances viz. of the BSP with the BJP and Congress and the overblown egos of the Dalit OBC leaders, seem to have put a crimp in the construction of a larger and inclusive Bahujan politics.[28] In addition to this the parties with which they have aligned, have ditched their issues. Rather Dalits votes have strengthened the agenda of caste with which they have aligned. Like in Bihar voters of RJD include a substantial section of Dalits. But ironically atrocities on Dalits during this regime has broken all earlier records of atrocities. Rank enemy of Dalits, the Ranbir Sena has become more ruthless and the culprits are seldom punished.

But howsoever progressive Dalit politics may seem today, it may not provide a permanent solution to the problems of Dalits because it cannot give birth to a national level movement (transcending narrow lines). That is why it has not only failed in protecting them against discriminations and ensuring equality of opportunity but also it has been unable to check the rising atrocities on them. Rather Dalit politics has given birth to a band of 'Dalit aristocrats.' Dalit politics has also dismayed the liberal outsider by fractions wrangling and intemperate speeches.[29] Moreover politics of Dalitism is done on the basis of identity which reinforces the institution of caste. Whereas the solution to their problems lie in going beyond identities and transcending categories because indignities and humiliation meted out to them is on the basis of identity. It has been a common experience that howsoever higher post Dalits get in bureaucracy and other services, some upper caste people continue calling them sarcastically with their caste names like S.P. is a Chamar and Commissioner is a Dhobi etc.

Thus we find that these identities have proved to be an obstacle in their integration with mainstream. And so there seems to be a need to look at the problems of Dalits by coming above identities.

Some other efforts have been also made by NGOs like Sulabh International of Bindeshwar Pathak, who claims to have freed the outcasts from the vagaries of scavenging. But it is also of limited success. Rajni Kothari claims that 'Satyashodhak' ideology of caste-class has been a success but even this has remained confined to a few districts of Maharashtra and even there it has been unable to evolve a common front between Mahars and other Scheduled Castes groups.[30]

A brief look at the above discussed approaches reveal that in one way or the other, these have not succeeded in freeing Dalits from the shackles of exploitation and indignities. D.R. Nagraj a noted Dalit social scientist in his book 'The Flaming Feet : A Study of the Dalit Movement', classifies the Dalit struggle in Karnataka for three rights.

(i) **Structural Rights**: A change of structures is possible only when Dalits acquire and own land because ownership of land is essential for the struggle towards equality.

(ii) **Right to Social Space**: Equality before law is not possible till the Dalits acquire the right to enter and use public places such as restaurants, public wells, recreation clubs and play fields etc.

(iii) **Right to Cultural Space**: This is related to Dalits right to enter temples and recite holy books and become priests of temples which was earlier denied to them.[31]

While class perspective overemphasizes the need for structural rights of Dalits, Gandhian perspective restricts itself to the demand of social and cultural space. Ambedkar's and BSP perspective too are of limited use and narrow in their scope. If anybody thinks that Harijans alone can fight and win their battle without the help of other democratic mass it will be a wrong way of thinking which will only result in the isolation of the Dalits and thus help their oppressors.[32]

6. **Human Rights Perspective**: It is here that one realizes to adopt the Human Rights Approach for the liberation of Dalits. This is the only approach which does not recognize any category or identity rather it thinks in terms of humanity. It believes in the mantra—People only live full lives in the light of Human Rights.

The movements of the oppressed and of the oppressed have enormous inherent potential to release creative intervention. But the movements for the oppressed need to consider several philosophical and operational questions. It is in this process that they not only develop a new vision and wider horizon but also direct a large number of humanistic and democratic groups in building a better social order where dignity, freedom, and decency—the philosophical base of Human Rights - would not only become the most dominant of human concerns but the governing norm of social relationship.[33] Human Rights Movement helps the Dalits to reform the system and to join the mainstream not as subordinates as they have been forced to be for centuries, but as equals. Proper type of movement can also help them to be self reliant and assist them in their search for a new identity, sense of dignity and. humanity that they are aspiring for. They should be ensured the right to development which is an inalienable right of every individual according to the UN Declaration on the Right to Development.[34] This development should be a comprehensive one in economic, social, cultural and political fields aiming at the constant improvement and the well-being of the Dalits on the basis of their active, free and meaningful participation in the development and distribution of benefits resulting therefrom should also be just and fair.

Given the historical context, the scope of human rights in India has to encompass all levels and structures of dominance. For power of the state rests on dominant structures of society which in turn, depends on the nature and the way the social relations are structured. While economic or property structure constitutes the base and source of dominance, the other relatively autonomous sources of dominance e.g. gender, religion, caste, institutions, ideology, mass media etc. cannot be ignored. Thus no Human Rights perspective can be complete without this comprehensive vision and no Human Rights activism is complete without an action oriented strategy against all structures and forms of dominance. The civil liberties and democratic rights movements in Indian context have been able to grasp this essence through not only very excruciating experience but sacrifice of a few of its own members. These movements have also realized that the gains of democracy or peoples movement should not only be consolidated but further extended as a part of overall transformative process. In the process democratic forms and institutions-decentralisation autonomy of academic institutions, judicial activism collective bargaining, anti-poverty programmes—can fully be exploited. The linkages with the international democratic public opinion may also have to be forged and fortified. The Human Rights activism should also explore all the democratic elements legacies and practices of the civil society that history has be queathed.[35] For this all right-thinking forces and organisations in the country and all those who believe in social justice and social equality should unitedly come to the aid of the Dalits in their struggle against atrocities and social oppression. This is not merely a humanitarian task, but the very interests of the country's development and national advance requires such cooperation and help from all progressive and democratic sections. As long as a considerable section of our people is forced to live a life of utter misery and is denied even the basic civic rights, there cannot be any national progress in the real sense, such a situation will act as a drag on the country's forward march.[36] Hence the issue is not only one of liberating the Dalits from the agony of what has been a painful marker of their identity, it is also the moral context, one of cleansing the soul of India of the evil of caste and caste based oppression that has besmirched it. At a material level it is one of preserving the integrity of India and ensuring that it dreams of prosperity are not turned into ashes. The Dalits search for a new identity is thus the search for a new India of equal citizens.[37]

References

1. Harsh Mander, 'Dalit Status and an Agenda for State Intervention' in Vijay K. Gupta (ed) *Perspectives on Human Rights*, Vikas Publishing House, New Delhi, 1996, p.81.

2. E. Zelliot, "Dalit : New Cultural Context for an Old Marathi Word", in contributions to Asian & African Studies, pp.1-2, quoted in E. Zelliot "*From Untouchable to Dalit*", Manohar, Delhi, 1992.

3. Manifesto of Dalit Panther Movement (Bombay, 1973), Quoted in Gail Omvedt, *Dalit Vision*, Orient Longman New Delhi, 1995, p. 72.

4. Concept given by La Fountain quoted in the *Fourth World: Appraisals and Aspirations* (ed) Radhakant Nayak, Manohar Publications, New Delhi, 1997, pp. 11-24.

5. Rajni Kothari, "Rise of the Dalits and the Renewed Debate of Caste", in Partha Chatterjee (ed) *State and Politics in India*, OUP, Delhi, 1997, p. 439.

6. P.K. Kodian, "Atrocities on Harijans and Weaker Sections" in A.R. Desai (ed) *Repression and Resistance in India*,

Popular Prakashan, Bombay, 1990, p. 320.

7. Sukhadeo Thorat, "Ambedkar and the Economics of the Hindu Social Order : Understanding its orthodoxy and legacy", in Walter Fernandes, (ed.) *The Emerging Dalit Identity : The Re-assertion of the Subalterns*, Indian Social Institute, New Delhi, 1996, ·p.23.

8. G.K. Ghosh and Shukla Ghosh, *Dalit Women*, APH Publishing Corporation, New Delhi, 1997, p.9.

9. Walter Fernandes, Op.cit., p.3.

10. Ibid.

11. The 28th Report (1987) of Commissioner of SC & ST, quoted in James Massey, *Down Troden : Struggle of India's Dalits for Identity, Solidarity and Liberation* WCC Publications, Geneva, 1997, p.26.

12. The Problem, Dalit, *Seminar* (monthly), November 1998, New Delhi, p. 12.

13. Thomas Mathew, *Caste and Class Dynamics : Radical Ambedkarite Praxis*, DeTech Publication, New Delhi, 1992, p.21.

14. Rajni Kothari, Op.cit., p.452.

15. 'The Problem', Dalit *Seminar* (monthly), op.cit., p.12.

16. Ibid.

17. Arundhuti Roy Choudhary, reviewing the book, "Dalits in India : Religion as a Source of Bondage or Liberation with special reference to Christians" by James Massey, in *Seminar* (monthly), Nov. 1998, p.71.

18. Jose Kananaikil, "*Scheduled Castes Converts and Social Disabilities : A Survey of Tamil Nadu*", Indian Social Institute, New Delhi, 1990, p. 41.

19. M.N. Srinivas, *Social Change in Modern India*, Orient Longman, New Delhi, 1972, pp.1-45.

20. Jose Kananaikil, *Scheduled Castes in Search of Justice, Part II, The verdicts of the Supreme Court*, Indian Social Institute, New Delhi, 1986, p.7.

21. Rajni Kothari, Op.cit., p. 453.

22. G. Hargopal, "Political Movements and Human Rights: The Case of Koyyur Kidnap," *Economic and Political Weekly*, December 4, 1993, p.73.

23. Rajni Kothari, Op.cit., p. 454.

24. G. Hargopal, Op.cit., p.74.

25. A. Gajendran, "Transforming Dalit Politics", *Seminar* November 1998, New Delhi, p. 26.

26. Ibid.

27. Gopal Guru, "A Critical Look at Dalit activism", *The Hindu*, January 12, 1999, New Delhi.

28. 'The Problem', Dalit, *Seminar* (monthly), November 1998, New Delhi, p. 13.

29. Ibid., p.12.

30. Rajni Kothari; Op.cit., p. 454.

31. D.R. Nagraj, *The Flaming Feet : A Study of the Dalit Movement*, South Forum Press, Bangalore, 1993, quoted in Walter Fernandes (ed.) Op.cit., p.118.

32. P.K. Kodian, "Atrocities on Harijans and Weaker Sections", in A.R. Desai (ed.) Op.cit., p. 320.

33. G. Hargopal, *Political Economy of Human Rights : Emerging Dimensions,* Himalaya Publishing House, Mumbai, 1997, pp.200–201.

34. *Declaration on the Right to Development*, 1986, UN Department of Public Information (Booklet) Art. 1, p.3.

35. G. Hargopal, Op.cit., pp. 26-27.

36. P.K. Kodian, Op.cit., p. 320.

37. P.S. Krishnan, "Untouchability and Atrocities", in Walter Fernandes, Op.cit., p. 139.

10

Basic Rights of Refugees: Issues in the Global and Indian Context

M. Afzal Wani

I. Introduction

The problem of refugees is one of the current complexities with numerous dimensions. It is globally spread and politically charged. Nonetheless it is humanly vital. It is basically a matter of whole humanity and human rights. Persecution or fear of persecution, creating feelings of trouble and turbulance, are at its roots. It involves the flight of people from regions of insecurity and instability to those of safety and stability. In other words, the problem of refugees is the problem of human rights involving flow of people from places of denial to the regions of guarantee. The issue has rightly attracted the attention of the global community and now a new branch of law called the refugee law, has evolved.[1] An agency known as the United Nations High Commissioner for Refugees (UNHCR) has also got established which is helping in the voluntary repatriation and assimilation of refugees besides providing them with facilities for nutrition, health, education and employment.[2] The vexed questions, however, are that who is entitled to the status of refugee; what is the position of internally displaced persons; and how long will a refugee have to remain as a refugee. The present paper is an attempt to look into these questions with reference to global-conventional practices and the judicial trends in India.

II. Persons Treated as Refugees

The persons to avail of the benefits of care by the UNHCR, according to clause 6 of the Statute of the Office of UNHCR and Article 1 of the Convention relating to the Status of Refugees done at Geneva on 28 July 1951 and the 1967 Protocol include any persons who have been considered as Refugees under the Arrangement of 12 May 1926[3] and 30 June 1928[4], or under the Conventions of 28 October 1933[5] and 10 February 1938[6], the Protocol of 14 Sept. 1939[7], or the constitution of the International Refugee Organisations. These also include any such person who as a result of events occuring before I January 1951 and owing to the well-founded fear of being persecuted, for reasons of race, religion, nationality or political opinion being outside the country of his nationality and is unable or owing to such fear or for reasons other than personal convenience, is unwilling to avail himself of the protection of that country,[8] or who, not having a nationality and being outside the country of his former habitual residence, is unable, or owing to such fear or for reasons other than personal convencience, is unwilling to return to it.

Any decision to the contrary regarding eligibility of refugee status taken by the International Refugee Organisation during the period of its activities shall not affect the import of the persons under this Clause or Convention.

For the purposes of the competence of UNHCR, refugee, therefore, includes any person who is outside the country of his former habitual residence, because he has or had well founded fear of persecution by reason of his race, religion, nationality or political opinion and is unable or, because of such fear, is unwilling to avail himself of the protection of the government of the country of his nationality 'or' if he has no nationality, to return to the country of his former habitual residence.[9]

Earlier under the League of Nations Treaty Series 1922–26 a group approach was adopted to define refugee. To declare a person as refugee it was sufficient that he was outside the country of his origin and without the protection of the government of that state. A refugee under the Arrangement of 12 May 1926 was defined as "any person of Russain origin who was not enjoying the protection of the Government of the Union of Socialist Soviet Republics and who had not acquired another nationality". It is worth noting that in this instance the presence outside the country of origin was not explicitly required but was implicit in the provisions providing that the certificates should cease to be valid if the bearer returned to their country of origin.

Group or category approach was adopted to define refugees in 1936 also in arrangements in respect of people fleeing from Germany. The same was later incorporated in 1938 Convention (Article 1) to cover: (a) persons possessing or having possessed German nationality and not possessing any other nationality and were proved as not having enjoyed in law or fact, the protection of the German Government; and (b) stateless persons not covered by previous Convetions or agreements who had left German territory after being established therein and who proved as not having enjoyed in law or fact the protection of the German Government.

The persons who left Germany for reasons of purely personal convenience were excluded from the definition by Article 1(2) of the Convention.

In the 1938 Evian Conference, an inter-governmental committee was established by participating States to facilitate involuntary emigration from Germany (including Austria) covering emigration on account of political opinions, religious beliefs or social origin.

The general criterion under these approaches to define 'refugee' appears as the *impossibility or intolerability of continued residence in ones own country*. According to the Constitution of International Refugee Organisation refugees include: (i) victims of the Nazi, Fascist, or Quisling regimes which had opposed the United Nations; (ii) certain persons for reasons of Jewish origin or foreigners or stateless persons who had been victims of Nazi persecution; (iii) persons considered as refugees before the outbreak of the Second World War for reasons of race, religion, nationality, or political opinion; (iv) displaced persons including those deported or expelled from their own countries, those unable or unwilling to avail themselves of the protection of the government of their country of nationality or former residence; (v) individuals having valid objections to returning to their country of origin, including persecution or fear based on reasonable grounds of persecution because of race, religion, nationality or political opinions, and objections of a political nature judged by the International Refugee Organisation to be valid.

Article 14 of the Universal Declaration of Human Rights declares that every person has a right to seek and to enjoy in other countries asylum from persecution save in the case of prosecutions generally arising from non-political crimes or from acts contrary to the purposes and principles of the United Nations. Any persons seeking benefit under this provision may be treated as a refugee entitled to care by UNHCR. Same is the position adopted by 1967 Declaration on Territorial Asylum.

III. Persons not treated as refugees

A person is not covered by the UNHCR statutory definition when : (a) he has voluntarily re-availed himself of the protection of the country of his nationality; or (b) he has reacquired his lost nationality; (c) he has acquired and enjoys the protection of the country of new nationality; or (d) he has re-established in the country of origin which he left or outside which he remained owing to fear of persecution; or (e) he can no longer, because the circumstances in connexion with which he has been recognised as a refugee have ceased to exist, claim grounds other than personal convenience for continuing to refuse to return to his country of origin or avail himself of protection of that country;[12] or (f) he is a national of more than one country but because of well founded fear of persecution is unable or unwilling to avail himself of the protection of either government of the countries of his nationality or to return to any of them; or (g) he is recognised by the competent authorities of the present country of residence as having the rights and obligations which are attached to the possession of the nationality of that country; or (h) he continues to receive protection or assistance from other organs or agencies of the United Nations; or (i) he has committed a crime covered by the provisions of treaties of extradition or a crime mentioned in Article VI of the London charter of the International Military Tribunal or by the provisions of Article 14, Para 2 of the Universal Declaration of Human Rights.[13]

The UNHCR Statute affirms that the work of the office shall relate as a rule, to groups and categories of refugees but proposes an individualistic definition of the refugee enabling a case to case treatment necessitated by the recent escalation in refugee crisis. This is an apparent contradiction in terms but the concept of refugees has attained very broad dimensions now. The UNHCR is supposed to address even specific refugee problems on the advice of Executive Committee of the High Commissioners Programme.[14]

IV. Broadened Dimensions of Refugee Definition

As a matter of fact there exist many examples of broadening of dimensions of the refugee definition and providing pragmatic solutions to refugee problems by UNHCR. Some such examples are :

(a) Authorization of High Commissioner by General Assembly to assist mainland Chinese in Hong Kong whose status as 'refugees' was complicated by the existence of two Chinas each of which might have been called upon to excercise protection.[15]

(b) Assistance to Algerians fleeing to Tunisia and Morocco to escape the effects of the struggle for liberation.[16]

(c) Assistance of Angolan refugees in Congo.[17]

The common factor that appears as being given recognition for treating the people as refugees is the need to cross an international frontier because of a conflict, or radical, political, social or economic changes in their countries of origin.

But in 1960 the General Assembly developed the notion of High Commissioner's 'good offices' to cover the refugees who did not otherwise come within the competence or immediate competence of United Nations.[18]

As regards the individual assessment of refugee status, it became impratical in 1960s because of the grave African refugee problem. Fear had to be taken as established where the whole group in question would move. As it did not remain possible to establish fear on the basis of individual cases, the determining of the refugee status of groups accordingly did not attract a strict application of the definition of refugees to them.

In 1975 when the UNHCR was first involved in the Indo-China peninsula, it referred to 'displaced persons' along with the refugees. 'Displaced persons' are not the same as 'refugees'. The term had a special meaning in the Constitution of the International Refugee Organisation but had otherwise been commonly employed to describe those displaced within their own country, may be due to the civil strife or natural disasters. In 1977 the High Commissioner sought advice from the Executive Committee on the refugee/displaced person distinction but no formal response did forthcome.

Again in 1975 about a million people got displaced in Kampuchea, Laos, and Vietnam. The UNHCR promoted, at the request of the Governments concerned, programmes for displaced persons undertaken within the framework of its 'good offices' and on 'humanitarian basis' viz. securing asylum, providing care and maintenance, facilitating resettlement and repatriation.

The displaced persons from Indo-China outside their country of origin and persons leaving the Indo-China peninsula in small boats were referred in UN documents first as Indo-Chinese 'displaced persons and boat people', and 'refugees and displaced persons'. Then the Executive Committee in 1976 spoke of those who had left their country in small boats as 'asylum seekers,[19] and in 1977 expressly called them refugees from Indo-China.[20] In 1980, the General Assembly referred those boat and land cases as 'refugees'.[21] This amounts to an extension of benefits to displaced persons as were primarily intended for refugees in true sense.

Maintaining the view that refugees are those who have crossed the international border whereas displaced persons have not, it becomes difficult, apart from purely humanitarian considerations, to determine in the case of massive exodus that each and every person has a well founded fear of persecution as is provided under the statute of UNHCR. Since lack of protection is an element of statutory definition of the refugee, this needs to be given precedence because of impracticability of individual determination in the case of a massive exodus.[22] This kind of approach has been followed in Afghan and Ethiopian crisis. In 1979 the representative of Afghanistan, commenting on UNHCR's report in the third committee, observed that assistance to 'Afghan refugees' in Pakistan contravened the UNHCR's Statute, the 1951 Convention and the UN Charter.[23] In 1980 the representative of Ethiopia opposed the extension of UNHCR's resources to the ethiopian refugees, who according to him, were either instruments of aggression and disruption or were nomadic groups on their seasonal movements.[24] Such kinds of protests have not affected the UNHCR from rendering protection and assistance to mass asylum seekers.

Thus refugees in broader sense include those who have a well-founded fear of persecution on certain specified grounds determinable on case to case basis as well as those large groups, categories of persons who have crossed an international frontier, without or unable to avail themselves of the protection of the government of their state of origin. The obligations with respect to the displaced persons may, however, be limited to temporary refuge, material assistance and the pursuits of voluntary repatriation. The refugees in the strict sense of the term may enjoy full spectrum of protection including resettlement.

The trend of flexible approach in defining the term refugee and extending benefits to larger numbers of people, individuals or groups, offer only one most justifiable, explanation, that is, the influence of Human Rights. States cannot claim an absolute right to return some one to persecution (refoulment). The asylum seekers are given benefits under the names of 'boat peoples', 'aliens', 'displaced persons' and so on.

Protection under refugee law is thus ordinarily available to those who have left their countries of origin. Those who quit their homes but remain within their national borders, do not become the subjects of concern under the International Refugee Law, though their position is generally not different from the former category of people. The benefits of the UNHCR can be extended to such displaced persons only through "good offices"[26] on the request of the UN General Assembly as was done in the case of Chad, Sudan, Guinea, Bissan, Mazambique, Angola, Laos, Ethiopia and the former Yugoslavia.[27] Governments, acting through the United Nations have created bodies like UNBRO (United Nations Border Relief Operation) to assist such displaced persons.[28]

Persons who leave their countries of origin under the fear of war and civil disturbances are also not covered by the international refugee law. They are supposed to have no sufficiently individualized fear of persecution.[29] People displaced by deforestation, desertification and other environmental factors are also not oridinarily covered by the International Refugee law.

V. An Assessment of the Policies

The Role of UNHCR:

The role of the UNHCR in the matters of refugees is wide and significant, broadly covering the aspects like,[30]

(a) development of conventions and their ratification by Governments for the protection of the refugees;

(b) execution of the measures to improve the situation of refugees and to reduce the number requiring protection;

(c) promotion of voluntary repatriation or assimilation within the new national communities;

(d) admission of refugees to the territories of States;

(e) obtaining permission for refugees to transfer their assets on and for their re-settlement.

(f) collecting information from Governments about the number, condition, laws and regulations concerning refugees in their territories; and

(g) keeping in touch with Governments, inter-governmental organisations and private organisations dealing with refugee questions and to facilitate their coordination.

The beneficieries:

The movement of people across an international frontier under a well founded fear of persecution is called refugee movement. The persons involved in such a movement are called refugees. They are a concern of UNHCR. Displacement of people within the borders of a country is called internal displacement. Those who are involved in such displacement are not called refugees but are known as internally 'displaced persons'. This has already been made clear that ordinarily they are not the concern of UNHCR and are not entitled to the benefits to which the refugees are. Sometimes favours are extended to them under the schemes called 'good offices'. There is no doubt in the fact that the refugees and the 'displaced persons' can be classified separately but there is again a glaring reality which is quite easily understandable that the two groups of people are equally disadvantageous. May be in case of displaced persons the States deemed as responsible for their protection but where the state fails to provide necessary support to internally displaced persons, who will come to their rescue. Will they not even then qualify for the status of refugees for the purposes of, at least, enjoyment of basic human rights or fulfilment of necessities of life? This is the basic question that has prompted the UN General Assembly to develop the concept of 'good offices' for displaced persons.

Now there exists the regime of human rights and the Sovereignty of human rights. States take birth so that the life is protected and human rights are respected. This is the essence of the establishment of a state. Where a State is not capable enough to provide security and stability to a particular group of subjects in their area of residence and does not provide them suitable residential and other facilities in the areas of displacement, within its own territory, how can the global community be expected to look as a mute spectator!

Generally internal displacements take place due to violence on the basis of ethnicity and political ideology. This is true of all places. Wherever the people expect to find an abode of peace within their country they shift to that place. Where no safe place is available in the country of origin the out flowing people try for obtaining asylum elsewhere in the world. So wherever they have a chance to go for safety, or take *refuge*, within or outside the country, there remains a need for protection and support. In either case they face dislocation and loss of home. Such people must be taken care of by all institutions and organisations working for the protection and advancement of human rights within or outside the country involved.

With the emergence of new problems new approaches to resolve them become indispensable. All over the world developmental activities are given the first priority. However, with the process of development we are witnessing the horrible scenes of enviromental degradation. Even states are contributories to enviromental problems through their 'schemes of development, which result into displacement of people. Constructions of dams, though to increase production causes not only deforestation but also displacements. Establishment of hazardous industries and the flow of industrial waste in a particular area cannot be without similar effects. The sufferers in these situations may either move to other places in the same country or move over the borders across. In either case the people may fall into an ethnic trouble or an economic conflict. Even, in certain cases, the displaced persons may not be having necessary skills of work and profession to get established at the new place. Thus, even the home country may not be able to manage the settlement of displaced persons. The role of international agencies in such cases may, therefore, not be denied just because someone has not crossed the international border.

Group and individual approaches to determine the status of displaced persons or refugees are in certain situations equally important. It is possible that the persecution is faced by an individual or a few of them and they shift to a different place. By adopting group approach we may find that most of the reformists and dynamic personalities working in different strata of a society without an exit whenever the persecution becomes intolerable. Thus, there must not be a total denial of refugee status when only individuals have shifted from the place of persecution.

Economic migrants pose another relevant question. Why should not they be treated as refugees? They also seek, after leaving their home, refuge at a particular place and want to be treated as refugees. What are the basic hurdles in recognizing them as refugees? Probably their admission to the group of refugees is denied on the basis that they are leaving their places of origin under their own volition for better prospects of their life. Since they are supposed to have opted to face a challenge and must therefore, bear the brent. The problem, however, has a different dimension also. The economic migration takes place either under the influence of push factors – when the conditions are adverse at a place, or pull factors – when the conditions are not adverse but the migrating person seeks for better avenues for development. In establishing a criterion for making differentiations between these two categories of displaced persons we may have to face many difficulties, but the fact remains that the economic migrants who have migrated because of 'push factors' must be categorised as beneficieries under the refugee law. This will help them to live with a better sense of security.

VI. Indian Scenario

India is yet to sign the 1951 Convention and the 1967 Protocol. It is only a member of the Executive Committee of the High Commissioners Programme. It is being generally stressed that India should accede to the 1951 Convention and the 1967 Protocol so that the refugees are given a treatment under these policy documents. Presently about 2.5 lakh refugees are in India most of them being from Tibet, Srilanka, Bangladesh and Afghanistan.[31] The main enactments relevant to the subject at the moment are the Foreigners Act of 1946 and Extradition Act, 1962. The Supreme Court of India has made some head way in laying down some principles for the benefit of refugees while dealing with some issues related to Chakma refugees who have shifted to India from Bangladesh.

According to the international standards all the refugees in India are entitled to be recognised as refugees in the 'conventional sense' of the term and their rights to be protected accordingly. The Supreme Court in the *People's Union for Civil Liberties (PUCL)* V. *Union of India*[32] has held that India being a signatory to the International Instruments like Universal Declaration of Human Rights etc., the Article 21 of the Constitution has, therefore, to be interpreted in conformity with the International law. Thus the refugees can avail of the benefits under Article 21 of the Constitution in the same way as the citizens of India. They cannot be exposed to threat to life and personal Liberty.

In the Indian Union, the State of Arunachal Pradesh homes about 65000 Chakma Refugees. Their position came for consideration before the Supreme Court in *Khudiram Chakma* V. *Union of India*.[33] They came to India on March 30, 1964 from erstwhile East Pakistan (now Bangladesh) due to distrubances prevailing there at that time. As refugees they were given shelter in Government Camps at Ledo in Dibrugarh (Assam) and later in 1966 shifted to Miao Camp (Arunachal Pradesh which became a State in the Union of India in 1987). The State has broadly speaking three cultural groups with their own socio-regional affinities: (i) The Monpas and Sherdukpens of Tawang and West Kemeng Districts; (ii) Khamptis and Singpos of the eastern part of the State, and (iii) the Neotes and Wanchos adjoining Nagaland in the Tirap District. Khudiram Chakma and 56 other families were alloted lands in villages at Gautampur and Maitripur. There were already a good number of Chakma refugees living in their alloted lands under the Chakma resettlements schemes (1966) drawn by the Government for them. Khudiram and his fellow families did not stay in the alloted lands but got through an unregistered deed some different piece of land from the local Raja, Ningrunong of Damba on Nov. 20 (1972). Such an acquisition of land, according to the contention of the State, was illegal because of the restrictions on land acquisition by non-natives of the District as provided by Section 7 of the Bengal Eastern Frontier Regulation 1873 (hereinafter BEFR 1873). The Chakma's contention was that since the date of donation they had been residing and cultivating the said land and had developed the area for habitation purposes. In 1973 he was during panchayat elections in Joypur village, appointed as the Gaon-Bura of the village. This was approved by the Government with a grant of *sanad*, dated Nov. 20, 1975. The appellant Chakma further contended that the Deputy Commissioner of Kenonsa approved the Transfer and the Extra Assistant Commissioner, Miao by a memorandum issued instructions against any eviction of the appellants from the said land.[34] Some Deori families who were allotted lands in the adjecent area of Joypur village attempted to encroach upon the lands of the appellant and on a complaint being lodged the Executive Magistrate at Miao by his letter dated May 30, 1977 issued instructions to Ningrunong Singpo Rajkumar to turn out the extra families from the appellants village with a direction to the Circle officer, Diyun, to report compliance. It was after such intervention that such outsider in due course were expelled. With their sweat and blood and the donation from the Raj, the Chakmas converted the uneven track of Jungle into a truely self sufficient village with tremendous agricultural success on which the Tirap District Authorities granted two Rice Hullar Units in the name of the appellant.

Then started the trouble. In view of the appellant's success and roses all the way, the nearby villagers sought to dislodge the appellant and the other families by raising various disputes. One of which was that the place cannot be utilised as refugee settlement and that they should be shifted to another place. As a bolt from the blue came an order of the Circle officer, Diyun, dated February 15, 1984 directing the appellant to shift to the vacant land at Gautampur and Maitripur villages latest by February 24, 1984. The Chief Minister of Arunachal Pradesh when approached did not interfere.

The appellant's contentions were appealing in their nature but the mischief of his opponents by way of repeated complaints led to the appointment of an inquiry committee against him which held the appellant and the other 788 Chakma, Deori and Bhutia refugee families guilty of having illegally encroached upon about 872 hectares of land in Miao Sub-division alone.

The other complaints were that the Chakma people were induldging in illegal activities, such as commission of offences under various lands, collection of arms and ammunition, establishing contacts with the extremist groups, encroachment of adjoining areas. Pursuant to these complaints the Government, by an order, dated 15.2.84, directed the appellant and other Chakmas of Joypur village to shift to the vacant land alloted at Gautampur and Maitripur villages latest by 25.2.1984. The order was challenged before the Gauhati High Court. The questions before the Court were:

(a) Whether the petitioner and the 56 Chakma families are the citizens of India or foreigners?

(b) If not citizens, could they be directed to move to another place from Joypur village, Miyo Sub-Division in Arunachal Pradesh.

(c) Whether the impugned order is *ultra vires* the Constitution?

As regards citizenship the High Court referred to Section 6-A of the Citizenship Act, 1956 which provides that persons who have come into Assam before January 1966 from the specified territory and who have been ordinarily resident in Assam since the date of their entry shall be deemed to be citizens. The court said that the petitioners stayed in Assam for a short while in 1964 and are not the citizens. The plea of the petitioners was that they came to Assam in 1964 and stayed there for some time. Then they shifted to Miao Sub-Division in Arunachal Pradesh. In 1964 the territory of Arunachal Pradesh was included in Assam. Since they stayed in Assam they must be deemed to be citizens of India within the meaning of Section 6-A of the Citizenship Act, 1955 as amended in 1985. They also contended that proviso to Section 2 of Immigrants (Expulsion from Assam) Act, 1950 would also protect them. But all these contentions were rejected by the High Court. As regards the second question the H.C. referred to Section 7 of the BEFR, 1873 which prohibits acquition of land by non-natives in the district without sanction of the State Government. Besides it referred to Clause 9 (2) (a) of the Foreigners Order, 1948 which prohibits acquisition of land or any interest thereon or within the prohibited area by any foreigner. Clause 9(2) (b) provides that the local authority may impose conditions regarding acquisition of land or any interest thereof or any other matter deemed necessary in the interest of public safety. The Chakmas were staying within the inner line of the notified area.

The High Court held that the petitioners have no right to seek a permanent place of abode in that area and the authorities had every right to ask them to shift.

With respect to third question that whether the order was

arbitrary the High Court found various complaints against these Chakmas alleging that they were indulging in procuring arms and ammunition and were actively associating with anti-social elements. The High Court accordingly held the order as not devoid of reason.

The High Court, however, directed the State Government to give adequate compensation to the petitioners in the event of their being evicted from the place. This was done on humanitarian grounds.

The matter ultimately came before the Supreme Court through petition by both parties. Before the Supreme Court, on behalf of petitioners, it was contended:

(a) that in 1947 the Chakmas were the citizens of India;

(b) that they returned in 1964 to erstwhile Assam State and stayed there for some time and then shifted to Arunachal Pradesh;

(c) that by mere accident of their going to Arunachal Pradesh, they could not loose their citizenship;

(d) that Raja Ningrunong Singpo of Damba donated lands in their favour, approved by the Deputy Commissioner;

(e) that the appellant was appointed Gaon Bura of Joypur village with a *sanad* from Deputy Commissioner ;

(f) that Executive Magistrate directed Raja to turn out the extra families occupying lands at Joypur in the area alloted to the appellants and other Chakmas;

(g) that they have been paying taxes including house tax;

(h) that they even if non-citizens, should have been given an opportunity of being heard as was the right given to Slum dwellers in *Scheduled Caste and Weaker Section Welfare Assn. v. State of Karnataka*[35], a case under the Karnataka Slum Areas (Improvement and clearance) ACT, 1973; and

(i) that the fundamental rights are available to foreigners as well, including Article 21 of the Constitution as was laid down by Supreme Court in *Louis De Raedt v. Union of India*.[36]

Against the appellant Chakmas it was contended that they claim to be the citizen of India by invoking Section 6-A of the Citizens Act as amended and incorporated on December, 7,1985 in pursuance of Assam Accord. In order to get the benefit of Section 6-A two conditions mentioned in Sub-Section (2) of the said Section must be satisfied simultaneously:

(i) The persons who are of Indian origin (viz. undivided India) came before January 1, 1966 to Assam from the specified territory; and

(ii) have been "ordinarily resident" in Assam (as it existed in 1985) since the date of their entry into Assam.

The appellants were residing in Miao Sub-Division of Tirap District, Arunachal Pradesh since 1968 they did not satisfy these conditions. The exact meaning of the expression "ordinarily resident" was explained by the Court in *Shanno Devi* V. *Mangal Sain*.[37] The appellants cannot claim citizenship of invoking Section 6-A of the citizenship Act.

It was further argued that, of course, this court in *Louis De Raedt*[38] took the view that even a foreigner has a fundamental right but that fundamental right is confined only to Article 21 and does not include the right to move freely throughout and to reside and stay in any part of the territory of India, as conferred under Article 19(1) (d) and (e). Such a right is available only to citizens. The appellants being foreigners cannot invoke Article 14 of the Constitution to get the same right denied to them under Article 19 since Article 14 cannot operate in regard to a right specifically withheld from non-citizens. In support of this submission reliance was placed on *Indo-China Steam Navigation Co. Ltd. v. Jasjit Singh, Addl. Collector of Customs* and *Louis De Raedt*.[40] The land donated in favour of the appellants by Raja Ningrunong Singpot of Damba by donation deed dated November 20,1972 is, therefore, illegal. Section 7 of the Bengal Eastern Frontier Regulation, 1873 and caluse 9 of the Foreigners Order 1948, which are applicable to Arunachal Pradesh, specifically prohibit such transfer without prior permission of state Government. No such permission, in this case, was obtained. The tribals of North-Eastern States are historically protected races. Part X of the Constitution of India contains provisions and law governing them. The decision regarding settlement of foreigners is a matter of policy. It is well-settled in law that the Court does not interfere in a matter of governmental policy since it is for the government to decide.

As regards the observance of natural justice in the matter of passing the eviction order against Chakmas it was pleaded against them that the relevant materials from the file show that it is not correct to state that the order came to be issued all of a sudden. There is abundant material to show that the question of eviction was an ongoing process, right from 1978. Many notices were issued over a period of years to shift to Villages Maitripur and Gautampur. There were protests from Chamkas. From the file it is seen that the appellant was aware of the shift order dated September 26,1983. There was also an oral hearing of the same. It was because of the complaints filed by the residents of the locality against the appellant and in view of the report that they were indulging in procuring arms and ammunition and were in close contact with anti-social elements. The impugned order was passed only after taking an overall view of the matter. The court upheld the impugned order. It, however, opted not to interfere in the matter of settlement of refugees in any particular area, considering it a matter of policy to be decided by the Government.

The Chakma problem came for consideration before the Supreme Court again in 1995-96 in National *Human Rights Commission v. State of Arunachal Pradesh.*[41] After the *Khudiram Chakma* judgment, relations between the citizens of Arunachal Pradesh and the Chakmas deteriorated further and the latter complained that they are being subjected to repressive measures with a view to forcibly expelling them from the State of Arunachal Pradesh. All Arunachal Pradesh Students Union (AAPSU) issued final notices to all 'illegal foreigners' including Chakmas to leave the state. The deadline was fixed as September 30, 1995. Concern was shown for them by the People's Union for Civil Liberties, Delhi and the National Human Rights Commission who brought the matter to the Supreme Court. Before the Supreme Court two issues were raised (a) grant of protection to Chakmas in the wake of threats; and (b) Conferment of citizenship upon them.

As regards the first question the Court observed that the State, being governed by Rule of law is bound to protect the life and liberty of every human being, be he a citizen or otherwise. It cannot permit any body or group of persons to threaten the Chakmas to leave the State. No State Government can tolerate such threats by one group of persons to another group of persons. The State is duty bound to protect the threatened group from such assaults and if it fails to do so, it will fail to perform its constitutional as well as staturory obligations. Those giving such threats would be liable to be dealt with in accordance with law. The State government must act impartially and carry out its legal obligations to safeguard the life, health and well being of Chakmas residing in the State without being inhibited by local policies. The Court relied on the *Louis De Raedt*[43] view and distinguished the *Khudiram Chakma*. In both these cases the court upheld the application of Article 21 to refugees.

As regards the question of citizenship the Court rejected the contention that the ruling in the *Khudiram Chakma* has for-closed the consideration of the citizenship of Chakmas. In that case the court was seized of a matter where 57 Chakma families were seeking to challenge an order requiring them to vacate land bought by them in direct contravention of Clause (7) of the Bengal Eastern Frontier Ragulation, 1873. The issue of citizenship was raised in a narrow context and was limited to Section 6-A (2) of the Citizenship Act, 1955, which is a special provision for the citizenship of persons covered by the Assam Accord. The Chakmas are now seeking to obtain citizenship under Section 5(1) (a) of the Act, where the considerations are entirely different. That Section provides for citizenship by registration. Its application is not limited to a specific group. It provides that the prescribed authority may, on receipt of an application in that behalf, register a person who is not a citizen of India, as a citizen of India if he/she satisfies the conditions set out therein. This can be invoked by any person who is not a citizen of Indian but is seeking citizenship by registration. Such applications would have to be in accordance with the prescribed rules. Under these rules the Chakmas can also advance their case and request for there consideration for citizenship through registration. Any person. who satisfies the requirements of Section 5 of the Citizenship Act can be registered as a citizen of India.

In the instant case when Chakmas made a representation to the Deputy Commissioner for grant of citizenship under Section 5 (1) (a) of the Citizenship Act 1995 he did not communicate any decision to them. Rule 7 for the Citizenship Rules 1956 requires the application to be made to the local collector, and the Rule 8 describes the registering authority who shall not be below the rank of a Joint Secretary to the Government of India in the Ministery of Home affairs. Rule 9 enjoins the Collector to transmit every application received by him under Section (1) (a) to the Central Government through the State Government with a report on the required matters. Rule 10 provides for issuance of certificates to the persons granted citizenship and the Rules 11 & 12 provide for maintenance of registers. It is clear that the Deputy Commissioner cannot take a decision in the matter. He has only to forward the matter with necessary report. The Supreme Court, therefore, held that by refusing to forward the applications for citizenship the Chakmas have been denied their constitutional and statutory rights. The court directed the State and the Central Governments to take necessary steps to protect Chakmas from every kind of threat and not to evict them from their homes. They also be not denied domestic life and comfort therein.

VII. Conclusion

The definition of refugees under the International refugee law is an outcome of the historical developments and political constraints. It suffers an apparent contradiction when it affirms that the work of UNHCR shall relate as a rule to groups and categories of refugees but proposes an individualistic definition requiring a case by case consideration of refugee status and fulfilment of elements. It now includes only those people who have crossed an international border. But benefits are extended sometimes to internally displaced persons also under the scheme of special offices called the 'good offices'. There is, however, a need to confer the status of refugees on all those internally displaced persons in whose case the home State is not able to provide them necessary support or is for any other reson (may be ethnic dominance) failing to provide support to them. Moreover, those kinds of economic migrants must also be provided support and assistance under the international refugee law who leave their homes under the influence of 'push factors' characterised by adverse conditions.

In the Indian context it is a just feeling that now the Government of India must sign the Universal Instruments like 1951 Convention and 1967 Protocol relating to the status of refugees. Appreciable is the role of judiciary for interpreting the Constitution in conformity with the principles of International law and Human Rights law. The Supreme Court has touched the highest mark on the scale of Human Rights relating to refugees by saying that the State is bound to protect the life and liberty of every human being, be he a citizen or otherwise, and it cannot permit anybody or group of persons to threaten others to leave the State.

References

1. The main components of the refugee law are the 1951 Convention on the Status of Refugees, relevant provisions of the Universal Declaration of Human Rights (especially Article 14), UN Declaration on Territorial Asylum, Protocol of 1967

relating to refugees, Convention on the Organisation of African Unity 1969, The Eurpean Agreement on the Abolition of visas for Refugees 1969, American Convention on Human Rights and the Catagena Declaration of 1984.

2. The UN General Assembly decided to establish High Commissioners Office for Refugees (UNHCR) on 3 December 1949, the statute of the office was adopted on 14 December 1950 and the Office took its birth on 1 January 1951. The Statute declares its work as humanitarian, social and entirely non-political in Character.

3. Arrangements relating to the issue of identity certificates to Russians and Armenian Refugees, 12 May 1926; 84 LNT (League of Nations Treaty) Series No. 2004.

4. 'Assyrian, Assyro-Chaldean, and assimilated refugees' as defined in the Arrangement of 30 June 1928; 89 LNTS No. 2006.

5. Article 1, 1933 Convention Relating to the International Status of Refugees and Reservations Thereto: 159 LNTS No. 3663.

6. Arrangement in Respect of Refugees from Germany, 10 February 1939; 191 LNTS No. 4461.

7. It refers to the Additional Protocol, 14 September 1939; 198 LNTS No. 4634.

8. In case of a person who has more than one nationality, the term, "The Country of his nationality" shall mean each of the countries of which he is a national, and person shall not be deemed to be lacking protection of the country of his nationality if, without any valid reason based on well founded fear, he has not availed himself of the protection of one of the countries of which he is a national.

9. See clause (6), Statute of the Office of UNHCR; and Article 1, 1951 Convention on the Status of Refugees and the 1967 protocol relating to the same matter.

10. This is evident from the wording of the certificates attached to the arrangement of 5 July 1922, Arrangement of 30 June 1928, and the Convention concerning the Status of Refugees coming from Germany, 10 February 1938.

11. Country of origin is the country of nationality or country of former residence.

12. Clause (6) Statute of the Office of UNHCR.

13. Sec NU General Assembly Resolution 217 A (III), 10 December 1948.

14. Established in 1957 vide General Assembly Resolution 1166 (XII) 26 November 1957.

15. Ibid: also Resolution 1784 (XVIII), 7 December 1962.

16. General Assembly Resolutions 1286 (XIII) 5 December 1958, 1389 (XVI) 20 November, 1959, 1500 (XV) 5 December 1960, 1672 (XVI) 18 December 1961.

17. General Assembly Resolution 1671 (XVI) 10 December 1961.

18. General Assembly Resolution 1499 (XV) 15 December 1960.

19. General Assembly Resolution 3455 (XXX) December 1975.

20. UN doc. A/AC 96/534, Para 87 (f).

21. UN doc. A/AC 96/549, Para 36 (b).

22. General Assembly Resolution 35/41, 25 November 1980, para B.

23. Protection implies internal as well as external protection–diplomatic protection, documentation for abroad and right to return.

24. UN doc. A/c 3/34/ SR 46, Para 58f.

25. Cf. General Assembly Resolution 35/180, 15 December 1980, and General Assembly Resolution 36/153, 16 December 1981, on assistance of refugees in Somalia.

26. A notion developed by UN General Assembly in 1960 on humanitarian grounds for treatment of those not covered by the ordinary definition of `refugees'.

27. Resolution 39/106/40/136.

28. UNBRO was created in 1982 along the Thai–Cambodian border to coordinate assistance to Cambodians held in border camps.

29. The definition of refugee adopted by the Organisation of African Unity (OAU) includes the persons displaced by war or Civil disorder—Article 1 (2) of OAU Convention.

30. Clause (8), Statute of the Office of the UNHCR.

31. *The Times of India,* January 25, 1999.

32. AIR 1997 SC 568.

33. (1994) Supp (1) SCC 615.

34. Memorandum No. MR8 (A) 75/8648–51, dated April 26, 1976.

35. (1991) 2 SCC 604.

36. (1991) 3 SCC 554.

37. AIR 1961 SC 58.

38. *Supra* note 36.

39. AIR 1964 SC 1140.

40. *Supra* note 36.

41. (1996) 1 SCC 742.

42. *Supra* note 33.

43. *Supra* note 36.

11

Human Rights Abuses in the Pre-Trial Detention: Sensitising Police and Judicial Personnel

Subhram Rajkhowa

Concept of Human Rights

Rights which are inherent in our nature without which we cannot live as human beings are generally termed as human rights. According to an United Nations publication[1] human rights allow us to fully develop and use our human qualities, our intellegence, our talents and our conscience and to satisfy our spiritual and other needs. They are based on mankind's increasing demand for a life in which the inherent dignity and worth of each human being will receive respect and protection.

The denial of human rights and fundamental freedoms not only is an individual and personal tragedy but also creates conditions of social and political unrest, sowing the seeds of violence and conflict within societies and nations.

However, the concept of human rights does not convey the same meaning and understanding to the matters of different systems of Government. It varies in a democratic government accepting the "Rule of Law" and totalitarian government or to an all powerful monarchy. It does not have the same meaning in India, U.K. U.S.A., C.I.S. and China and it is differently understood in the military and semi-military areas. In fact, all the 190 odd countries of the United Nations deny violation of human rights.[2]

International Instruments

Among the various human rights are the one not to be subjected to torture or other cruel, inhuman or degrading treatment of punishment and the right to freedom from arbitrary arrest or detention. In other words, one is not to be subjected to physical or mental pain or suffering with a view to extracting a confession or information, or to intimidation or punishment for any act allegedly committed. In fact, there are over 30 instruments provided under various United Nations Agencies, concerning crime prevention, specifying and securing human rights in response to specific problems perceived by the various member states. These include the Universal Declaration of Human Rights, the International Covenant on Civil and Political Rights, the Convention Against Torture and other Cruel, Inhuman or Degrading, Treatment or Punishment, the Standard Minimum Rules for the Treatment of Prisoners, the United Nations Standard Minimum Rules for the Administration of Juvenile Justice (Beijing Rules) and the Body of Principles for the Protection of All Persons under Any Form of Detention or Imprisonment[3].

The United Nations programme on crime prevention and criminal justice system has focused on pre-trail detention in dealing with the treatment of detained and imprisoned persons, although no comprehensive standards for the protection of persons in pre-trial detention,whether in Police or Judicial custody can claim protection under the national legal system as well as under the respective instruments, provided the concerned State adopts any such instrument. Not only absence of torture and ill-treatment are the guiding principles behind the standards on the treatment, but also prosecution of the perpetrators of torture are provided for.

While guaranteeing detainees freedom from torture and

arbitrary arrest, the UDHR and ICCPR provides for the presumption of their innocence of any criminal charges till trial, under Article 11(1) and 10(2) respectively. Similar provisions are also contained in Rule 84(2) of the Standard Minimum Rules of 1955, as well as under General Comment 13(7) of the Human Rights Committee under Article 40 para 4 of the ICCPR.

Article 5 of the UDHR, Article 7 of the ICCPR, Principles 21(1), (2) and Principles 23 of Body of Principles for the Protection of All Persons under Any Form of Detention or Imprisonment, in short the Principles of Detention as well as the General Comment 7(1) and 7(2) of the Human Rights Committee provide that statements found to be obtained by tortures should not be used as evidence against any one and that the allegations of torture should be vigorously investigated and perpetrators prosecuted. It is significant to observe that Article 4 of the ICCPR prohibits the States from derogating under any circumstances of the right of individuals not to be tortured or to be subjected to cruel, inhuman or degrading treatment or punishment.

In order to prohibit the torture and ill treatment of detainees for the purpose of compelling them to confess to crimes or divulge information under fear or threat by the Torturer, the General Assembly[4] adopted a Declaration on the protection of All Persons from being subjected to torture and Other Cruel, Inhuman or Degrading Treatment in the year 1975. This Declaration was given legal sanction by way of the Convention in 1984.

The Convention not only provides that the States parties will outlaw torture in their national legislation, but also notes explicitly that no order from a superior or one under exceptional circumstances may be invoked as a justification of torture and other cruel, inhuman or degrading treatment or punishment.

The Convention also introduces two new elements of particular importance to combat torture. The first is that a torturor may be prosecuted where ever he is found in the territory of any State Party, since the convention specifies that persons alleged to have committed acts of torture may be tried in any State party or be extradited for trail in any State Party where they have committed their crimes. The other new element is that the Convention contains a provision allowing for an international inquiry if there is reliable information indicating that the torture is being systematically practised in the territory of a State Party. Such an inquiry may include a visit to the State Party concerned, with its agreement.

The State Parties to the Convention also pledge to take legislative, administrative, judicial and other measures to prevent acts of torture in any territory under their jurisdiction. No exceptional circumstances whatsoever, whether a sate of war, internal political instability or any other public emergency, may be invoked as a justification of torture[5].

The Convention also provides for a Committee Against Torture, to oversee implementation by the State Parties and to resolve any allegations brought to it. This Committee comprising of 10 members are required to consider on measures taken by the member States of the Convention to honour their undertakings. Further, the Committee is also empowered to make confidential inquiries.

In addition, the Committee on Human Rights has a special rapporteur on torture who acts in individual cases and reports to the Commission on the action he has taken with regard to instances of torture in particular countries. There is also the "thematic mandate" on arbitrary detention, besides the right thematic special rapporteurs on related matters. Their reports are submitted to the General Assembly, which are placed for discussion in public sessions and constitute an important element for any decisions the Committee may take on the relevant item.

Further, in the year 1990, the 8th U.N. Congress on the Prevention of Crime and the Treatment of Offenders also called upon the U.N. bodies to assist countries in improving conditions of pre-trial detention, and in developing non-custodial measures as an alternative to the use of pre-trial detention, and request the Secretary General to assist in the task.[7] The Congress inter-alia observed;[8]

(b) Pre-trail detention may be ordered only if there are reasonable grounds to believe that the persons concerned have been involved in the Commission of the alleged offences and these is a danger of their absconding or committing further serious offences, or a danger that the course of justice will be seriously interferred with if they are left free;

(i) All proceedings concerning persons in custody should be conducted as expeditiously as possible so as to reduce the period of pre-trail detention to the minimum.

The following year, the Human Rights Committee created a working group with the task of investigating cases of detention, imposed arbitrarily or otherwise inconsistently, with the relevent international standards.[9]

Apart from the above Declarations and Conventions the Declaration on Basic Principles of Justice for Victims of Crime and Abuse of Power calls upon the States for providing remedies by way of restitution and compensation, and for providing necessary material, medical, psychological and social assistance to victims of official abuse, as well as for providing access to justice.[10] There are also the Principles on the Effective Prevention and Investigation of Extra Legal, Arbitrary and Summary Executions, adopted by the ESCOC in 1989 and the Declaration on the Protection of All Persons from Enforced Dissappearances, adopted by the General Assemby in 1992.

The dignity and humanity of persons in detention is also sought to be maintained through the Basic Principles on the use of Force and Fire Arms by Law Enforcement Officials,[11] two of which being considered significant are quoted in extensio;

Principle 15 - Law Enforcement Officials, in their relations with persons in custody or detention, shall not use force, except where strictly necessary for the maintenance of security and order within the institution, or when personal safety is threatened.

Principle 16 - Law Enforcement Officials, in their relations with persons in custody or detention, shall not use fire arms, except in selfdefence or in the defence of others against the immediate threat of death or serious injury, or when strictly necessary to prevent the escape of a person in custody or detention presenting the danger referred to in principle[9] (the danger of the perpetration of a particularly serious crime involving grave threat to life.)

Problem of Enforcement

Inspite of the various international instruments, pre-trial detention in Police and judicial custody continue to be a cause of concern to the international community. Although, countries claim of observing the norms of human rights through their domestic legal systems, many countries have not matched the international requirements. The international conventions, particularly the one on torture remains to be ratified by many a state. Inspite of the general agreement to incorporate the basic provisions in the domestic legal systems, many a State have not taken any step towards that end, although signatory states incur a legal obligation to implement the human rights standards to which they subscribe at the international level. This has resulted in the detainees being subjected to the worst conditions of confinement, in antiquated, over crowded, unsafe detention centres. Not to speak of the lack of distinction between convicted and pre-trial detainees, at times three to four times the capacity are confined in the prisons. What is more appaling is that in many a country, persons arrested are never brought before a judicial authority, often times being held in-communicando[12]. Apart from the national prison systems, suspects held are often tortured during Police custody, to extract confession towards their incrimination and to divulge information. This has on occasions resulted in cruel fatalities.

Violation of Custodial Rights

Large number of men, women and children continue to be the victims of torture in custody, due to the lawlessness of the law enforcement machinery. Many of such victims have no remedy for want of corroboration of their torture in police custody, for physical injuries at times do not surface on their bodies. The Police machinery [13], continue to employ the policy of regression, often by the use of third degree methods, in the form of beating, use of cigarattes butts to burn the skin, denying food, water, sleep drinking urine, putting ice on naked part of human body, head down suspension, electric shock treatment, hot water bottle treatment, parading naked in public, inserting steel or live wires into body crevices[14]. Sereve beating to the extent of fracturing of limbs, hanging upside down and inserting of pins and nails in the sensitive parts of the body, including the private parts, are some of the methods used by the police against women prisoners in custody. Some such victims of torture suffer mutilation or paralysis, for remaining period of their life for want of proper and timely medical treatment[15].

Factors which contribute to torture include lack of transparency about what happens in Police custody; Police disregard of legal safeguards regarding policy custody, absence of adequate safeguards regarding interrogation of suspects, lack of accountability; lack of support for police professionalism and prolonged remand in Police custody.[16]

The demand for dignity of the individuals and security of the State at the same time, in the context of rights and liberty of citizens, has to be protected and distinguished from challenges of terrorism and insurgency. Yet, preventing a national institution from investigating violence committed by the Police, severly reduces any such institutions potential effectiveness as a protector of human rights. Similarly, the defence personnel as exempt from the complaint mechanisms may also have a detrimental effect on the institution's effectiveness, particularly in view of the strength of the defence services in many States, and its corresponding potentials to violate human rights by way of torturing the suspects in various ways[17].

At times victims of torture die in custody, unable to bear the third degree torture of the law enforcement machinery. Such loss of life is a serious cause of concern to the world community. The Human Rights Committee has observed that when a death occurs in custody the State may take steps to ascertain how it occured. In a case where autopsy was given by the military authorities, but the State did not submit any information on the circumstances of death, or the inquiries it had made into there circumstances the Human Rights Committee had held that the State had violated Article 6(1) of the ICCPR by not taking appropriate measures to protect the detainees life in detention (*Wellemmo Igna Cio Dermit Barbato and Hugo Haroldo Dermit Barbuto Vs. Uruguways 21.10.82*) The Committee held that while it could not determine whether the detainee committed suicide or was killed by others, the State authorities had violated Article 6(1) by not protecting and detainee's life and not investigating how his death occured[18].

Custodial death may be equated with murder perpetuated by the over enthuastic guardians of law, whose legal duty is to interrogate and keep accused under custody on behalf of the State. The death of a detenu generates some suspicion about the extend of the use of third degree methods of interrogation by the Police all over the world. It amounts to a flagrant violation of human rights in its extreme form which no executive officer should violate under any pretext. It is a disgrace to the entire police profession which is put under a cloud and therefore, calls for condemnation and punishment of those guilty law enforecement officers. Those who exist to protect the freedoms cannot be allowed to indulge in a breach of trust. It calls for strict vigil of the human rights activists all over the world, to ensure the basic liberties to women, children, suspects and even to the proclaimed terrorists.[19]

No nation is free from human rights abuse and therefore, can claim a pre-trial detention system that could not be improved upon. But at the same time issues of torture are ofter politicised, giving it an exaggerated form.

Therefore, government should respond to situations of such abuses by streamlining the police force as well as incorporating various provisions of international instruments into their domestic legal system. States have a responsibility to conform to human rights standards setting of the United Nations, by removing the incompatibility of its law with the convention standards[20].

Situation in India

Coming to the situation in India, it has to be observed that human rights standards find place both in the Constitution Itself as well as various legislations adopted from time to time. Among the significant Constitutional provisions are those incorporated in Articles 14 to 16, 19 to 23, 25, 29 to 32, 136 and 226. Important provisions in the Code of Criminal Procedure are to be found in Sections 173(3), 207, 208, 218, 228(2), 235(2), 238, 240(2), 248(2), 273, 304, 306, 313, 314, 317, 374, 379, 380 and 381 etc. However, the Police Act of 1861 is very ancient and needs to be amended to meet the present day demands. Yet, inspite of various provisions, the country is yet to ratify Optional Protocol of ICCPR.

Custodial crimes and Police brutalities are reported to be practiced in various States in India. Due to lack of transparency to the desired extent, the Government has come in for criticism from various national and international organisations, within the country and abroad. Among the international organisations, Amnesty International has been reporting widely on the allegations of human rights violation in certain states in the country.

Amnesty International's current concerns are centred round the use of torture and ill treatment,which is considers to be widespread, leading to deaths of over 50 people in Police custoday each year, as a result of such practices. Of the 43 cases of reported deaths in Andhra Pradesh, Karnataka and Uttar Pradesh between 1986 and 1989, 12 Policemen were reported suspended and only one convicted[21]. However, because of the prolonged procedure of Courts, cases take a long time to be disposed off.

The torture inflicted is often with a view of extract information or towards self incrimination. In the case of women, most allegations of torture concern rape in police custody[22].

Amnesty International received reports of 517 custody deaths since 1.1.1985 upto 1.3.1994. By November, 1992 it had submitted 455 cases to the Government for their opinion. However, the government submitted fact sheets in respect of 230 of those cases, stating that in more than a third of those cases, there was primafacie evidence that further action was needed against the police allegedly responsible for torturing and killing suspects in police custody[23]. 36 deaths were reported to Amnesty International in 1993 and 64 deaths in custody in 1994. Delhi along accounting for 10 of the 36 deaths during 1993[24]. Although 12 deaths in custody were reported in Kerala between March 1992 and December 1993 the State Police Chief while denying most of them to be caused by torture neverthless, condemned torture by observing deaths in custody as "the work of devils".

Earlier, in 1992 Amnesty International report on India had observed:

> "Yet torture is pervasive and a daily routine in everyone of India's 25 States, irrespective of whether arrests are made by the police, para military forces or the army—In all 415 (deaths in custody) there is evidence that the victims who include women and children are brutally beaten or otherwise tortured until they die!"

In the State of Jammu and Kashmir, the Amnesty International listed 706 cases of torture as on 31st January, 1995 but the government has brushed aside the allegations by observing that "generalisation cannot substitute facts". The government held 273 of the 519 listed cases to militants killed in encounter and cross firing. In respect of 81 others go it held that no reports were ever lodged with the police, while 32 persons were considered as intraced. Another 14 were reported to have died due to accident or sickness. Only 85 cases were said to be found involving custodial violence and were said to be under police investigation. However, only in 8 cases charges were framed.[25]

Even though the government has admitted of some custodial deaths having taken place, these are considered to be few and far between. The government has maintained that 225 security forces have been proceeded against.[27] As against this 400 army officers and other ranks are reported killed and over 1000 injured in the hands of the extremists during the last five years[28]. However, provocative grave abuses committed by armed separatists groups can never justify the security forces resorting to arbitrary detentions, torture, extra-judicial killings or "disappearences". It has to be remembered that such practices are prohibited in Indian law and clearly contravenes international human rights standards which the Indian Government is bound to uphold.[29]

The Government facts sheets, responding to the Amnesty International's allegations of "lack of systematic procedure for the independent and impartial investigation", has condemned the use of torture, terming the incidents as mere abberrations, while denying that the use of torture is wide spread in India. The very fact that the Government has been responding to the allegations of the Amnesty International that the government is taking the issue of custodial violence seriously, by pointing to the action taken to investigate cases of custodial deaths, and prosecute those respondible, is an indication of the problem being addressed to by the Government. Yet, the fact that the situation calls for action is reflected from, the report of the United Nations Special Rapporteur on Extra-Judicial Summary or Arbitrary Executions[31] as observed at Geneva in February, 1995:

> "The special Rapporteur notes with concern that, while in most cases investigations are said to be initiated, reports brought to its attention suggest that such proceedings virtually never appear to conclude with a judgment convicting the security forces personnel involved.

The length of the investigation procedures is also working in a number of cases, inquiries opened more than two years ago and are still said to be in progress."

But one has to accept that under the existing legal system, the investigative procedures are lengthy and time consuming, resulting in delay in the disposal of cases against police and para-military personnel. Of late, however, the interrogation methods of the army are reported to be streamlined with the imparting of necessary training. Further, the policy of providing some amount of transparancy is also much welcome. In the case of Srinagar, the Amnesty International and others had claimed that there existed a torture camp at Papa Two where captured militants were being tortured, but foreign groups visiting and interviewing the foreign mercinaries lodged at the improvised lock up belie such allegations[32].

Surprisingly apart from the disturbed frontiers of the country, even in other States there have been allegations of torture (Chart). In the case of West Bengal, 12 custodial deaths are reported to have occured during the current year (1995), taking the total to 217 custodial deaths since 1977. This has invited a strong reaction from the Chief Minister of the State, who has cautioned the police to handle the problem with utmost restraint. Because of the strong public opinion against police excesses, the government initiated action against most of the guilty officials and in others, charge sheets have been submitted and the cases are pending trial.[34]

According to the National Human Right Commission[35], between April 1994 and May 1995 out of total of 108 custodial deaths, 30 have occured in West Bengal, 14 in Assam, 9 in Rajasthan and 7 in Uttar Pradesh. Around the same time between April 1994 and June 1995 a total of 75 persons lost their lives in Judicial custody, with Delhi accounting for 46 of them. Infact, during the month of June, of the current year alone Delhi has accounted for 10 such deaths, leading the Human Rights Commission to institute an inquiry.

Responding to the situation in the country, the Prime

Minister observed on 14.09.92, that action had been taken against 230 officers and security forces personnel for violation of human rights in Punjab and Kashmir, and prosecution was being initiated against many others. He observed -

> "There can be nothing more revolting and reprehensible than the betrayal of custodial trust by the guardians of law and those appointed to protect the individual. We have to deal with such cases with alacrity and in an exemplary manner and also to ensure that the victims obtain possible and quick response".

He reiterated the nation's commitment in another statement a few months later, on 17.02.93, ensuring that excesses are not committed, specially in custody, stating that "human rights are of paramount importance in a democracy, like ours". According to the Amnesty International this demonstrates that torture practices are not government policy and that there is a recognition at the highest governmental level that India faces a major problem of custodial violence in respect of pre-trial detainees which needs to be addressed is called for, while at the same time, the existing safeguards are to be properly implemented. For instance, magisterial inquiry into allegations of custodial deaths is provided for mandatory under the law, but is often observed in its breach. Further the Commissions of Enquiry Act, 1952 provids discretion upon the government not to make public, report of nay inquiry commissions, which leads to a feeling of protecting the guilty. A happy augary has been the decision of the Govt. to amend the Criminal Procedure Code, making it mandatory for institution of judicial inquires into cases of custodial deaths. Further jail reforms need to be urgently addressed to as well.

Role of Judiciary

The Constitution has assigned a significant role to the judiciary in our legal and constitutional system. It has been playing its role as a sentinel of human rights, not to speak of the constitutional and legal rights. The concept of Public Interest litigation through the process of liberalisation of the concept of *locus standi* has played a humanising role in the sphere of custodial violence, pertaining to pre-trial detainees. This is also evident from the second periodic report of the UNHCR[37], which has stated that:

> "The Supreme Court in India and the various High Courts of the individual states ensured the effective implementation of Human Rights through a liberalisd review of administrative action. Such liberalisation has led to the growth of Public Interest Litigation and seizure of Court's jurisdiction in such matter even on the basis of post-cards or telegrams received from individuals or of stories or reports published in magazines or newspapers and the provisions of compulsory legal aid to the needy".

An important role is taste upon the judiciary to see that the police cannot succeed in concealing evidence of custodial violence by falsifying or destroying police records or putting pressure on doctors to manage post mortem reports. Till such time the various conventions are not ratified, the judiciary while implementing the existing legislation in a firm manner should explore the spirit of the international conventions through humanitarian interpretation, atleast under the existing constitutional provisions.

The judiciary is the basic structure for protection of human rights at the national level. The helpless victims of custodial crimes consider it their only ray of hope. Therefore, a duty is cast upon the judiciary to help preserve the judicial process for the protection of the rights of individuals in detention.[38]

As observed by the Committee of Ministers of the Council of Europe:[39]

> Custody pending trial should be ordered only if there is reasonable suspicion that the accused has committed the alleged offence and that he is likely to absconds, interfere with the course of justice, or commit a serious offence.

The Supreme Court as well as the different High Courts have awarded compensation, even in writ proceedings for violation of human rights. Some of these important rulings in recent years should certainly help prevent human rights violations, and facilitate effective relief being granted to the victims of custodial violence as well as to the dependents of the victims of custodial death.

On March 24, 1993 the apex court awarded examplary damages of Rupees one and half lacs to the mother of Suman Behera, a victim of custodial violence from the State of Orissa, who died on 1.12.87[40]. Similarly, on 19.3.93 the Court awarded monetary compensation of Rupees three lacs to the widow and two children of Joginder Kumar who died in police custody on 6.8.90. The Supreme Court emphasised that the puling did not prejudice the Woman's right to claim further compensation through other legal avenues, and directed to Delhi administration to sanction the prosecution of five police official and a Sub-Divisional Magistrate. The apex Court has even gone to the extent of holding that payment of compensation to a victim of rights violation should be personal liability of the offender and not that of the State. The Court[41] has considered the right against torture, cruel or unusual punishment or degrading treatment and the right against custodial violence as emanated rights, though unenumerated in the Constitution.

Such steps by the apex Court are indeed a positive indication of its serious view on instances of torture and custodial violence. Sentensing the culprits to prison terms and awarding compensation to the victims or their dependents is certainly to have its effect on the law enforcement machinery. But this has to be matched by the government with equally effective measures to expeditiously bring to book the erring members of the law enforcement machinery. Diseased brains who derive sedastic pleasure in human torture, obviously need to be weeded out of the police force.[42]

The Role of the National Human Rights Commission

The National Human Rights institutions have an important role to play in protecting and promoting human rights, aimed at ensuring that they are enjoyed by one and all. In consonance with such objective, the National Human Rights Commission was set up in India on the 1st of October, 1993 under an ordinance, subsequently replaced by the Protection of Human Rights Act 1993, the range of functions being provided under Section 12 of the Act. This is in part a response to the changing social realities and emerging trends in the nature of crime and violence. The Act is also a reflection of the Vienna Declaration of 1993[43], which expressed the desirability of drawing up a national action plan for the promotion and protection of human rights through a set of priorities and appropriate vehicles for implementation.[44]

Among other activities, the commission has been particularly engaged, either suo-motto or on the basis of complaints, with instances of custodial deaths/violences such as custodial death and rape, disappearance from custody, cruel, inhuman or degrading punishment and torture[45]. Taking a serious view of such violations the Commission has observed that such instances must be boldly and swiftly dwelt with, and accordingly has issued instructions to all State Governments and Union Territories asking for reports from the District Magistrates and Superintendent of Police within 24 hours of the occurance of any such activities. The Commission has further observed that failure to comply will be considered as an attempt to suppress knowledge of any such incident[46]. It has further called for immediate deterrent action against police staff indulging in custodial violence.[47] Going a step further it has also intervened in Court proceedings, apart from holding sitting to probe alleged custodial crimes.

The Commission has given a new direction and added a meaningful perspective in the realisation of human rights in the country. To cite an example/instance in the case of custodial death of Basudeo Shah a case under Section 302 of the Indian

Penal Code has been registered on the direction of the Commission. The erring officers have been arrested and investigation is in progress. Besides, the Commission has also recommended payment of Rs. 50,000/- to the next of kin of the deceased. The 12 illustrative cases as provided in its 1994-95 annual report indeed reflects a depressing situation with regard to custodial deaths due to police torture, killings of innocent civilians in cross fires between the security forces and the terrorists in the North-East, besides rapes in custody and so on.[48]

While recommending implementation of the recommendation of the National Police Commission, 1979 it has stressed the need for separating the law and order function from the investigative role of police. Another significant recommendation of the Commission relates to accession to the 1984 Convention Against Torture. The Commission has also recommended change in the system with regard to post-mortem in custodial deaths. X Ray analysis has been made mandatory and it would be required to conduct the entire process with video cameras in vigil. Scene of death should be preserved for forensic examination.

The Commission has further been urging the respective State Governments to initiate serious action against allegations of custodial deaths and violence. The data collected by the Commission is being constantly monitored and follow up measures initiated to prevent custodial deaths and ensure that human rights of citizens are not violated.

Further, the Commission has been taking a serious view of deaths in judicial custody. While visiting certain jails, it has made some significant observations besides important recommendations. It has observed that some of the jails are very much over crowded, lacking in proper medical facilities. While citing the instance of Tihar Jail in the capital, it has observed that 30 to 40 persons die in Tihar eveyr year due to TB which is a curable disease. Besides ordering an inquiry into the death of Rajan Pillai, it has also ordered a general probe in respect of deaths in Tihar jail to cover all deaths which have occured in the jail during the last two years. According to the Commission, deaths were related to reasons which could be controlled and the cause removed or properly checked.

In fact, the Chairperson of the Commssion has been repeatedly stressing upon the need to sensitise police officials through proper inculcation of human rights values. Towards this end a meeting of 10 Director General of Police was arranged by the Commission in May 1995 to consider, in particular the question of Police training and human rights. This was followed by a recent training programme of police officers of the rank of Deputy Inspector General and above. Further, the Commission has been advising the National Police Academy and the various State governments on various aspects of sensitising the police personnel.

To match the efforts of the Commission, it has also been suggesting to the respective State governments to constitute State Human Rights Commission, who are yet to set up the Commission. Moreover, it has also been emphasising upon the need to sensitise the judicial officers towards human rights values, besides calling upon the States to constitute human rights courts.

The Commission has also called upon the Government to effect certain changes in the Act to enable the Commission to compel attendance of witness, besides allowing it to initiate proceedings for prosecution as well as for providing interim relief to victims of their dependents. Such measures would enable the Commission to conduct effective investigation through trained personnel and effective and judicative functions.

Sensitising the Police and Judicial Personnel

Prevention of human rights abuses can be properly effected through awareness rising both amongst the public and the law enforcement machinery. This has to be supported through legal measures to counter human rights abuses, particularly in the sphere of custodial violence

While internal vigilence can be instilled by sensitising an individual to his or her own potential for vindictive behaviour[49] through legal awareness, that of the Police force can be instilled by a behavioural reorientation through training to effect attitudional change in the police force. In fact, a complete restructuring of the police is called for[50]. Training courses concerning law enforcement personnel should be developed which transform knowledge about human rights into operative skills[51]. These courses should aim at fast values and attitudes pertaining to national and international standards, particularly relevant to day to day activities. In other words, the police personnel should be taught to encounter their problems perfectly in consonance with the various instruments relating to torture and other forms of custodial abuses. The process of training and education should aim at motivating the targetted group to continue the training process after completion of course for dissemination of information and free and post course evaluation[52].

The training process should focus on sensitivity towards observance of human rights, scientific investigation and more intense teaching of the provisions of law dealing with custodial violence and consequences of the policemen. The performance of the officials should be regularly monitored to ensure that they are sensitive to human rights considerations[53], and that they strictly comply with the relevant provisions of law during the course of investigation. The superior officers should pay surprise visits to police stations to find for themselves any instances of violation of the rights of the accused.

Preventive and punitive measures should be inflicted by way of stringent disciplinary action. For the aforesaid purpose the service rules should suitably incorporate provisions for stringent punishment for violation of human rights. Guilty officials should also be proceeded with under the relevant penal provisions, apart from being made liable to compensate the victim or his family[54], besides other relief to be provided by the State. Besides the reformative and punitive measures, preventitive measures are also called for. A person under custody should be sent for medical examination and make the reports available to relatives of the accused. Further, the police immediately upon arresting a person should be obliged to provide information of such detention to relatives or any one nominated by the arrested person[55].

> Persons arrested should not be subjected to interrogation for more than a specified period at a stretch. Scientific methods should be adopted by the investigating agency to collect evidence. All modern infrastructure should be made available to the investigation agency. Conditions of police lock ups should be improved without any further delay, and all basic amenities should be provided therein.
>
> ....As soon as an accused is produced before a magistrate, he shall enquire from the detenue if he has any grievance pertaining to physical torture during his police custody. If any complaint is made, he shall take cognisance of the offence and take all other necessary action as may be deemed just and proper."[56]

Thus apart from sensitising the police personnel, the judicial officers should also be provided training, to accord recognition to humanitarian considerations. In fact, as observed by Amnesty International[57] in respect of India, a series of court decisions that have established clear police responsibilty for some custodial deaths and have provided relief to the victims of families, are a further indication of a move towards ending impunity.

The judicial officers should make a conscious effort to prevent torture or maltreatment in police lock-up, or by reducing the length of police custody for investigation, legal asisstance should also be provided to the needy at State expense when an accused under custody is produced for the first time before a judicial officer[58]. Further, judicial enquiry in all cases of rape, death and grievious hurt in police custody should be got conducted by Senior Judicial Officers, till such time state level human rights courts are established.

Besides sensitising the police and judicial service

personnel to bring about commitment and understanding, increse of public awareness of human rights, particularly matters relating to pre-trial detainees has to be achieved through a process of information and education[59] as envisaged by the Paris principles.

Crimes perpetrated on pre-trial detainees need to be officially condemned[60] and international instruments to be ratified in order to put a stop to custodial violence, besides providing transparency in the functioning of the governmental machinery. Periodic steps are required for implementation of existing standards on the treatment of offenders under a responsive legal system. The lot of the pre-trial detainees would be greatly improved even if existing standards set forth are respected.

Number of Persons Dead in Police Custody

During 1993 and 1994

(Upto the available months)

State & Union Territory wise

State/U.T.	1991	1992	1993	1994	Remarks (Figs. of 1994 are upto the month of)
1	2	3	4	5	6
STATES					
Andhra Pradesh	5	12	7	0	May
Arunachal Pradesh	0	1	0	0	April
Assam	1	4	1	NA	January
Bihar	2	7	4	NA	-

1	2	3	4	5	6
Goa	0	1	1	0	May
Gujrat	8	1	2	0	January
Haryana	0	0	0	NA	-
Himachal Pradesh	0	0	0	0	May
Jammu & Kashmir	2	0	14	NA	-
Karnataka	0	1	3	0	April
Kerala	2	0	0	0	May
Madhya Pradesh	3	1	0	1	May
Maharashtra	11	20	31	NA	-
Manipur	0	1	0	0	May
Meghalaya	0	0	0	0	March
Mizoram	0	1	0	0	June
Nagaland	0	0	0	0	May
Orissa	0	0	1	NA	-
Punjab	2	1	1	NA	April
Rajasthan	5	3	0	2	May
Sikkim	1	0	0	0	April
Tamil Nadu	5	1	3	1	March
Tripura	0	0	1	0	May
Uttar Pradesh	3	5	6	2	April
West Bengal	4	8	1	NA	-
TOTAL	54	68	76	6	

UNION TERRITORIES

A & N Island	0	0	0	0	May
Chandigarh	0	0	0	0	May
D & N Haveli	0	0	0	0	May
Daman & Diu	1	0	0	0	May
Delhi	3	2	0	0	May
Lakshadweep	0	0	0	NA	-
Pondicherry	1	0	0	0	May
TOTAL (All India)	59	70	76	6	

Source: Monthly Crime Statistics :

Note: 1. Figures exclude January and February data due to its non-availability.

2. Figures of 1993 are upto April only.

3. NA stands for figures not available.

4. Figures are provisional.

References

1. United Nations Publication, *Human Rights: Question And Answers*, New York, 1987 p.4.

2. Phukan R. (1994) *Right to Adequate Environment and the Indian Scenerio*, Unpublished Dissertation, Gauhati University p.43.

3. 1994 *Human Rights and Pre-trial detention-A Handbook* International Standards relating to Pre-trial Detention, Centre for Human Rights, Geneva, p. iii.

4. General Assembly resolution No.3452 (XXX) of 1975.

5. 1994 *Human Rights and Social Work*, A Manual for Schools of Social Work and the Social Work Profession, Centre for Human Rights, Geneva p. 16 ibid. p. 21.

6. *ibid* p. 21.

7. *Supra* note 3, p. iii.

8. *Supra* note 3, p. i.

9. Resolution No. 1991/92 of 5.3.1991.

10. General Assembly Resolution No. 4/34 of 1985.

11. Report of Eight Congress, Supra 3, p. 31.

12. *Supra* note 3, p. 5.

13. Majumdar S.R., Lawlessness in Law Enforcement, *Police Research and Development Journal,* Jan-Mar 1995 New Delhi p. 19.

14. ibid.

15. Desai A.R. (ed) *Violation of Democratic Rights in India*, Popular Prakashan, Bombay, 1986 pp. 242-43.

16. Amensty International's suggestion to Maharashtra Goverment, *Police Research and Development Journal*, July-Sept, 1994, New Delhi, p. 13.

17. National Human Rights Institutions-A Hand Book on the Establishment and Strengthening of National Institutions for the promotion and Protection of Human Rights, Centre for Human Rights, Geneva 1995 p. 29.

18. *Supra,* note 3, p. 36.

19. Sharma P.D. Anatomy of Custodial Deaths, P.T.I. Feature.

20. Sanajaoba N. (ed) Human Rights Standard Setting Prerogatives, Human Rights Overseas, New Delhi, 1994, pp. 5626.

21. Amnesty International India Summary of Amnesty International's Current concerns in India, October 1994 A I Index ASA 20/21/90 P-5.

22. *ibid*, p 7.

23. Amnesty International, India, Rising reports of custodial

deaths in Delhi, June 1993 (summary) AI INDEX: ASA 20/26/93.

24. Amnesty International, India, Deaths in custody in 1993 June 1994, Summary AI INDEX AXA 20/07/94.

25. Amnesty International, India Deaths in custody in Kerala March, 1994, AI INDEX AXA 20/07/94.

26. Amensty International, India, Analysis of the Government of India's response to Amnesty International's report on torture and deaths in custody in Jammu and Kashmir March 1995 summary, AI INDEX ASA 20/05/95 p. 32.

27. *ibid* p. 11.

28. Pal N.K. Insurgency and the Indian Army, *Assam Tribune*, Guwahati 30.09.95.

29. *Supra,* note 26 p. 10.

30. Scores of Custody Deaths in India Assam, *Tribune*, Guwahati dtd. 3.11.95.

31. Report of UN Special Rapportuer.

32. Bhargava G.S. U.N. Convention Against Torture, Need for Transparency, *Indian Express*, New Delhi, 13.10.95.

33. *ibid.*

34. Custodial deaths in West Bengal, *Assam Tribune*, Guwahati, 10.11.95.

35. Commissions asks States/UTs with high incidence of custodial deaths to take corrective steps, *Human Rights Newsletter*, National Human Rights Commission, New Delhi, Vol.2, No.10, October, 1995.

36. *Supra,* note 23.

37. New York, 1991.

38. *Supra,* note 3, p. 3.

39. Recommendation No. R(80) concerning custody pending trial.

40. Unnikrishanan Vs. State of Andhra Pradesh, 1993 ISOC 645.

41. *Supra*, note 23, p. 8.

42. *Supra*, note 19.

43. Part II para 71.

44. *Supra*, note 17, p. 27.

45. National Human Rights Commission, New Delhi, Annual Report 1993-94, p. 9.

46. *ibid, p.* 10.

47. *Supra*, note 35.

48. Pal R. M., National Human Rights Commission must live upto expectation, *Indian Express*, New Delhi 21.10.95.

49. *Supra*, note 17, p. 18.

50. Mathur K. M. 1994 Role of Police in Changing Social Scenerio, Supra note 16, p. 11.

51. *Supra*, note 17 p. 20.

52. *ibid* p. 21.

53. Study of Custodial deaths in India, *Assam Tribune*, Guwahati, 18.9.95.

54. Reformative, Punitive and Preventitive measures for Human Rights violations - Syndicate Group Paper of Workshop on Human Rights (unpublished) Assam, Administrative Staff College, Guwahati.

55. *Supra*, note 23, p. 23.

56. *ibid*.

57. *Supra*, note 24.

58. Recommendation at National Police Academy, Hyderabad.

59. 1991 International Meet in Paris (Principles), *Supra* note 17, p. 5.

60. 12 Point Programme for Prevention of Torture-Torture in the Eighties, London, 1984 p. 249.

12

Human Right To Environment In India: From Legality To Reality

Md. Zafar Mahfooz Nomani

I. Enviro-Human Right: The Genesis

The normative abundance of international environmental law appears to be quite considerable[1] still the desideratum of human right approach to ecological sustainability and planetary viability among municipal legislatures are well discernable and documented[2]. The prolixity of national enactments on environment mostly gravitate around technocentric approaches wherein the inherent tendency of looking at environment from technological and developmental paradigm dominates over the scene.[3] In contrast to it ethnocentric approach *i.e.,* 'all human being have the fundamental right to an environment adequate for their health and well being' has either suffered a serious setback or not brought to fruition in modern environmental legal ordering. While entering into the the third generation of human right[4] it is nothing but imperative to grapple the complementarity of economic growth and environmental sustainability in human right discourse[5]. This becomes germane on the matrix of complexity of poverty, population, depleting resources, food insecurity, energy crisis, urban gloom, industrial catastrophe and other related problems.[6] Because of marine pollution, eutrophication of lakes, denudation of forests, soil acidification, acid raining, global climate change, ozone hole, extinction of tropical rain forests in the next millenium the rapid depletion of natural resources will culminate into some planetary catastrophe of irreversible character.[7] Therefore, it is important to understand the extent to which environmental warfare is linked to overall tactics of high technology counter insurgency warfare carried on against people to the land itself. Just as counter insurgency warfare tends towards genocide with respect to people, so it tends towards ecocide with respect to environment.[8] In such a desperating atmosphere it is high time to come out of traditional doctrinaire limits to the domain of pragmatic discourse so that global and national careful 'public ordering' of ecological sustainability can be seriously undertaken[9].This goes without saying that a resilient legal regime always endeavours for development with social and human face. Under this legitimate persumption the ontological status of environmental law both international and national level summons for a close scrutiny from human right perspective. In the context of theoritical and conceptual postulates of human right approaches to environmental protection the present paper scans the imperatives and viabilities of nascent enviro-human right jurisprudence in Indian perspective. This remains sayable at this juncture that enlightened opinion making of NGO community alongwith judicial articulation led to the proliferation of human right jurisprudence transcending even repressive legalism. The paper also endeavours to appraise the promise and pitfalls of human right approach and submits for the exploration of traditional environmentalism and indigenous human right ingrained in the historical roots of the country.

II. Human Right Approaches: Theoritical Cross-Currents

An inquiry into the philosophical foundations of environmental human right seems germane to arrive at a jurisprudential basis. To tune further innovation it will be useful to set the new right against the backdrop of existing theories and approaches to human right. The volumnity of literature makes a comprehensive efforts to integrate philosophy, law and jurisprudence still a vibrant approach needs to be dexeterously carried out for environment sustainability. Jurists opined variously but in near unanimity voiced that areas of international law, united nations law, international human right law, international labour law and law of sea should explore the broad rubrics of environmental law and recast through constant appraisal and unification[10]. A panormic survey of some of the theoretical approaches runs quite in order.

The *jus cogens,* that is, the '*customary law approach*' entails that traditional norm of international law as state responsibility can resolve various environmental controversies alongwith new rules of law, institutions, standard and localised regimes. The legal rehabilitation bordering around fishing zone, contiguous zone, economic zone and continental shelf can be refurbished on the customary rule of international law[11]. The emphasis on treaty law under *jus cogens* approach may sometimes come in conflict with environmental right as evidenced in *French Nuclear Test* case where peremptory norm of international law are violated even though specific treaty commitments' are not at issue. Therefore, a balancing test might be applied at such time as and when a state act threatens the ecology. It is widely submitted that better approach will be amalgamation of certain aspect of environmental law and human right law as *jus cogens*[12].

The *traditional international law* approach however can be substituted by a '*global public order approach*'. The fast denudation of physical and natural base may endanger the survival of human being that is why there is a need for a clarion call to look at environmental human right from the 'world public order' perspective. Based on the assumption that in the next millienium some planetary catastrophe of irrevesible character is imminent, new enviro-human right world ordering must assure survival potential of world civilisation by overcoming fundamental challenge of war, poverty, pollution and oppression[13].

'*State sovereingnty*' is yet another approach which has regrettably resulted in tardy growth of human right to environment.[14] Under unilateral approach of state, bilateral and regional normative order were not allowed to operate properly. This has led to flagrant violation of human right to environment and put the common heritage on the brink of disaster. *Fisheries case*[15], *Nuclear Test case*[16] and *Tory Canyon case*[17] are pointer to this effect. Even *Stockholm Declaration* has been forced to memorialise in a fashion reminiscent of Article 2 (7) of the *United Nation Character.*[18] Principle 21 of *Stockholm declaration* and *Declaration on State Sovereignty of Natural Resources*[20] were framed more under historical legacy than of legal expediency of contemporary human right conscience.

'*Spring Board approach*' juxtaposed to sovereignty principle has been somewhat a precise approach towards empowerment of individual right to clean environment[21].A resonant voice echoed against debilitating Principle 21 of Stockholm Declaration by USA and Netherland. They favoured for greater international supervision and role play of individaul, state and international community in environment management system[22]. In due course of time the spring board approach came in prominence by empowering the real stakeholders, indigenous communities and traditional identities in the arena of enviro-human right world across[23].

As a logical extension to 'sovereignty approach' is the '*property approach*' which equally proved prejudicial to the right to access to natural resources. Civil and Common law achieved notoriety in according dominant position to property owners to exploit resources for maximum economic gain. In the wake of industrial revolution in UK and USA blatant disregard to natural entities were experienced resulting into uprooting of poor and countryside people[24]. However, the property notion is not always oblivious to environmental values and human right since in UK this approach served as a handy tool[25]. In a broader notion of property individual right to pure and healthful environment is implicit. A more realistic approach seems to be blending of equity law and human right with the concept of property.[26] This entails some restriction on absolute onwership by imposing public order, nuisance and peaceful enjoyment of natural resources by non-owners.

The '*right to life approach*' is yet another potential instrument of realisation of environment right. Ingrained in numerous international conventions, regional charters and national constitutions the sacrosanct nature of right to life can not be derogated[27]. In fact this approach has been utilised more often as a handy tool in anticipatory and executory breach of environmental human right.

Under the backdrop of north-south inequity and inter-governmental disparities in use, access of natural wealth, the 'social justice approach' to enviro-human right is coming to the fore under Jenkinian and International Labour Organisation (ILO) model[28]. Many regional institutions are engaged in drafting of social character inclusive of environmental rights[29] under the supervisory machinery of ILO. In the absence of any specialised broad based U.N. agency to protect environment akin to ILO and its tripartite structure such as International Labour Conference, ILO Labour office and Commission of Inquiry expeditious promotion of rights has not been made a reality. It is high time that United Nation Environment Programme (UNEP) should revitalise its organisational structure similar to ILO model,[30] for the promulgation of enviro-human right charter by blending together social and eco-justice.

The '*universalist and particularlist*' propensities discernable at human right approaches also holds great promise. However, proponents are quite divided over the feasibility of universalist and particularlist models. Prof. Richard N. Gardner maintains that UN is the only framework available for cooperation on both an east-west and north-south basis. While environmental cooperation through forum like *North Atlantic Treaty Organisation (NATO) and Organisation for Economic Cooperation and Development* (OECD) can be useful supplement to UN efforts.[31]

This view however didnot find favour in Robert E. Stein's particularistic model. He is of the view that regional organisations can achieve great success in their respective ecological regions.[32] The value of experiences and legal precedent under particularist model will always be beneficial experiments for the international organisation. A compromising but tangentially pertinent approach finds mention in Wolfgany Friedmann's '*international cooperative model*'.[33] He pleads for a international law of cooperation in which regional organisation can pursue more intensive cooperation in natural resource conservation which may not be attainable on a universal scale because of varying degree of hetrogenity of values. Professor Faweett, president of the *European Commission on Human Rights* also favours regional and local approach. He maintains that regional approaches are productive in approximating the dominant features of natural and man-made environment in an identifiable ecosystem[34].

The competing set of approaches displayed above partially mirrored into international and municipal legal promulgations and pronouncement. An analytical scrutiny of most of declarations and conventions follows that they are more honoured in breach than practice. One of the fundamental reasons is the vagueness shrouded in thrashing out of a cogent legal strategy.

III. International Enviro - Legal Regime

This tardy growth further owes to the failure of *Stockholm* Declaration in drafting 'universal declaration on environmental human right'. The declaration of conservation year by Council of Europe and *Founex* report have generated enlightened opinion making for the recognition of enviro-human right. In the wake of apparent clash between environment and development, the anxiety and concerns regarding vulnerability of people of developing countries, found expression in the report as under:

> If, by miracle all these person were to be brought up to the standards fo living now enjoyed by the people of United States...(the extraction of resources to achieve this desirable goal will deplete the earth resources) their

> extraction would virtually deplete the earth of all high grade mineral resources and would necessitate our living off the leanest of the earth substances the water of the sea and ordinary rock[35].

Perhaps under this backdrop *Stockholm* Declaration proclaimed that 'man is both creature and moulder of environment which gives him physical sustenance and affords him the opportunity for intellectual, moral, social and spritual growth. Under exuberence of technocentric approach 'in the long and tortuous evolution of human race on this planet a stage has reached when, through rapid acceleration of science and technology man has acquired the power to transform his environment in countless ways and on an unprecedented scale.'[36] Affirming faith on human right to environment the Declaration maintains that 'mian has the fundamental right to freedom, equality and adequate conditions of life, in an environment of a quality that permits a life of dignity and well-being'[37]. At the same time it enjoined a solemn duty *'to protect and improve the environment for present and future generation'*. This will go along with 'economic and social development which is essential for ensuring a favourable living and working environment for man and creating conditions on the earth that are necessary for the improvement of the quality of life'[39]. Since *Stockholm* Conference rejected the proposal for a *Universal Declaration on the Protection and Betterment of the Environment* as a counter part to *Universal Declaration of Human Right* it called upon the states that 'the sovereign right to exploit the natural resources should be in confirmity with the *Charter* of *United Nation* and principles of international law.'[40] It was not conscientised at that time but well realised afterwards that monopolisation of natural resources by states most often than not have led to the environmental abuses, flagrant violation of human right to environment, and deprivation of ecological resources. It is quite astonishing to note that *General Assembly Resolution on Permanent Sovereignty over Natural Resources* passed almost a decade ago to *Stockholm* declaration balances the right of states and people in far greater specificity. An assertion to this effect merits a mention here:

> The right to people and nations to permanent sovereignty over their natural wealth and resources must be exercised *in the interest of their national development and of the well being of the people of the state concerned.*[41] (emphasis added)

By making 'fundamental right to freedom, equality and adequate conditions of life, in an environment of a quality' subservient to 'Charter of UN and the principles of international law', the *Stockholm* Conference lost a unique opportunity to explicate the human right approach to decent environment in a subtle manner. Under these circumstances, to map out the range of such a right, an inquiry into the Covenants on Human Rights serves a logical purpose. *The Universal Declaration on Human Right* has no direct reference to environmental human right *per se* none the less it reflects the paediatric conscience in the framework of right to health and proper working environment:

> Everyone has the right to a standard of living adequate for the health and well-being of himself and for his family, including food, clothing, housing and medical care and necessary social services...[42]

Article 1 of *International Covenant on Economic, Social and Cultural Rights and Civil and Political Rights* in analogous content corroborates the significance of environmental human right in the following words:

> All people may, for thier own ends, freely dispose of their natural wealth and resources without prejudice to any obligation arising out of international co-operation, based upon the principle of mutual benefits, and international law. *In no case a people be deprived of its own means of subsistence.*[43] (emphasis added)

To make it more substantive and logical it further maintains:

> Nothing in the present covenant shall be interpreted as impairing the ***inherent right of all peoples to enjoy and utilize fully and freely their natural wealth and resources.***[44] (emphasis added)

Concurrent to these explicit specification the concept of right to life which under its broad sweep encapsulates the fundamental human right to environment. Everyone has right to life, liberty and security[45] and shall not deprive of his life[46] is an assertion to this effect. To remove environmental inequity under the presumed notion of state sovereignty and property approach to ecology, the *Declaration on Right to Development* obligates that the state 'to undertake all necessary measures for the realization of the right to development such as equality of opportunity for all in their access to basic resources, education, health services, food, housing, employment and fair distribution, right of freedom equailty and adequate conditions of life in an environment of quality' is further stretched and explicated under the *Rio Declaration on Environment and Development*, 1992. Of significance here is the anthropocentric approach which runs as under:

> Human being are the centre of concerns for sustainable development and are therefore entitled to a healthy and productive life in harmony with nature.[48]

This is indeed a paradigmatic shift which tuned the organic growth of environmental human right. The Declaration rightly perceived that statisation of natural resources and paternalistic framework of state sovereignty and platonic concept of distributive justice will probably not be beneficial for fostering human right. An endorsemnet to 'spring board' and 'particularalist' aproaches to environmental human right by recognition to real stakeholders[49] well finds support under Declaration:

> Indigenous people and their communities and other local communities, have a vital role in environmental management and development because of their knowledge and traditional practices. State should recognise and duly

> support their indentity, culture and interests and enable thier effective participation in the achievement of sustainable development.[50]

Entitlement to 'healthy and productive life in harmony with nature' and recognition of centrality of a man in sustainable development is articulated in *Vienna Declaration on Human Right*, 1993, Deriving sustenance from *Basel Convention*, 1989, *Bamco Convention*, 1991 and *Rio Declaration*, 1992 it reiterates the faith that the '*right to development should be fulfilled so as to meet equitably the developmental and environmental needs of present and future generations*'[51]. But most notably *Vienna Declaration* focussed on the serious violation of human right in the wake of indiscriminate proliferation of hazardous waste and pernicious dimensions of science and technology[52]. Therefore, it gives a clarion call to states to adopt and vigorously implement existing conventions relating to dumping of toxic and dangerous substances constituting serious threat to human right to life. The community of concerns expressed in Declaration adheres to the right to life approach in the framework of inter-generational equity and sustainable development. Thus we see that the desideratum created by *Stockholm Declaration* to arrive at seperate but concurrent 'universal declaration to right to environment' has been removed to great extent by subsequent international legal instruments. It is also appreciated to note that theoritical and juridical concerns of competing set of human right approaches are being adequately reflected and accommotated in the existing international legal framework.

IV. Legality to Reality: Indian Perspective

As a logical outcome it is worthwhile to explore the conscience of international environmental law, international human right law and judicial crosscurrents of enviro-human right under the existing Indian legal and judicial policies. The ontological status of environmental law is an impressive display of wide range of environmental right inclusive of enviro-human right in metaphorical connotation[53]. Most of the articulation of these rights follow from extra-constitutional and extra-environmental statutes. Notwithstanding the prolixity and volumnity of ciriminal law, tort law, environmental law and even constitutional law the judicial sagacity are often guided by the procedural gateway available under suit for declaration and injunction[54], representative suit, class action, public interest litigation,[55] *suo moto* cognizance of court, *amicus curie* and court sponsored commissions[56]. The ambivalent but resilient movement of judicial appratus aimed to fulfill international enviro-human right obligation in cases of serious derogation of civil, political, social, cultural and environmental rights. India has been an active participant in international environmental negotiation often assuming a leadership role among developing states by acceding to number of treaties[57]. But the absence of enabling legislation deprives the aggrieved party of specific treaty based remedies.

The umbrella legislation, *Environment Protection Act*, 1986 in its metaphorical connotation is quite progressive sounding. In the backdrop of human right approaches, the delineation of the scope of environmental right not only encompasses human environment but also includes biological entity, flora and fauna and property. Adumberation of welfarist tone of animal rights, plant rights and rights of other ecological entities is quantum leap from human right perspective. The holistic view of biotic and abiotic entities such as animals, flora and fauna, river, atmosphere and land can be interpreted beyond the shooting range of modern day human right to environment[58]. But on reality side the explicit recognition to human right to environment follows from extra-constitutional and extra-environmental statutes. Notwithstanding the prolixity and volumnity of customary law, criminal law, tort law, environmental law and even constitutional law, the judicial machinery are often moved by the procedural gateway available under public law remedies under civil and constitutional law. The procedural right in public law as a gravitational pull took a new vitality with the rise of public interest or social action litigation in actualisation of enviro-human right. Emboldened by human right oriented judicial initiative India's robust environmental movement in an adversorial atmosphere of repressive policing and bureaucratic red tapism has ushered third generation human right regime[59]. This was made possible by insulations of inspiration underpinned in *Stockholm* Declaration into our constitutional body. In 1976 *Forty Second Constitutional (Amendment) Act* obligated on the 'state to protect and improve and to safeguard the forest and wildlife of country'[60]. Though adopted as directive principle the court generally interpreted it in broad and long range ecological sustainability perspective. Encourged by the liberal atmosphere of freedom in the aftermath of emergency the right to life approach guaranteed under Article 21[61] articulated to include right to live in decent environment. 'Right to life is not mere animal existence'[62] but 'to live with human dignity'[63] and 'all that goes alongwith it'[64] encapsulated an environment free from polluted air,[65] vehicular pollution,[66] radiation pollution,[67] contaminated water,[68] noisy inhabitation[69] industrial hazard,[70] haphazard urban planning[71] deficated urban landscape[72] and right to ecological balance[73] health and decent environment. The right to life approach not only implicates absence of polluted environment but also the quality of environment[74] by attractive enumeration of justiciable entitlements such as clean river[75] and lakes,[76] coastal resource zone,[77] afforestation[78] preservation of wetland,[79] healthy growth of wildlife and orinthology[79a].

V. Human Right To Environment: Judicial Interpretation

This notional extension to right to life was recognised even without specific reference to actual and specific violations of fundamental right. A critical survey fo catena of cases exhibits two broad tendencies. The first approach seems heavily concerned with perilious consequences of environmental pollution and immediate threat to sustenance and survival. Whereas the second approach strives to enhance the quality of environment, health and sanitation, safety and security from hazardous processes, ecological balance, preservation of eco-system and bio-diversity, sustainable development and inter-generational equity. This often resulted in the closure of environmentally malign industries such as lime stone and stone quarrying in

Doon [80] and Saproon [81] valleys, tanneries at Kanpur, [82] Vellore [83] and Calcutta, [84] hazardous industries in Delhi [85] Rajasthan [86] and elsewhere, banning of aqua culture[87], prawn farming [88] and others. Most often than not the Supreme Court and High Courts have recognised these rights without an attendant fundamental right by issuing set of directives under their writ jurisdictions under Article 32 and 226 of the Constitution respectively. In *Dehradun Quarrying case* where the illegal limestone mining in the Mussorie-Dehradun region was devastating the fragile ecosystems, the Supdreme Court in an activist tone and tenor held:

> we are not oblivious of the fact that natural resources has got to be tapped for the purposes of social development but one can not forget at the same time that tapping of resources have to be done with requisite attention and care so that ecology and environment may not be affected in any serious way...It has always to be remembered that these are permanent assets of mankind and are not intended to be exhansted on one generation.[89]

The Supreme Court passed at least five comprehensive interim orders recognising right to ecological balance as fundamental right.[89] But none of these orders, articulate the actual fundamental right infringed inspite of the copious reference to Articles 21 and 32 of the Constitution. Since the exercise of jurisdiction under Article 32 presupposes the violation of a fundamental right, it becomes necessary to reasonably derive the fundamental right that the Supreme Court had in view when it issued orders.[90] This reasoning finds a peripheral mention in Justice K.N. Singh's concluding observations justifying the closure of polluting tanneries in *Ganga Pollution* (*Tanneries*) case :

> We are conscious that closure of tanneries may bring unemployment, loss of revenue, but *life, health and ecology have greater importance to the people* (emphasis added).

Dealing with the environmental ramification of haphazard

urban planning the Andhra Pradesh High Court construed the right to ecological balance as under:

> [I]t would be reasonable to hold that the enjoyment and fulfillment guaranteed by Art. 21 of the constitution embraces the protection and preservation of nature's gifts without (which) life cannot be enjoyed. There can be no reason *why practice of violent extinguishment of life alone should be regarded a violence of Article 21 of the Constitution. The slow poisoning by the polluted atmosphere caused by environmental pollution and spoilation should be regarded as amounting to violation of Art. 21 of Constitution.* [92] (emphasis added)

'It, therefore, becomes the legitimate duty of courts as the enforcing organs of constitutional objectives to forbid all actions of the state and citizen from upsetting the environmental balance'.[93]

Similar approach was adopted in *Kinkri Devi V. State of Himachal Pradesh*,[94] wherein the limestoning activity was banned on the ground of being violative of Article 21 alongside Articles 48-A and 51A (g).[95] It ruled that 'to ensure the attainment of the constitutional goal of the protection and improvement of the natural wealth and environment ... from the hazardous consequances of the arbitrary exercise of power of granting mine lease ... without due regard to life, liberty and property *the court will be left with no alternative but to intervene effectively by issuing appropriate writs order and direction*'.[96] Extinguishment of life due to slow poisoning under the arbitrary exercise of power attracted condemnation of Supreme Court in *Subhash Kumar* V. *State of Bihar*.[97] The court justified the applicability of writ jurisdiction on the ground of derogation of right to enjoyment of pollution free water and air under Article 21. In *Koolwal* V. *State of Rajasthan*, a petition to enforce improved sanitation measures in Jaipur met favourable disposition based in part on the expended right to life argument. No specific injury was alleged but 'poor sanitation and preservation of the environment due to slow poisoning of Jaipur resident was held to be violation of right to health.' In this case a direct nexus with human health and injury has not been demonstrated at all. The court further ruled that 'fundamental duty enshrined under Article 51A (g) extends not only to citizens but to instrumentality of state'.[98] Dovetailing the environment and health conditions the Supreme Court in *Virender Gaur V. State of Haryana* [99] delinated that 'the word environment is of broad spectrum which brings within its ambit hygienic atmosphere and ecological balance'. The citizen can not exercise the fundamental right unless the corresponding constitutional duty is being carried out by municipality'.[100]

The broad sweep of right to decent environment as a part of right to life extended even to those cases where mere apprehension to environmentally deleterious activities were anticipated but not committed. *In Law Society of India V. Fertilizers & Chemicals Tranvancor Ltd.* [101] is a case in point where mere likelihood of leakage of ammonia storage tank at Cochin amounted to dark shadow of genocide. The court ruled:

> A state of perpetual anxiety and fear of extermination of life is not an environment adequate for the health and well being of human race. *(I)t is the plain and clear negation of most basic human right guaranteed under Article 21.*[102] (emphasis added)

The human right to decent environment was recognised in *Ratlam Municipality*[103] case where neither the writ jurisdiction was involved nor any breach of fundamental right was alleged. While hearing an appeal under special leave petition from the municipality against High Court's approval of magisterial order under section 133 CrPC to remove fibth, menacing state of public health, malodorous fluids from the discharge of alcohal plant, breeding of mosquitos, snakes and scorpions, the Supreme Court speaking through Justice Krishna Iyer in an unmistakable terms developed an alternative ratio:

> A responsible municipal council constituted for the precise purpose of preserving public health and providing better facilities can not run away from its principal duty, by

> pleading financial inability. *Decency and dignity are non-negotiable facets of human right and are a first charge on local self governing bodies.* [104] (emphasis added)

The judgement invigorated fresh stamina into the seemingly dull legislation of public nuisance having wider ramifications in controlling enviro-health derogation at grass root level. None the less it is quite astonishing to note that the plea for human right was developed without any specific reference to Articles 21, 48-A and 51A (g). Rather the court preferred to be guided by the notion of social justice [105] and public health.[106] Giving a clarion call to rejuvenate public law glossed with human right values Justice Krishna Iyer further held:

> There is an urgent need to focus on ordinary man and a radical change in the hierarchy of values served by civil procedure. The municipality should come to terms of paramount principle of governance by improving public health provisions.[107]

In *Bayer India Ltd. V. State of Maharashtra*, [108] a human habitation proximate to hazardous chemical process was thought to be confronted with perilious demensions of chemical exposure and consequential threat to life. The court formulated the view that:

> Nothing can be more fundamental than the issue of public safety and right to life and where these are infringed upon, *the courts will have to act in general interest of the citizen and not the Government and public bodies.*[109] (emphasis added)

Another quantum leap in the arena of promotion of enviro-human right is the enforcement of these entitlements not only against state, instrumentality of state, statutory bodies but also to private entities. Cases are not rare where the courts have issued writs against many major industries in private sector.[110] Even where the cause of environmental harm emanates from a private entity, a writ petition against the state may be successful if the court finds that a designated governmental authority has not taken sufficient action to protect a healthy environment for the people. In *Ganga Pollution (Tanneries)* case the Supreme Court issued orders under article 32 of the Constitution to a number of private tanneries although the legal basis for issuing orders against private entities was not explained. [111] Under the pretext of lack of time the Supreme Court in *Sri Ram case* postponed the subtle delineation of applicability of writ jurisdiction against private entities.[112] The position, however, firmly crystalised in *Consumer Education and Research Centre*[113] case. The Supreme Court issued orders against thirty asbestos mines and seventy four asbestos related industries relating to occupational health and safety measures under Art. 32. Justified on the ground of right to life approach the constitutional bench clarified that '*even private persons or industries are bound by the direction issued by this court under Article 32.*[114] A concurrent justification for such an approach derived from the judicial obligation underpinned under article 142.[115]

The zealously guarded attitude of the court has not only cut short the want of proof, specific infringement of fundamental right, non-existence of statutory remedies but also given effect to international environmental law to promote enviro-human right. In the absence of specific treaty law commitment, such an approach led to filling of gap of municipal environmental and constitutional statutes with that of international standard. *Calcutta Wetland case* is a pointer to this effect. Since the court believed that 'environmental degradation is a social problem having far reaching ramifications on society it is nothing but incumbment on law court to discharge social duty to preserve wetland as per *Ramsar Convention.*[116] This line of thinking has percolated down deeply in numerous recent rulings of Supreme Court. In. *H-Acid* and *Vellore Citizens cases'* the 'polluter pays principle' incorporated under Article 130-R (2) of the *European Community Treaty and European Community Fourth Action programme* was judicially recognised.[117] *In Jagannath case* the Supreme Court has given effect to *UN Convention on Law of Sea* (UNCLOS) 1982 to protect coastal area and marine environment.[118] Similarly the soft law principles such as 'precautionary principle' and 'sustainable development' are held to be part of law of land in *Vellore Citizen Forum, Badhkal* and *Suraj Kund Lake,* [119] *Calcutta Tanneries, Taj Trapezium* and *Kamal Nath* [120] cases. Building of sewer in Ahmadabad[121], protection of Doon and Saproon valleys, hygienic conditions at Ratlam, sanitary condition in Jaipur, fear of death from the escape of deadly gas are the cases where substantive and concrete orders were passed without any specific attendant fundamental right. In *Chilka Lake* case the fishermen's traditional method of fishing as against the modern method amounted to violation of Article 21 on the ground of deleterious environmental impact of blue revolution.[122].

VI. Beyond Reality: Implication And Conclusion

Placed in nutshell the human right culture has percolated down to Indian human right regime within short period of time. With an active working partnership with an enlightened NGO community, and public spirited movements, sweeping judicial innovations were put forth. This emerging enviro-human right scenario has almost set at naught the paternalistic, authoritarian and repressive legal regime.[123] In the wake of country's extinctive ecosystem and endangered bio-diversity the well thought and conscientised judicial intervention left a mark of wisdom in overall planning, policy and legal discourse.[124] It is indeed surprising but remain sayable that despite environmental malign policies, repressive legal regime, bureaucratic slackness, official secrecy, and non-tolerant political culture, enviro-human right movement received renewable impetus. A careful jurisprudential analysis of specific content and scope of these rights reveals a conceptual quagmire and a sort of enigma. This is more noticeable when we attempt to locate appropriate dimension on the matrix of varying degree of articulated right. One connotation tantamounts to 'right to human health free from environmental pollution, unhygienic conditions and poor sanitation.' Even in the absence of substantive injury the court are willing to enforce these right under writ jurisdictions. *Secondly*, these right relate to principally to 'pollution free environment' than health *per se*. *Thirdly*, the scope of the rights can be extended to an 'entitlement of ecological balance, sustainable development' and right to live in perfect harmony with nature. The probable specification of these rights are not exhaustive in content and doors of interpretation are still open. However, the preponderance of balance tilts towards absolutist and relativist approaches. In this releneless pursuit of paradigmatic course, the traditional remedies in crime, tort and civil and customary laws are fraught with under utilisation. Viwed telescopically at disperate time and context, human right rehabilitative regime appears to perform the supplementary role in the enforcement of existing statutory provisions. Most often than not, instead of straight forward enforcement of existing statutory provisions an alternative ratio in human right perspective is generally advanced. As a natural sequal to this ambitious approach creation of extra executive and concurrent infrastructure are witnessed. The emergence of compensatory jurisprudence in public law constitutional domain[125] appears to be an amplified version of damages under tort. None the less the PIL has a galvanising effect in promotion of the enviro-human right and eco-justice in India. The procedural attraction, low cost device, speedy hearing, low evidentiary compliance, comprehensive remedy and non-appealability are some of the reasons for its frequent use. That is why inspite of substantive ambiguity, human right approach in realisation of environmental justice can be tailored to suit the need of complex ecological problem. Last but not the least it remains to be safely concluded that a strong indigenous tradition of environmentalism ingrained in historical roots[126] should also be explicated in subtle principles and popularised in the mainstream of political,[127] legal and judicial thought alongwith the modern developments in enviro-human jurisprudence.

References

1. *See* B. Simma & B. Ruster (ed.) *International Protection of the Environment: Treaties and Documents*. 33 vols. (1970); See also: W.E. Burhenne, *International Environment;*

Multilateral Treaties, 6 vols. 1974; H. Hohmann (ed.), *Basic Documents of International Environmental Law*, (1992).

2. A.O. Adede, 'International Environmental Law From Stockholm To Rio; An Overview of Past Lesson And Future Challenges, 22 (2) *Journal of Environmental Law and Policy*, 88-105 (1992); Jaro Moyda, 'Recent Developments In Environmental Law Making' XXIII (5) *Journal of Environmental Policy and Law*, 204-10 (1993).

3. *See* generally: Arne Naess, *The Shallow and Deep Long Range Ecology Movement. A Summary*, (1973); E.F. Schumacher, *A Study of Economics As If People Mattered. The Small Is Beautiful*, (1993); R.Elliot & A. Gare, *Environmental Philosophy*, (1983). Md. Zafar Mahfooz Nomani, Book Review, XII *Aligarh Law Journal* , 271-73 (1997).

4. P. Alston, A Third Generation of Solidarity Rights: Progressive Development or Obfuscation of International Human Right Law?. VXVIII (29) *Australian Law Journal* 1993.

5. Eibe Riedel, 'Change of Paradigm In International Environmental Law' 57 *Law and State* 28-29 (1998).

6. D. McGoldrick, 'Sustainable Development and Human Right: An Integrated Conception', 45 *International and Comparative Law Quarterly* (1996).

7. W. Paul Gormley, *Human Right and Environment: The Need for International Cooperation*, 34 (1976).

8. *Id*. at 14.

9. *See* R. Falk, *This Endangered Planet: Prospects and Proposal for Human Survival*, (1972).

10. *Supra* note 7 at 33.

11. *Id* at 43.

12. *Ibid*.

13. *Supra* note 9.

14. Sohn, The Stockholm Declaration On Human Environment, XIV *Harvard International law Journal* 423, 406 93 (1973).

15. Fisheries Jurisdiction case: *United Kingdom* V. *Iceland* (1974) ICJ3 *Germany* V. *Iceland* (1974) ICJ75.

16. Nuclear Test case: *Australia* V. *France* (1974) ICJ 253 & *Newzealand* V. *France* (1974) ICJ 457.

17. *See* E.D.Brown, The Lesson of Tory Canyon, 21 *Current Legal Problem* 113 (1969).

18. *Article* 2 (7) of U.N.Charter runs as under: 'Nothing contained in the present Charter shall authorize the United Nations to intervene in matters which are essentially with in the domestic jurisdiction of any state or shall require the Members to submit such matters to settlement under the present charter; but this principle shall not prejudice the application of enforcement measures under Chapter vii.'

19. *Infra* note.40.

20. Principle 1, 2 & 7, *General Assembly Resolution on Permanent Sovereignty Over Natural Resources*, A/RES/1803 (XVII), 14 Dec. 1902.

21. *Supra* note 14 at 448: The earlier draft of Netherlands elaborated upon a three level relationship: man, state, and international community. This approach serves as the spring board for protection of individual rights.

22. *Supra* note 7 at 37.

23. *Infra* note 50.

24. *Supra* note 7 at 37/22.

25. *See* also: Michael R. Anderson, 'Individual Right To Environmental Protection In India', in Alan E. Boyle *et al.* (eds.) *Human Right Approaches To Environmental Protection*, 215 (1996).

26. *Supra* note 7 at 39.

27. *Id* at 42.

28. C. Jenks, *Social Justice In The Law of Nations: ILO Impact After Fifty Year*, (1970): *See* also:C. Jenks, *A New World of Law? A Study of Creative Imagination In International Law,* 53-54 (1959).

29. *See* Tennfjord, 'The European Social Charter. An Instrument of Social Collaboration in Europe', VII *European Year Book*, 71 (1962).

30. *Supra* note 7 at 39, 45-6.

31. R. Gardner, 'The Role of U.N. In Environmental Problems', XXVI *International Organisation* 237, 239 (1972).

32. R.E. Stien, 'The Potential Of Regional Organisation In Managing Man's Environment', in J.L.Hargrove (ed.) *Law, Institution And The Global Environment*(1972).

33. W. Friedmann, *International Law of Co-operation: Regional Groupings In The Changing Structure of International Law*, 62-3 (1964).

34. J. Fawcett, Book Review, XII *Columbia Journal of Transnational Law*, 404, 409 (1973). *See* also: M.F. Strong, 'The United Nations and the Environmental Crisis', XXVI *International Organisation*, 169 (1972).

35. *Environment and Development, The Founex Report,* (International Con. No. 586) 44 (1972).

36. Proclaimation 1, *Declaration of the United Nations Conference On The Human Environment*, 1972.

37. *Id* Principle 1.

38. *Ibid.*

39. *Id* Principle 8.

40. *Id* Principle 21.

41. Article 1, *General Assembly Resolution on Permanent Sovereignty Over Natural Resources*, A/RES/1803 (XVII), 14 Dec. 1962.

42. Article 25, *The Universal Declaration of Human Rights,*, 1948.

43. Article 1(2), *International Covenants on Economic, Social and Cultural Rights & Civil and Political Rights,* 1966.

44. Articles 25, *International Covenant on Economic, Social and Cultural Rights* and Article 47, *International Covenant on Civil and Political Rights*, 1966.

45. Article 3, *The Universal Declaration of Human Rights*, 1948.

46. Article 6, *International Covenant of Civil and Political Right*, 1966.

47. Article 8 (1), *The Declaration On Right To Development*, (A/RES/41/128) 4 Dec. 1986.

48. Article 1, *The Rio Declaration on Environment and Development*, 1992.

49. Md. Zafar Mahfooz Nomani, 'Environment Protection Under Indian Federalism: A Review of Legal And Institutional Mechanism', XXI (1&2) *The Academy Law Review,* 146-8 (1997).

50. Principle 22, *The Rio Declaration On Environment And Development*, 1992.

51. Article 11, *The Vienna Declaration and Programme of Action: World Conference on Human Right*, (A/Conf. 157/24, 25 June) 1993.

52. *Ibid.*

53. *See* Chhatrapati Singh, 'Legal Policy For Environment Protection In India', in P. Leelakrishnan (ed.) *Law and Environment,* 31-33 (1992).

54. Michael R. Anderson, 'Public Nuisance and Private Purpose: Policed Environment in British India', 1860-1947 *SOAS Law Department Working Paper No.*1 (1992).

55. Md. Zafar Mahfooz Nomani, 'Community Action And Public Participation In Environmental Protection: A Review of Administrative Legal And Judicial Mechanism' (mimeo) *Paper Presented at International Mountain Meet*, 1998. Rishikesh (India). *See* also: Md. Zafar Mahfooz Nomani, 'Water Pollution Control And Public Participation: Legal Dimension', XXIII(1) *Indian Bar Review* (1996).

56. Krishna Mahajan, 'Enforcing Environmental Laws: Some Issues' 41(8) *The Yojna: Special Issue on Development and Environment,* 119-21 (1997).

57. Michael R. Anderson, 'International Environmental Law In Indian Courts', VII (1) *RECIEL* 22 (1998).

58. Section 2 (a), *The Environment Protection Act*, 1986 defines environment as under; "Environment" includes Water, air and land and the inter-relationship which exists among and between water, air and land, and human beings, other living creatures, plants, micro-organism and property.

59. *Supra* note 25.

60. Article 48-A of the *Constitution of India*, 1950 mandates: 'The State shall endeavour to *protect* and *improve* the environment and to safeguard the forest and wildlife of the country.'

61. Article 21, *The Constitution of India* reads as: 'No person shall be deprived of his life or personal liberty except according to procedure established by law.'

62. *Maneka Gandhi* V. *Union of India*, AIR 1978 SC 597, 623-24.

63. *Francis Coralie Mullin* V. *The Administrator, Union Territory of Delhi*, AIR 1981 SC 746, 749-50.

64. *Id* at 752-3.

65. *Navin Chemicals Manufacturing And Trading Co. Ltd.* V. *New Okhla Industrial Development Authority*, 1987 All L.J.13 *Chaitanya Pulverising Industry* V. *Karnataka State Pollution Control Board*, AIR 1987 Kant 82; *D.D.Vyas* V. *Ghaziabad Development Authority*, AIR 1993 All. 57; *P.C.Cherian* V. *State of Kerala*, 1981 KLT 113; *Krishna Gopal* V. *Madhya Pradesh*, 1986 Cr.L.J. 396; *Ajeet Mehta* V. *State of Rajasthan*, 1990. Cr.L.J. 1596.

66. *M.C.Mehta* V. *Union of India*, 4 SCC (1996) 351.

67. *M.K.Sharma* V. *Bharat Electronics*, AIR 1987 SC 1792; *Shiva Rao Shantaram Wagle* V. *Union of India*, AIR 1988 SC 952.

68. *M.C.Mehta* V. *Union of India*, AIR 1988 SC 1037; *M.C.Mehta* V. *Union of India*, AIR 1988 SC 1115; *Attakaya Thangal* V. *Union of India* 199 (1) KLT 580; *R.R.Singh* V. *State of Bihar*, AIR 1992 Pat.86.

69. *Rabin Mukherjee* V. *State of West Bengal*, AIR 1985 Cal 222; *Om Biranjana Religious Society* V. *The State*, 1996 CWN 57; *Burra Bazar Fire Workers Dealers Association* V. *The Commissioner of Police*, 1997 CWN 1983.

70. *M.C. Mehta* V. *Union of India*, 1987 SC 982; AIR 1987 SC 982; AIR 1987 SC 1086; *Union Carbide Corporation* V. *Union of India*, AIR 1990 SC 273; *M.C.Mehta* V. *Union of India*, (1996) 4 SCC 750.

71. *L.K. Koolwal* V. *State of Rajasthan*, AIR 1988 Raj 2; *T. Damodar Rao* V. *S.O. Municipal Corporation of Hyderabad*, AIR 1987 AP 171; *Sachinand Pandey* V. *State of West Bengal* AIR 1987 SC 1109; *Bombay Environmental Action Groups* V. *State of Maharashtra*, AIR 1991 Bom. 301.

72. *Municipal Council, Ratlam* V. *Vardichand*, AIR 1985 SC 1022.

73. *Rural Litigation & Entitlement Kendra* V. *State of U.P.*, (1985) 2 SCC 431; (1985) 3 SCC 614; (1986) SUPP. SCC 517; (1987) SUPP. SCC 487; (1989) SUPP. (1) scc 504.

74. Section 3, *Environment Protection Act*. 1986 mentions about 'quality' of environment: (1) Subject to the provision of this Act, the *Central Government shall have the power to take all such measures as it deems necessary and expedient for the purpose of protecting and improving the quality of the environment* and preventing, controlling and abating environmental pollution.

75. *Supra* note 68.

76. *Kholamuhana Primary Fisherman Cooperative Society* V. *State of Orissa*, AIR 1994 Ori. 191.

77. *Indian Council for Enviro-Legal Action* V. *Union of India* (1996) 5 SCC 281.

78. *Banwasi Sewa Ashram* V. *State of U.P.* AIR 1987 SC 374; *D.N.Pandey* V. *Union of India* AIR 1987 SC 359; *State of H.P.* V. *Ganesh Wood Product*, AIR 1996 SC 149; *M.C.Mehta* V. *Kamal Nath*, (1997) I SCC 388; *T.N.Godavaran Thirumnlkpad* V. *Union of India*, (1997) 2SCC 267.

79. *People United For A Better Living In Calcutta* V. *State of W.B.*, AIR 1993 Cal. 215.

79a. *Tarun Bharat Sangh* V. *Union of India*, AIR 1992 SC 514.

80. *Supra* note 73.

81. *General Public of Saproon Valley* V. *State of H.P.* AIR 1993 HP 52.

82. *Supra* note 68 (AIR 1988 SC 1037).

83. *Vellore Citizens Welfare Forum* V. *Union of India,* AIR 1996 SC 2715.

84. *M.C.Mehta* V. *Union of India,* (1997) 2 SCC 411.

85. *M.C.Mehta* V. *Union of India*, (1996) 4 SCC 351; (1996) 4 SCC 750.

86. *Indian Council for Enviro-Legal Action* V. *Union of India* AIR 1996 SC 1446.

87. *S. Jagannath* V. *Union of India,* (1997) 2 SCC 87.

88. *Supra* note 76.

89. *Supra* note 73: (1987) SUPP. SCC 487

90. Armin Resencranz *et al.*, *Environmental Law and Policy in India*, 57 (1992).

91. *Supra* note 680.

92. *Supra* note 71: AIR 1987 AP 171 at 181.

93. *Ibid.*

94. *Kinkri Devi.* V. *State of H.P.* AIR 1988 HP 4 at 7-9.

95. Article 51-A (g) reads: 'it shall be duty of every citizen of India to protect and improve the natural environment including forests, lakes, rivers and wild life, and *to have compassion for living creature*'.

96. *Supra* note 94 at 9.

97. AIR 1991 SC 420 at 424.

98. *Supra* note 71. AIR 1988 Raj 2 at 4

99. (1995) 2 SSC 577.

100. *Id* at 580.

101. AIR 1994 Ker. 308.

102. *Ibid.*

103. AIR 1980 SC 1622.

104. *Id* at 1629.

105. *Id* at 1628: Justice V.R.Krishna Iyer quoting extensively some of the authorities in subject held that 'the judiciary must be informed by broader principle of access to justice necessitated by conditions of developing countries and obligated by Article 38 of the Constitution'.

106. *Id* at 1631: 'The State shall realise that Article 47 makes it a paramount, principle of governance that steps are taken for the improvement of public health as amongst its primary duties'.

107. *Id* at 1629.

108. AIR 1995 Bom. 290.

109. *Id* at 291.

110. *Som Prakash Rekhi* V. *Union of India,* AIR 1981 SC 212; *Bihar State Harijan Kalyan Parishad* V. *Union of India* (1985) 2 SCC 644; *Central Inland Water Transport Corp. Ltd. V. Brojo Nath Ganguly*, (1986) 3 SCC 156.

111. *M.C.Mehta V. Union of India*, AIR 1988 SC 1037.

112. *M.C.Mehta V. Union of India*, AIR 1987 SC 1086.

113. *Consumer Education & Research Centre V. Union of India,* AIR 1995 SC 922.

114. *Id* at 941.

115. Article 142 of the *Constitution of India,* 1950 reads as: (1) The Supreme Court in the exercise of its jurisdiction may pass such decree or make such order as is necessary for doing complete justice in any cause or matter pending before it, and any decree so passed or order so made shall be enforceable throughout the territory of India...'

116. *Supra* note 79 at 227.

117. *Supra* note 86.

118. *Supra* note 87 at 95.

119. (1997) 3 SCC 715.

120. (1997) 1 SCC 388.

121. *Janki Nathubahi Chhara* V. *Sardarnagar Municipality,* AIR 1986 Guj. 49.

122. *Supra* note 76.

123. Upendra Baxi, 'Environmental Law; Limitation And Potential For Liberation' in J. Bandhyopadhya *et al.*, (ed.) *India's Environment: Crisis and Response* 307 (1985) *See* also: Michael R. Anderson, 'Classification and Coercions: Themes in South Asian Legal Studies in 1980's, *South Asia Research*, 168-9 (1990).

124. M.C.Mehta, 'Human Right and Environment', 42(2) *The Yojna,* 28 (1998).

125. *Nilabati Bahera V. State of Orissa* (1993) 2 SCJ 487 at 497.

126. *See* generally: D. Arnold & R. Guha (eds.) *Nature, Culture And Imperialism: Essay On Environmental History of South Asia* (1995). *See* also: Md. Zafar Mahfooz Nomani, 'Indigenous People And Natural Resource Management: A Search For A Socio-Legal Framework' (mimeo) *Paper Presented In All India Sociological Conference*, Aligarh, Dec.1998.

127. *See* generally: Anil Agarwal & Sunita Narain (eds.) *The Dying Wisdom: Rise Fall And Potential of India's Traditional Water Harvesting System,* (1997); Ashish Kothari *et.al.* (eds.) *Commanities And Conservation: Natural Resource Management In South And Central Asia*, (1998).

13

Healthy Environment: A Human Right

Mohiuddin Ahmad Farooqui

The environment protection since centuries is a world-wide issue. Environmental crisis has propagated a movement which is undertaken by scientists, social workers, political leaders even International Organisations. In this regard role of International Cooperation has also assumed tremendous significance. World political leaders took part in International Conferences with a sincereity to curb down environmental problems of their own countries. The severity of the environmental problem has now been proved a major threat to human life. Meaning of protection of life under various national and international documents was only eradication of poverty but later years it also encompasses the clean environment for human being. Rapid degradation of environment by industrial development which were in fact opted to achieve economic flourishment for poverty eradication has caused a great problem to existence of human life. Clean environment has now became essential to human life. Therefore, on account of multidimensional effect of pollution, right to healthy environment is universally accepted as a human right.

International Concern

Concrete concern towards rational use and conservation

of natural resources of the biosphere was first of all raised in 1968 from the platform of the United Nations, Educational, Scientific and Cultural Organisation (UNESCO), held a special inter governmental conference where experts had determined the scientific principles of this rational problem. The results of this conference are closely related to a number of important proposals on the environment which are being given high level consideration by International Organisations. Later on an international conference was held in Stockholm, Swedon in 1972. One of the result of this conference was the adoption of a Declaration on the Human Environment. In a major inter-governmental conference on environment programme (UNEP) in 1977, the Executive Director warned that 'Environmental Education is now a matter of life and death'[1]. In 1981, African Charter on Human and Peoples Right was promulgated of which Article 24 lays down that:

> "All people shall have the right to general satisfactory environment favourable to their development."

African Charter was first International instrument of Human Rights Law. It declares 'right to environment' as a human right and emphasizes the importance of environment being "general satisfaction' and favourable to .... development."[2]

United Nations Conference on Environment and Development (Earth Summit) at Rio Dejenerio (Brazil) in June, 1992 minutely reached to the observations that, every citizen has the right to live in environment worthy of human existence. This is natural as the concept of Human Rights is also expanded from its social ambit. Prior to the realisation of environmental degradation human rights were interpreted in terms of social development. But later on when the sporadic industrial development started rapid environmental pollution affects the survival of life. Thus, development and polluted environment both have upset the rights to life and health in other aspects. Obviously human rights have to be interpreted in terms of healthy environment. Rio-declaration proclaims that: "Human beings are the centre of concerns for sustainable development.

They are entitled to a healthy and productive life in harmony with nature."[3]

India took part a leading role in Stockholm Conference on Human Environment in 1972. This shows India's realisation of deadly portens of pollution and commitment to eradicate the pollution for well being of the people. Such conference held under the aegis of United Nations to establish the natural environment as a basic right. The right to a healthy environment is natural, inalienable and fundamental right of the people. Therefore, the Declaration acts as an eye opener to mankind and the people in the world. On the essential and imperative need to protect the environment Declaration can be viewed from any direction and finally prove an important milestone for International environmental movement. The proclamation felt that protection of environment is an important need of the time. It is recapitulated in a part as under:

> "Man is both creature and moulder of his environment which gives him physical sustenance and affords him the opportunity for intellectual, moral, social and spiritual growth. In the long and tortuous evolution of the human race on this planet a stage has been reached when through the rapid acceleration of science, and technology, man has acquired the power to transform his environment in countless ways and on an unpresidented scale. Both aspects of man's environment, the natural and the man made, are essential to his well being and to the enjoyment of the basic human rights. Even the right to life itself."[4]

United Nations proclamation also adopted that all governments of the world must realise human environment a major issue. Appropriate actions must be taken by these governments in this regard. In a better environment more needs and hopes of human can be achieved. Apart from governmental initiatives man himself must be committed to build a better environment by using his knowledge in collaboration with nature. There should be a goal of whole mankind to defend and improve the human environment for present and future generations.[5]

United Nations conference of 1972, calls upon the mankind of a goal of protection of environment to be pursued together with, and in harmony with the established and fundamental goals of peace and world wide-economic and social development. At the same time proclamation demands an infliction of responsibility to citizens, communities, enterprises and institutions at every level on achieving the said goal.

The conference has burdened upon the governments and people to exert common efforts for the preservation and improvement of the human environment for the benefit of all the people and for their posterity.

The agreed action plan of this U.N. Conference included three major components, viz. detailed environmental assessment so as to make rational judgments about priorities for action, organised environmental management and supportive action in the form of laws, manpower institutions, and finances to implement the decisions so reached.[6]

Since early 1970's man has become aware of the facts that the rapidly growing conditions of stress on his environment threaten not only his welfare but even his survival, Man's ambition of everlasting enjoyment and comfort had led him to exploit natural resources to the extent of reducing its natural capacities for self stabilisation. As a consequence of the outright disregard of the impact of the these activities, numerous environmental problems have arisen which seem to be the bare of modern scientific thought and technological advancements. It is only recently that man has come to realise that the environment is an unbroken totality which includes everything that affects the air, water, surroundings and other factors that affect the quality of life on earth.

National Concern

Mere declaration of environment a human right at the floor of United Nations was not enough. In consonance the nations have to take some objective steps in this larger issue of mankind. India in 1976, have brought many constitutional amendments in one go, through which environment as a whole is placed at the position of human right. Originally Constitution of India did not contain any provisions having a direct bearing on environment. However, some of the provisions do make tangential reference to the problem like article 47, 48 and 49 contain directives to government. India was one of the few countries that has provided constitutional safeguards to preservation of the environment. Article 48-A, 51-A(g) and entries in three Legislative lists are inserted in the Constitution. These provisions contain a clear mandate to the citizens to protect and improve the environment. Therefore, they constitute the basic policy framework for all the legislative and executive programmes in this regard.

Constitutional Development

First and foremost amendment of the Constitution with regard to the environment has paved the way to do liberal & socialists attitude towards environmental development. In the preamble of the Constitution for the words "Sovereign Democratic Republic," the words "Sovereign Socialists Secular and Democratic Republic" were substituted. The importance of this amendment can easily be visualized. Though India has always been following the ideal of socialist pattern of society, yet it was for the first time this ideal was given a constitutional recognition by the 42nd constitutional amendment Act 1976. The problem of environmental pollution is a social problem affecting, as it does the society at large socialistic pattern of the societies imposes a number of new obligations on the state. Inversely state have to eradicate social hazards and social evils and to ensure social justice. The environmental pollution is one of the most important social problems that a nation is called upon to face.

Part II of the Constitution deals with the Directive Principles of State Policies. Art 47 says that the state shall regard the raising of the level of nutrition and the standard of living of its people and the improvements of public health as among its primary duties... This article provides for the improvement of the public health as one of the primary duties of the state and it could very well include by implication of the protection and improvement of the environment, for the control and prevention of environmental pollution necessarily and primarily comes within the concept of the improvements of the public health.[7]

New insertion of Article 48-A as "the State shall endeavour to protect and improve the environment and to safeguard the forests and the wild life of the country," has directly intervened to casts an obligatory duty on the state to endeavour to protect and improve the environment. To make it effective few insertions are made in the legislative lists enshrined in the seventh schedule of the Constitution.

Addition of new chapter, IV-A of fundamental duties in the Constitution has proved deep concern of the state to protect and preserve the natural environment. Article 51A (g) enjoins that "it shall be duty of every citizen of India... to protect and improve the natural environment including forests, lakes, rivers and wild life, and to have compassion for living creatures." 'The principles enunciated commands to live together based on an environmental law to violate which is to gamble with civilized life itself.'[8] Addition of an exclusive state directive in the voluminous list of directive principles would be meaningless unless the legislative steps are not taken in conformity with it.

Thus the policy goals have been laid down in directives and fundamental duties through 42nd amendment Act, 1976. The inclusion of Article 48-A, 51-A (g) entries to legislative list and the word 'Socialist' in preamble have widened the concept and meaning of the 'life' as enshrined in Article 21 of the Constitution. In absence of healthy and clean environment existence of life is not possible. Even political, social and economic rights are questioned in presence of polluted environment. On increasing pollution hazards environment of man is grossly polluted. Healthy environment is going to become scarce in the regime of increasing industrial, agricultural, chemical and domestic activities of pollution. This menace is found abundantly in the third world countries. On such account the right to healthy environment has been recognised as a 'third generation human rights'. Particularly, in India with the innovative legislative activist as well as judicial activist approach it can be manifestly said that the expansionist meaning of Article 21 can lead us to draw the conclusion that deprivation of right to human life is not the only activity remains to be accomplished but to vigorously enforce the legislations enacted under the national policy for the protection of ecology.[9]

Legislative Development

In accordance with National Policy for Environment state has promulgated environmental laws to deal environment directly. These are the water (prevention and control of pollution) Act 1974, The Air (prevention and control of pollution) Act 1981, and the Environment (Protection) Act 1986. Prior to these laws existing local provisions were neither adequate nor satisfactorily dealt increasing tendency of pollution. Therefore, comprehensive legislations have been laid down to establish unitary agencies in the centre and states.

The objective of Water Act, 1974 is to prevent, abate and control the pollution of rivers and streams for maintaining or restoring wholesome of such water courses. With regard to preservation of the quality of air and control of air pollution the Air Act, 1981 is promulgated. An integrated approach for tackling the environmental problems relating to pollution is necessary. Therefore, the Boards (Central and States) are constituted by the Acts and deputed to perform the functions assigned under the Acts. Lately, in 1986 environment (protection) Act was passed. Object of this act is to deal environmental problems effectively. Although, there are existing laws dealing directly or indirectly, with several environmental matters, it is necessary to have a general legislation for environmental protection. Existing laws generally focus on specific types of pollution or on specific categories of hazardous substances. Some major areas of environmental hazards are not covered.[10]

Thus, in view of reflecting total considerations taken in Stockholm in 1972, India has promulgated a comprehensive legislation to protect and improve the environment. It is therefore, promulgated to confer decision taken at conference of human environment relating to the prevention of hazards to human beings other living creatures, plants and property. This Environment Act of 1986 is comparatively proved better in approach than the other laws enacted for prevention and control of specific factors.

Direct environmental legislations have promulgated in conformity of the directive principles. The fundamental duties must also be mandatory, state should not think its endeavours have come to an end when it has acted on its part i.e. by enacting laws. State as well as citizens both have obligations to protect and promote natural environment in order to have right to environment vis-a-vis right to life.

Inspite of all said constitutional and legislative provisions, rape of the earth, brutal exploitation of our forests, indiscriminate quarrying, and pollution of our water and air is unabated. It is in India only that one of the wonders of the world the Taj Mahal at Agra is suffering form stone cancer due to the damage caused by neighbouring 510 industries.[11] Millions of people on the banks of the river Ganga are heading towards an environmental catastrophe[12] (the water of the river of Kanpur consisted 29.200 units mg/ml of iron when the maximum limit is 0.3 units, and manganese was found to be 0.900 mg/ml when the WHO limit is 0.5 mg/ml[13]. Every six months more top soil gets washed away than has been used to build all the bricks houses across the country.[14] Seventy percent of all the available water in India is polluted.[15] About 73 millions workdays are lost due to water related diseases.[16] Cherrapunjee is no more wettest spot on the earth.[17] Calcutta – the most polluted city in the country where suspended particulate matter (SPM) in the air rose alarmingly from 800 micrograms per cubic meter in 1987 to 1325 micrograms per cubic in 1994.[18]

Judicial Response

Judiciary through various cases has illustrated the increasing importance of private rights of action in environmental litigation. Judicial attitude in this direction is worth considering because this is a question of enforcement of right to life. A Private right of action might better be termed a "citizen enforcement action." Promoting the purpose of legislative policy through citizen initiative is an important policy goal behind a private right of action may be defined a right under a substantive statute as a private party's action to enforce a regulatory standard.[19]

The judiciary has exhibited an enlightened judicial creativity and foresight whenever it had an opportunity, to decide issues relating to environment. The judiciary has been very active in taking up the cause of the environment. Judicial verdicts have brushed out the technical hindrances by devising new tools of legal interpretation and construction. It is the judiciary by giving directives to the government have accelerated the environmental considerations. In M.C. Mehta V. Union of India[20], following observations are made.

> "Having regard to the grave consequences of the pollution of water and the need for protecting and improving the natural environment which is considered to be one of the fundamental duties under the constitution (vide clause (g) of Art. 51-A of the constitution) we are of the view that it is the duty of the Central Govt. to direct all the educational institutions throughout India to teach atleast for one hour in a week lessons relating to the protection and the improvement of the natural environment including forests, lakes, rivers and wild life in the first ten classes. The Central Government shall get text books written for the said purpose and distribute them to the educational institutions free of cost. Children snould be taught about the need for maintaining cleanliness commencing with the cleanliness of the house both inside and outside, and of the streets in which they live, clean surroundings lead to healthy body and healthy mind. Training of teachers who teach this subject by the introduction of short-term

courses for such training shall also be considered. This should be done throughout India".[21]

Supreme Court has thus, opened the door for realisation of fundamental duties with regard to preservation of environment to both government and citizen. Judicial dynamism with regard to environmental matters are appeared due to failure of executive's duty towards protection of environment. The dynamism of an institution is an indication of its responsiveness and effectiveness. When the executive fails in its constitutional duties and is considered to be suffering from "executive inactivism," there is no other recourse for the people but to turn to the judiciary.[22]

Judicial responses in various cases raised the opinion that law is what the law does. Law is meant to eradicate inequalities and human sufferings. There should be a social goal for implementation of laws. Judiciary in India therefore, has interpreted fundamental rights as enshrined in the Indian Constitution as a repository of human rights and the fountain source of law for a just society.

The right to life as enshrined in Article 21 of the Constitution has been expanded to right of healthy environment. This interpretation is done by Supreme Court in Delhi Gas leak case. The apex court in this case expressed its concern over other hazardous technologies carrying in Delhi and cumulatively violating the standard of life. It lays as:

> There are many other plants in Delhi which are employing hazardous technology or are engaged in manufacture of hazardous goods and if proper and adequate precautions are not taken they too are, likely to endanger the life and health of the community.[23]

In the same case Supreme Court has declared that right to life is incomplete without right to healthy environment. The apex court stated:

> This is a question which heeds serious attention of the government of India and we would request the government of India to take the necessary steps at the earliest, because

> the problem of danger to health and well being of the community on account of chemical and other hazardous industries has become a pressing problem in modern industrial society."24

Thus, Delhi Gas Leak case, for the first time raised the question of far reaching importance concerning the true scope and ambit of Article 21 vis-a-vis the private corporation. The apex court was requested to evolve norms and principles for determining the liability of large private enterprises engaged in manufacturing and sale of hazardous products and the basis on which damages in case of such liability should be qualified. The Supreme Court has assumed violation of the right to life under Article 21 in this case.

In a developing country like India facing with problems of poverty, illiteracy and socio-economic inequalities, judiciary cannot be concerned merely with the isolationist character of human rights. But this norm is first time broken and environmental pollution was controlled through the apex court in Rural litigation and Entitlement Kendra Dehradun V State of U.P.[25] It is discernable from the attitude of the apex court in this case that on the one hand it realised the importance of the preservation of environment and ecological balance and on the other hand, it also recognised the rights of the affected persons. In this case order of closure though has caused loss of large investment of money, time and effort and also caused hardship to them. Supreme Court has observed that:

> 'It is a price that has to be paid for protecting and safeguarding the right of the people to live in healthy environment with minimal disturbance of ecological balance and without avoidable hazard to them and to their cattle, homes and agricultural land and undue affectation of air, water and environment.'[26]

The judiciary has played a pivotal role in interpreting and expanding the scope of fundamental rights, especially that of 'Right to life' enshrined in Art 21. of the Constitution to establish human rights.

In Ratlam Municipality v. Verdichand, Supreme Court has announced healthy environment as a right to life which must be respected at any cost. The apex court hold that 'even as human rights under part III of the Constitution have to be respected by the state regardless of budgetary provision.'[27]

It further holds that:

> "Decency and dignity are non-negotiable facts of human rights and are a first charge on local self governing bodies. Similarly, providing drainage systems – most pompous and attractive but in working condition and sufficient to meet the needs of the people cannot be evaded if the municipality is to justify its existence[28].

The Supreme Court has strengthened Art. 21 in two ways, First, it required laws affecting personal liberty to also pass the tests of Art. 14 and 19 of the Constitution, thereby ensuring that the procedure depriving a person of his or personal liberty be reasonable, fair and just. Second, the court recognised several unarticulated liberties that were implied by Art. 21. It is by this second method that the Supreme Court interpreted the right to life and personal liberty to include the right to a wholesome environment.

The fundamental right to life of people in Article 21 of the Constitution has prefered over sight to life of individual. This view is supported by justice Singh's concluding observations in Ganga Pollution case, where he justifies the closure of polluting tanneries are as:

> "We are conscious that closure of tanneries may bring unemployment, loss of revenue, but life, health and ecology have greater importance to the people"[29].

Regarding maintainability of the petition in Ganga Pollution Case Supreme Court has allowed by giving the reasons of its nature of protecting life of other... Supreme Court in this case observed:

> "The petitioner in the case before us is no doubt not a riparian owner. He is a person interested in protecting

the lives of the people who make use of the water flowing in the river Ganga and his right to maintain the petition cannot be disputed".[30]

Besides it, the Supreme Court has imposed pollution fine on polluters under polluter pays principle and has provided compensation to the citizens affected.

Thus from above few cases we can gather the findings that scope and ambit of right to life also explained even on the ground of private corporation. Directive to stop polluting the river stream is issued because of the fact that the case involved the restitution of right to life (Article 21), implementation of Social Policy (Article 48-A) and enforcement of fundamental duty. It was alleged that leather industry discharges waste water containing putrescible organic and toxic inorganic materials in sewage which will deplete and dissolve the Oxygen content of the receiving water course, resulting in emanation of foul adoure and the death of all acquatic life. Lastly, Supreme Court by considering nuisance of river pollution as a public nuisance has been given a kiss of life on question of the application of the provisions of Article 32,21,48-A, and 51-A (g) i.e. the co-relation of fundamental human rights to human environment.

Conclusion

Human rights are those rights which are inherent in nature and without which we cannot survive. Human rights and fundamental freedoms allow us to fully develop our intelligence, our dealings and our conscience to satisfy our spiritual and other things. These minimal natural rights are available to each and every human beings against the state or other public authority. However, these rights have yet not been created by any legislation. The judicial interpretation has widened the scope of right to life in relation with human right to healthy and clean environment. Therefore, express announcement of a legislation making environmental right as a human right is the need of the hour.

International and National studies of human environment and law reveals that there is a need to develop human environment rights code. It is seen that there is no dearth at International and National level to pay the foundation of human environmental law. It can be concluded that policy goals enforcement of environment is very much present in the judicial responses. Therefore, it becomes evidently clear and certain that for the declaration of the right to healthy environment as a human right we need effective, efficient environmental laws.

On the basis of some cases Supreme Court has acted as a saviour of environmental rights. Significant contribution to environmental causes is made by higher courts and they shows much dynamism in respect of protection of environmental rights. Dynamism of courts is obvious because they themselves stand as a protector of human rights. Citizens of India may contribute to this task in a way to secure other area, which are still remain unpolluted, by launcing a movement. Various non-governmental organisations may also support to the government as well as judiciary to reach upto real problem of pollution. Human rights organisation like Amnesty International and Peoples Union of Civil Liberties may take up the environmental issues like other issues of civil liberties.

For rapid and sincere solution of environmental pollution the National Environmental Commission and Environment Ombudsman is needed. Judiciary has issued directives for affirmative action by various agencies and instrumentalities to make environment healthy and clean. Ways and means should be devised for follow up of these actions. Environmental awakening among the people will make the environmental laws more enforceable and also lead to develop more purposeful laws in this subject. Sense of environmental rights and duties will make right to healthy environment more strengthful human right.

References

1. B.P.Singh Sehgal, *Human Rights in India: Problems and Perspectives*, Deep & Deep 1995 New Delhi, p.427.

2. Paul Sieghart, *The International Law of Human Rights* (1985) p.376.
3. Emphasis added.
4. *Encyclopaedia*, United Nations, p.780.
5. Emphasis added.
6. G.H.Lalvani, 'Law and Pollution Control', J. Bandyopadhyaya (ed.) *India's Environment Crisis and Responses*, Natraj Publishers, Dehradun 1985, p.284.
7. Lal's Commentaries on Water & Air Pollution Law, 3rd Ed. 1992 (reprint) Law Publishers India (P) Ltd. Allahabad p.364-65.
8. V.R.Krishna Iyer, 26 (1986) *IJIL*. p.628.
9. K.L.Bhatia, 'Human Rights and Human Environment. A study in the Policy Perspective, *ALJ*, X (1990) p.48.
10. Lal's Commentaries on Water & Air Pollution Laws. 3rd Edition 1992, (reprint) Law Publishers India (P) Ltd. Allahabad, p.255.
11. M.C. Mehta V. Union of India, AIR 1996 SC 734.
12. M.C.Mehta V. Union of India, AIR 1988 SC 1037.
13. Report of Industrial Toxicology Centre, Council of Scientific and Industrial Research (for Ganga Action Plan).
14. "A Citizens Report", in justice V.R.Krishna Iyer, *Environmental Pollution and the Law* (1984) p.87.
15. Ibid.
16. Ibid.
17. Ibid.
18. Soutik Biswas, "Facing Fire Over Smoke", *India Today,* Feb.28, 1995, p.149.
19. For detailed and critical study see, William H. Timbers and David A.Wirth, Private Rights of Action and Judicial Review in Federal Environmental Law", 70 (3) *Cornell Law Review*, 1985, p.408.

20. AIR, 1988 SC. 1115.
21. M.C.Mehta V. Union of India, AIR 1988 SC 1115 (1127).
22. M.C.Mehta, Judicial Activism: Unexpected Saviour, *The Hindu Survey of the Environment*, 1996, p.205.
23. M.C.Mehta V. Union of India, AIR 1987 SC 965 (981).
24. M.C.Mehta V. Union of India, AIR 1987 SC 965 (981).
25. AIR 1985 SC 652, and AIR 1985 SC. 1259.
26. R.L.& E. Dehradun V. State of U.P. AIR 1985, SC 652 (656).
27. 1980 *Cr.L.J.* 1075 (1081).
28. 1980 *Cr. L.J.* 1075 (1082).
29. M.C.Mehta V. Union of India, AIR 1988 SC 1037 (1048).
30. M.C.Mehta V. Union of India, AIR 1988 SC 1037 (1126).

14

Human Rights in North-East India: A Contemporary Perspective

Kunja Medhi

The concept of human rights since its inception to the present time has undergone tremendous changes in its meaning and application. In the threshold of the 21st century also the concept does not carry the same meaning and content in all the countries of the world. Even the countries with democratic Governments and proclaiming the adoption of the principle of the "Rule of Law" differ in the application of the concept, not to speak of the countries with monarchical, totalitarian and the military regimes. About the countries with religious fundamentalism, the least said the better. Even most of the Member-countries of the United Nations while accepting the U.N. Declaration of Human Rights, seem to have followed different meanings for different groups of people. However, few countries admit violation of human rights overtly or covertly.

India, a democratic country with twenty five component States have numerous groups of Ethno-tribal people through the length and breadth of the country. In the North-East India alone in its quarter million square kilometer of land, there have been more than two hundred groups of ethnic people, belonging to six major racial groups.[1] The tribal population belongs to the Palaco-Mongoloids group—a group of the Mongoloids.

Most of the socio—ethnic groups of people of North-East India have of late experienced human rights violations due to political uprisings, staged by several prominent ethnic groups. These groups since prehistoric times down to the modern times, especially the British administration, enjoyed autonomous powers in their localities. However, after the independence of India despite elaborate provisions of the Constitution, namely, the Sixth Schedule relating to the administration of Tribal Areas in the States of Assam. Meghalaya and in Mizoram, several groups of people both of the hills and the plains who found the logistics inadequate for their development embarked upon the path of peaceful as well as violent agitations, thereby forcing the authorities to carve out separate territories, with Constitutional Governments within Indian Union. Some of the other underdeveloped ethnic groups suffering long years of economic deprivation and backwardness found the formation of several insurgent groups spear heading the cause of their ethnic groups demanding economic sufficiency, political powers and even a few of them sovereign status. Although the U.N. Charter has provided for the Right to Self-determination,[2] the Government machinery resorted to army operations on and off resulting thereby wanton violations of human rights.

Army Operations: Certain code names were given to the combing operations that were conducted to flush out the known and unknown insurgents in the North-East India, namely, Operation Bajrang, Operation Sher-E-Dil, Operation Rhino (1), Operation Rhino (II), Operation Tiger Heart[3] and all these took place from late 1990s onwards. These operations were conducted under two Acts:- (i) The Assam Disturbed Areas Act 1955 and the (ii) The Armed Forces (Special Powers) Act 1958 as amended in 1972.

During such operations, for example, that of Operation

Rhino alone about Fifty thousand soldiers of Indian Army aided by about a lakh of paramilitary personnels belonging to CRPF, BSF, Assam Rifles and the State Police let loose a reign of terror especially in the rural areas. Mass raids accompanied by various types of torture and humiliation, merciless beating, kicking, submarine treatment, punching and trampling on the ground were some of the ways of committing atrocities by the Security Forces. As usual womenfolk became the easy prey for the prowling Armed personnels. Several cases of rape of young girls and married women tarnished the record of human rights of this region. Apart from the encounter killings, wherein insurgents died, other types of killing took place as a result of (a) Army raids; (b) Custody in Army camps; (c) Point-blank shooting; (d) Gangrape and mental shock; (e) Torture; (f) Suicide at the time of arrest.

The Armed Forces virtually sidelined the Civil administration and the Co-ordination Committees that were formed between the Army and the Civil authorities remained non-functional. The highhandedness of the Armed Forces was clearly demonstrated when their raids did not spare even the residences of the Members of the Parliament, Magistrate, Police Officers and those of the Armed Forces. The arrested persons had to face interrogation by the Army personnel, although the aforesaid Acts clearly limited the role of the Armed Forces to that of providing necessary aid and not to that of usurping the powers and functions of civil administration. The Army however, after handing over the persons to the police forced the latter to hand over the persons back to the Army camps for interrogation and torture.[4] In all the cases of Army operations, the Armed Forces relied on its own actionable hard intelligence. However soon it became clear that it had neither worthwhile information nor actionable intelligence. Wanton torture, interrogation and large-scale raids were the only ways, resorted to by the Army in their search for the insurgents, leading to widespread violation of human rights and massive atrocities on the common people.[5] The Police also made several worthwhile leads to the rescue of hostages as well as top leaders held by the Army.

Indiscriminate mass raids : Section 4 (d) of the (Assam) Armed Forces Special Powers Act 1958 which empowered Commissioned Officers, Warrant Officers, NCO or any other person of equivalent rank in Armed Forces to enter and search without warrant, any premises could make any such arrests as mentioned above.[6] The characteristic features of such raids were that (a) these raids were conducted more or less on the basis of mere suspicion of harbouring armed insurgents; (b) The places suspected to have been the residences of known hardcore terrorists; (c) Information provided by local touts to the Army personnel to avenge any personal feud or grudge. Apart from these grounds of Army raids, in various cases raids were conducted at the whims and caprices of the Armed personnel.[7]

The arrested persons were humiliated and subjected to various punishments such as : (a) Forcing them to kneel down facing the sun; (b) Making them run in circles or do frog jumps till they fell down exhausted. (c) Keeping them without food or water and at the sametime inflicting various types of physical torture. The motive of such atrocities seemed to terrorise common people with a common question thrown in on and off : "Where is ULFA"[8]? (Member of United Liberation Front of Assam). Some people were kept under lock and key for days together in small cages. The Army camps on the bank of the river Ghagar virtually turned to be a hell with screams of the suffering people. Each day around 500 people were arrested, they were either released by evening or night or kept till the next day or handed over to the police. The overall situation proved beyond doubt that the sadistic sinister ulterior motives led the tormentors to create a sense of terror among the people.

One important feature of the interrogation procedure was that the interrogation procedure was illegal and moreover it was incommunicable to the villagers due to language barriers. It was a futile and cruel exercise forcing the suspects to lead to the insurgents or to the hidden arms. Despite the mass raids, torture and interrogation the Army could not capture even a single hardcore militant. Random and indiscriminate raids by the Army, roaming through the villages in plain clothes, arresting youths even while they were buying foodstuff or listening to sports commentaries or going to schools and libraries were the common features. Most of the tortured persons lost mental balance and became permanently disabled for the rest of their lives. A number of people lost their lives in the so-called "encounter" deaths. Several people died due to (a) long period of torture; (b) gangrape and subsequent mental shock; (c) During Army raids; (d) shooting at point blank range; (e) death in Army custody; (f) suicide at the time of arrest; (g) encounter deaths.[9] A sample is given in Table No. 1.

Table No. 1

Army atrocities	Torture	Persons killed
1. Army raid	A few persons died	Mr. Purna Das, a teacher of Goalpara was beaten to death in the courtyard of his home on 24.9.91.
2. Gangrape	- do -	Miss Raju Barua & Miss Bhanimani Dutta.
3. Shooting at point blank range	-do-	Nitu Rajbansi of Dhekiajuli, Nagen Kalita, a member of Armed Forces was detained and killed. Sarat Kakoty of Bhutiagoan was similarly killed.
4. Death in Army custody	A number of people died	Biren Doley, Dibakar Handique, Khireswar Bora, of Lakhimpur District, Kiron Saikia of Sonitpur, Raj Kamal Choudhury of Hajo.
5. Suicide at the time of arrest	-do-	Ajit Medhi, Abhijit Phukan, Manoranjan Haloi, Ranjit Buragohain.
6. Torture	-do-	Babul Barua, Brajen Moran, Nagen Kalita, Dibakar Handique, Kiran Saikia.
7. Mental shock	-do-	Wife of Phatva Moran died due to mental shock when her husband was severely tortured before her eyes.

8.	Rape	-do-	Undibala Roy, Dwijumoni Nath, Numali Baniya, Labanya Barua, Basanti Mazi, Pabitribala Nath, Chitralekha Das.
9.	Torture in Army	-do-	Ranjit Tanti, Jadu Bora, Anupam Barua, Mridul Kalita, Gautam Saikia, Prafulla, Mukunda Mohan Bania, Dipak Bania, Jayanta Nath, Barun Roy Choudhury, Soneswar Gogoi, Mogeswar Mudoi, Nomal Saikia, Rajen Phukan, Bogai Doley, Gangakarta Bora, D. Saikia.
10.	Encounter deaths	-do-	Ratul Tanti, Hemanta Rabha, Hirokjyoti Mahanta, Lakhi Nath, Sagar Das, Jogeswar Timung, Ragea Orang, Abhoy Hatikakoty, Bulbul Basumatary, Sukleswar Deka, Bhai Kanta Saikia, Poona Basumatary, Pabitra Deka.
11.	Villages affected by Army Operations	-do-	Dibrugarh District...Five villages. Sibsagar District....Fourteen villages. Nalbari District....Thirty two villages. Darrang District....Eight villages.
12.	Number of persons permanently maimed	-do-	As many as forty two persons have been suffering till the present time as a result of severe torture.

(Source : Azir Asom, Assam Tribune,Azir Batori, North-East Times) 1991-92; other local papers.

"Operation Bluebird" : Manipur, one of the seven States of North-East India was declared a disturbed area on September 1979 and the Armed Forces (Assam and Manipur) Special Power Act 1958 was extended to the whole of Manipur State. Under this Act the Army was given sweeping power to conduct search so as to destroy the insurgency. Since quite sometime past insurgency has been a common feature as a number of ethnic-tribal groups have been demanding independence. Human rights violations took place right from 1950s in that region, especially Nagaland and Manipur when Armed Forces were sent to these places. In several cases Judiciary held the Government responsible for violation of human rights and granted compensation to the families of the victims. People's protests against the imposition of this Act was vehement. Newspapers also took a leading role in criticising the imposition of the Act:

"This law is a means to suppress people's rights and insurgency is a political problem, it needs political solution..." "....To suppress the democratic rights of the people of Manipur in the name of maintaining law and order, and to scare the mass." ".....Army operation is using a sledge-hammer to kill a fly."[10] During 1974-1992 as many as ten army operations were conducted in various parts of Manipur, which consisted of combing operations and subsequent indiscriminate killing of villagers. Several cases of rape of young girls and married women, disappearances of arrested persons from Army custody, opening of fire indiscriminately on common villagers, illegal detention of lawyers and newspaper editors were some other features of the Army operations that marked the worst kind of human rights violations in North-East India. A short description of the combing Operation resorted to by the Armed Forces in retaliation of an attack by the insurgents on an Army outpost would make the example clear. The National Socialist Council of Nagaland (NSCN), an insurgent group killed nine soldiers and looted arms and ammunitions after mounting an attack of an outpost belonging to Assam Rifles at Oinam village in July 1987. The incident was followed by Combing Operation, code named "Operation Bluebird", combined with arbitrary arrests of villagers in and around Oinam and execution of 11-15 persons in the Army camps. The encounter killings included old people, teachers, women and children.[11] It was regarded as one of the worst cases of human rights violations by the national and international organisation.[12] Altogether twenty two villages suffered from inhuman torture in the hands of the security forces. The people were held in open or in the churches for upto 12 hours at a time day after day for several weeks. No one was produced before the Magistrates as required by the law under the Constitution of India. Several women were raped including a seventeen years old school student whose brother was suspected to be in NSCN. The Army devastation included 125 houses, looting of granaries, domestic goods and live-stock. Villagers were forced to sign false affidavits denying all that had taken place under threat of torture.

The Central Government condoned the abuses by the Army and resisted several appeals for ordering an investigation into the allegations, although the Government was called upon by various organisations to make a full impartial investigation, to review and withdraw certain sections of the Armed Forces (Special Powers) Act which empowered the security Forces to shoot to kill. The Act without doubt contravened the right to life as it provided immunity from prosecution to the Army. Demands for compensation for the victims of torture as well as for those killed in Army custody also were made.

Local Civil Liberties Groups as well as their Lawyers worked relentlessly for redressal of grievances. The Gauhati High Court rejected two claims for compensations. There had been widespread resentment against the thwarting measures adopted by the Government, since the Government of India was even a supporter of International Covenant on Civil and Political Rights. It was expected that the Central Government would assist the villagers in securing effective remedies rather than obstructing their efforts. The noteworthy efforts were made by several other organisations to help the affected people. For instance :

(a) Civil Liberties and Human Rights Organisation (CLAHRO) submitted Habeas Corpus petitions;

(b) Manipur Baptists' Convention submitted petitions against the abuses of women during the combing operations;

(c) Naga People's Movement for Human Right (NPMHR)

filed a petition in Gauhati High Court on behalf of the villagers against the Assam Rifles.

Security Forces attempted to discredit the Human Rights Organisations by bringing legal proceedings against some of their members. A few lawyers were threatened for their role in upholding the human rights of the common people. The Gauhati High Court directed the Sessions Court in Imphal to record evidences from the affected villagers but only 32 were examined instead of 700. The people were between the devil and the deep sea for the fact that several extremist groups, namely National Socialist Council of Nagaland (NSCN), The People's Liberation Army (PLA), People's Revolutionary Party of Kangleipak (PREPAK), The Kangleipak Community Party (KCP), the United Liberation Front (UNLF) and Manipur Revolutionary Party (MRP) had been and are still very active in the region. Generally Human Rights violations take place by the Armed Forces as a follow up of the attacks on their units by the extremists groups. During 1974-92 severe cases of human rights violations were recorded which were rather unprecedented.[12] Several rape cases resulted either in the death or suicide of the victims. Miss Rose, a Tankhul Naga young girl committed suicide after she was raped by the Deputy Commandant D.S. Pundir on March 4, 1974. Several cases were registered against the officers after the military operations were over.[13] Another 25 year old disabled Tankhul Naga girl, Miss K.S. Marth was raped by a sepoy of 4th Assam Rifles, Ganesh Prasad on 9 July 1981.[14] A Meitei pregnant woman Mrs. Memcha Devi was raped by the army on September 9, 1980.[15] In 1987 three women were sexually abused by the Army during the Oinam operation in July 1987.

A good number of persons disappeared during their custody in the Army camps. Killing of arrested persons and suspects in the Army custody was a routine matter in Manipur.[16] With the delayed legal proceedings, hundreds of people suffered from widespread fear psychosis. As mentioned earlier indiscriminate and wanton firing on and killing of common people including school children and players of a volleyball match was another black example of Army brutalities, apart from the usual shooting down to death of the insurgents, known and unknown. Firing and killing of the processionists,[17] firing by CRPF on the defenceless inmates of the Manipur Central Jail, killing of Radio artistes and the members of a cultural group had been other features of the combing operations. The mode of punishments were similar to those mentioned elsewhere in this paper.

Certain sections of the Armed Forces (Assam and Manipur) Special Power Acts, 1958 could be mentioned just to cite example of the unrestricted powers of the Armed Forces:

Under the Act the Central Government can declare an area as "disturbed" even without consulting the State Government. Sections 4(a), 4(c) and 6 facilitate flagrant human rights violations.

Section 4(a) : "A Commissioned Officers, a Warrant Officer, a non-Commissioned Officer or other ranking officers have power to "arrest, without warrant, any person who has committed a congnisable offence or against whom a reasonable suspicion exists that he has committed or is about to commit a cognisable offence..."

Section 4(b) :- This section empowers the above-mentioned officers (Section 4(c)) to "fire upon or otherwise use force, even to the causing of death against any person, who is acting in contravention of any law or order for the timebeing in force in the disturbed area, prohibiting the assembly of five or more persons or the carrying of weapons or, of things capable of being used as weapons or of fire arms, ammunition or explosive substances."

Section 6 :- This section of the Act provides immunity from prosecution to the Armed Forces - "No prosecution, suit or other legal proceedings shall be instituted except with the previous sanction of the Central Government, against any person in respect of anything done or purported to be done in exercise of the powers conferred by this Act."

In this backdrop CLAHRO has been working at the moment also for the restoration of democratic norms and "Rule of Law" in Manipur by challenging the draconian Act. The Amnesty International made ten recommendations to the Government of India in this respect.

Apart from the Army operations, in usual times also this part of India has seen violations of human rights as provided by Articles 21 and 22 of the Constitution of India. The Terrorist and Disruptive Act (TADA) which has been on the track of the Preventive Detention Laws of pre-independence period has put thousands of people behind the bar[18] in the wake of the insurgency. Under this Act a person could be detained indefinitely without trial. Several hundreds are still languishing in various jails. The cumbersome judicial process makes people very often shudder to go to the courts.

Irrespective of political ideology, caste, religion, language and education, women in North-East India still face wanton violation of human rights whose life, position, status are governed by conservation and religious orthodoxy despite modernisation and advance of science and technology. Women have suffered as a result of militancy as well as in the hands of the Army personnels. The society in this part of the world is yet to realize the women's rights are human rights and women's problems[19] are human problems. Women who constitute an integral part of the patriarchal value system have to face the challenges of redefining themselves in their search for alternatives while fighting for their human rights.

A new beginning could be made by the people across the globe, despite cultural diversities, to contain human rights violations. A new paradigm is to be developed to educate one and all, right from childhood to understand the concept of human rights, the modalities of which could be decided in such highly prestigious international forums of human rights.

References

1. The present major racial groups of Indian people are (i) The Negrites; (ii) The Proto-Australoids; (iii) The Mongoloids; (iv) The Mediterranean; (v) The Brachycephals; (vi) The Nordics.

2. Article 1 of the International Covenant of Economic, Social and Cultural Rights and Article 1 of the International Covenant of Civil and Political Rights, 1966 provide. "All peoples have the right of self determination. By virtue of that right they freely determine their political status and freely pursue their economic, social and cultural development."

3. Operation Rhino 1 was imposed on 27 November 1990. It continued till 19 April 1991. Operation Rhino II was imposed on 1st April 1992 which continued till 25 June 1992. The former covered the districts of Upper Assam whereas the latter covered the districts of lower Assam. Along with these, two other operations, namely, "Sher-E-Dil" and "Operation Tiger Heart" were conducted in Upper Assam. Operation Bajrang was conducted in 1991. Another Operation, "Operation Bluebird" was conducted in and around Oinam district of Manipur by the Assam Rifles. This was in retaliation against the action of the Armed Secessionists belonging to National Socialist Council of Nagaland (NSCN), which attacked on Assam Rifles' outpost in July 1987 killing nine soldiers and removing arms and ammunitions. Report of Amnesty International: India "Operation Bluestar" - A case study of torture and extrajudicial executions in Manipur. Amnesty International Secretariat, 1 Easton Street, London WC IX BDJ U.K., January 1990.

4. Report by MASS, 1991-92, Guwahati.

5. The query in general by the Armed personnel has been, "Where is ULFA? (Member of United Liberation Front of Assam). If they were not satisfied with the answer/and or they

hardly waited to get an answer, the follow-up action was house search without any search warrant. Their sudden encounter with overwhelming and decisive firepower resulted in the killings of several youths branded as insurgents.

6. Section 4 (c) of the (Assam) Armed Forces Special Powers Act 1958 empowered the Army in respect to indiscriminate mass raids in the villages of North-East India. About 4000 villages had been subjected to this form of search, according to estimates from newspaper reports, Government press releases and actuals on site reports.

7. On 4 October 1992 a large contingent of Rajputana Rifles surrounded a large village, named Bodhakora of Lakhimpur District, inhabited by a mixed population comprising poor, daily wage earners and marginal farmers. In the house to house search, all male members were dragged out, some even from bed and subjected to manhandling and beatings. Women were abused, slapped, hit by rifles and many of them were subjected to sexual molestation. Youths were arrested and taken to the Army camps. (Reports based on field surveys of a good number of villages depredated by the Army.)

8. The ULFA-Members of the United Liberation Front of Assam—this organisation has been banned by the Government, as it has demanded separation of Assam from the rest of India, so that it could exercise sovereign powers. The ULFA and its supporters have ample proof to show that Assam has been used by the Central Government more or less as colony for its oil, tea and timber, while giving only a checked feed in return for development purpose.

9. The methods of torture included:

   (i) Beating in public view, at home before the family members and inside the Army camps with hand, lathi (rod), rifle butts and whips: punching on face, head and abdomen; trampling and kicking, making people to lie down on ground then beating on the soles of feet with rod.

   (ii) Hanging people from calling boams by hands: hanging from tree in upside down position; hanging by one hand, the other hand tied behind the back. After such hanging severe beatings or other forms of tortures were carried out.

(iii) Wet submarine treatment was a method of torture when the head of the person was immersed in a water bucket or drum till drowned to death

(iv) Pouring water continuously over the mouth and nose of a person after tying and immobilising till he was suffocated.

(v) Staking a person by making him lie down on ground with the face either up or down, hands and feet tied in a spread eagled manner to stakes driven to ground. After immobilising a person in such a manner he was beaten, kicked or trampled under boots or tortured in other ways. Sometimes a rod was rolled forcefully over his back by two soldiers causing blood vomitting and evacuation of bowels in severe pain.

(vi) Keeping tied to a stake in uncomfortable sitting position for days together.

(vii) Frame treatment—persons bound spread-eagled to a vertical rectangular wooden frame to immobilise and then tortured.

(viii) Applying electric shock from a 12 volt car battery or directly from domestic mains to all parts of the body including the private parts.

(ix) Uprooting hairs by pichers from head, eyebrow, armpit and even from private parts.

(x) Applying chilli powder to eyes and anus with the hands bound behind the back.

(xi) Forcefully pulling apart the legs by two soldiers resulting in tear of the anus.

(xii) Pushing a stout rod smeared with chilli powder and petrol through the anus.

(xiii) Burning with lighted cigarette butts in all parts of the body including the private parts.

(xiv) Sticking pins all over the body.

(xv) Burying in ground upto neck and covering the head with a bucket.

(xvi) Denying food and water for days together.

(xvii) General physical punishment and humiliation. Usually large groups of people were subjected to such treatment. People were lined up in a field or in camps, sometimes in full view of womenfolk and were forced to do the following:

(a) to kneel down facing the sun for hours;

(b) to stand naked in sun and rain;

(c) to stand in waistdeep or neckdeep water for hours;

(d) to perform frog jumps till the person was exhausted;

(e) to run in circles;

(f) to carry army personnels on back over long distances;

(g) to perform sit ups holding the ears;

(h) forcing to eat sand, earth or to drink alcohol and filthy water.

All these punishments were accompanied by filthy abusive language of the Army personnels and most of the times they were in drunken conditions. *Human Rights* : Dr. N. Sanajaoba (ed.) Omson Publications, New Delhi, 1994.

Detailed list of the persons killed as a result of Army brutalities during the Operation Rhino is available with the MASS, an organisation formed for protection of human rights and to fight for restoration of justice.

10. *Resistance*, English Weekly, 11 September 1979, Imphal, Manipur.

11. *73-pages document of Amnesty International ; India: Operation Bluebird* : A case study of torture and extrajudicial

executions in Manipur. Amnesty International, International Secretariat, Easton Street, London WC IX BDJ, UK. 1990.

12. Only a local inquiry was held confirming some torture allegations; ibid.

13. 4 March 1974; 11 November; 7 September 1979; 26 April 1980; 9 September 1980; 8 July 1981; 19 February 1982; 14 March 1984; 9 July 1987; 14 March 1992.

14. *Resistance*, ct. above, 18 October 1977.

15. ibid, 13 September 1980.

16. ibid, 21 October 1980.

17. *Amnesty International*, ct. above, 1990, London.

18. An organisation of Kuki people, named Kuki National Assembly (KNA) demanding the creation of a separate hill district. One person was killed in Army firing; Resistance, 1 December, 1981.

19. A number of meetings/interviews and field surveys was attended/conducted by the author of the paper to ascertain facts.

Appendix-I

Basic Instrument Concerning Human Right

(i) Instruments covering overall dimensions

1. *Charter of the United Nations* (1945) is the first international instrument/multilateral treaty to "reaffirm faith in fundamental human rights, in the dignity and worth of the human person, in the equal rights of men and women..." Although the Charter does not elaborate the meaning and varied dimensions of human rights (this task was taken up subsequently by adoption of various instruments), it lays down the basic principles and also that one of the "purposes of the United Nations shall be to promote universal respect for, and observance of human rights and fundamental freedoms for all without distinction as to race, sex, language or religion".

2. *Universal Declaration of Human Rights* (1948) represented the highest aspirations of humankind by drawing together, for the first time, ideas shared by many political, cultural and religious traditions, and spelling out of the contents of human rights.

K.P. Saxena, Teaching Human Rights, Lancer, New Delhi.

In its 30 articles, the Declaration sets out the basic rights and freedoms for all peoples, covering civil, political, economic, social and cultural rights. Yet, in itself, the Declaration has no legal force. It is a set of moral rules. The power and impact of these moral rules, and their applicability, may be judged by their widespread acceptance and incorporation into domestic legislations and jurisdiction of various countries.

The Universal Declaration was adopted on 10th of December 1948 and ever since then 10th of December is observed as the Human Rights day all over the world.

3. *International Covenants on Human Rights*, derived from the Universal Declaration, set out an internationally recognized standard, in legal terms, against which human rights violations can be judged. The Covenants (one dealing with civil and political rights, the other with economic, social and cultural rights) were adopted in 1966, but it took 18 years for the two Covenants, to come into force in 1976.

The Covenants are of critical importance. They have three common elements: (a) the right to self-determination, a right which has led to decolonization and to many new States joining the United Nations; (b) the principle of equality between men and women, and non-discrimination on grounds of gender, race or religion; (c) the principle of indivisibility-the essential interdependence of civil and political freedoms with economic, social and cultural standards.

International Covenant on Civil and Political Rights include:

(a) the right to life, liberty and security (art.6)

(b) the right not to be subjected to torture or to cruel, inhuman or degrading treatment or punishment (art.7);

(c) the prohibition of slavery and slave-like practices,

forced or compulsory labour (art.8);

(d) the right not to be arbitrarily arrested or detained (art.9);

(e) the right to equality before law and to a fair trial (art.14);

(f) the right to freedom of expression (art.19), religion (art.18), assembly (art.21) and association, including the right to form and join trade unions (art.2);

(g) the right to freedom of movement and residence (art.12); and

(h) the right to take part in the government of one's country (art.25).

International Covenant on Economic, Social and Cultural Rights include:

(a) the right to work (art.6 and 7);

(b) the right to social security (art.9);

(c) the right to protection of the family (art.10);

(d) the right to an adequate standard of living (art.11);

(e) the right to education (art.13);

(f) the right to health (art.12);

(g) the right to join trade unions (art.8); and

(h) the right to social security (art.9).

(ii) Instruments re-emphasizing some specific dimensions

1. *International Convention on the Elimination of All Forms of Racial Discrimination* adopted by the UN General Assembly in 1965, contains provisions for eliminating racial discrimination in all its forms and manifestations, for preventing and combating racist doctrines and practices and for building an international community free from

all forms of racial segregation and discrimination.

The States Parties to the Convention undertake to prohibit and to eliminate racial discrimination in all its forms and to guarantee the right of everyone, without distinction as to race, colour or national or ethnic origin, to equality before the law, notably in the enjoyment of a long list of human rights and fundamental freedoms. The Convention lists specifically among these the right to work, the right to join trade unions and the right to housing. Measures for the implementation of the Convention include the establishment of the Commitee on the Elimination of Racial Discrimination (see "Implementation mechanism", below).

2. *Convention on the Elimination of All Forms of Discrimination Against Women* was adopted on 18 December 1979 and entered into force in 1981.

In article 1, the Convention defines discrimination against women as meaning:

> any distinction, exclusion or restriction made on the basis of sex which has the effect or purpose of impairing of nullifying the recognition, enjoyment or exercise by women, irrespective of their marital status, on a basis of equality of men and women, of human rights and fundamental freedoms in the political, economical, social, cultural, civil or any other field.

Under article 2, States that become parties to the Convention agree to pursue, by all appropriate means and without delay, a policy of eliminating discrimination against women, and to that end undertake:

(a) to embody the principle of equality of men and women in their national constitutions and to ensure, through law and other appropriate means, the practical realization of this principle;

(b) to adopt appropriate legislative and other measures, including sanctions where appropriate, prohibiting all discrimination against women;

(c) to establish legal protection of the right of women on an equal basis with men and to ensure, through competent national tribunals, the effective protection of women against any act of discrimination;

(d) to take all appropriate measures to eliminate discrimination against women by any person, organization or enterprise;

(e) to modify consequently or abolish laws, regulations, customs and practices which constitute discrimination against women.

In part V, the Convention establishes the Committee on the Elimination of Discrimination against Women (see "Implementation mechanism", below).

3. *Convention Against Torture and Other Cruel Inhuman or Degrading Treatment or Punishment* (1984) not only provides that the States parties will outlaw torture in their national legislation, but also notes explicitly that no order from a superior or exceptional circumstances may be invoked as a justification of torture or other cruel, inhuman or degrading treatment or punishment. The Convention also introduces two new elements of particular importance to combat torture. The first is that, henceforth, a torturer may be prosecuted wherever he is found in the territory of any State party, since the Convention specifies that persons alleged to have committed acts of torture may be tried in any State party or be extradited for trial in the State party where they have committed their crimes. The other new element is that the Convention contains a provision allowing for an international inquiry if there is reliable information indicating that torture is being systematically practised in the territory of a State party. Such an inquiry may include a visit to the State party concerned, with its agreement.

The States parties to the Convention also pledge to take effective legislative, administrative, judicial and other measures to prevent acts of torture in any territory under their jurisdiction. NO exceptional circumstances whatever, whether a state of war, internal political instability or any other public emergency, may be invoked as a justification of torture. The implementation of the Convention is monitored by the Committee against Torture (see "Implementation mechanisms", below).

4. *Convention on the Rights of the Child* (1989) is the result of long negotiations between representatives of countries with different social and economic systems and various cultural, ethical and religious approaches; non-governmental organizations; and United Nations agencies. It has as its guiding spirit the best interests of the child and call on States which ratify it to create conditions in which children may take an active and creative part in the social and political life of their countries.

In the Convention, a child is defined as a person under the age of 18, unless national laws determine an earlier age of majority. Encompassing the whole range of human rights— civil, political, economic, social and cultural — the Convention recognizes that the enjoyment of a given right cannot be separated from the enjoyment of others. It emphasizes that the freedom a child needs to develop his or her intellectual, moral and spiritual capacities is dependent on a healthy and safe environment, access to medical care, and minimum standards of food, clothing an shelter, among other things. Non-discrimination is and important principle of the Convention: children shall enjoy all their rights without discrimination of any kind, irrespective of the child's or his or her parents' or legal guardians' race, colour, sex, language, origin, property, disability, birth or other status.

The Convention enlarges the legal coverage of human rights by protecting children from all forms of exploitation in dealing with the question of children of minority and indigenous groups and the problems of drug abuse and neglect. Specific provision is made for protection of the human rights of children involved in the criminal justice system. The Convention acknowledges the primary role of the family and parents in the care and protection of children, and the obligation of the State to help them carry out these duties. The implementation of the Convention is entrusted to the Committee on the Rights of the Child (see "Implementation mechanism", below).

(iii) **Implementation Mechanism**

The Convenants/Conventions, noted above, have also instituted "international mechanism" to monitor and oversee that the obligations, which State parties have accepted, are observed by them. However, this international mechanism merely is meant for exercising supervisory role and exerting of political and moral pressure on State parties which remain solely responsible for the protection of human rights. This supervisory role is generally provided in the form of examining the reports received from the State parties; in certain circumstances complaints of non-observance or violation by a State party are also examined.

1. *Human Rights Committee* established in 1977, the Human Rights Committee monitors the implementation of the International Covenant on Civil and Political Rights.

It is composed of 18 members, elected by States parties to the Covenant from among their nationals, who serve in their personal capacity. The Committee generally meets three times a year in New York (March) and Geneva (July and October). The functions of the Committee as set out in articles 40 to 45 of the Covenant (see in Appendix 'C') are; to study reports on the measures States parties have adopted to give effect to the rights recognized in the Covenant and on the progress made in the enjoyment of these rights.

States parties to the International Covenant Civil and Political Rights are invited to send representatives to be present at the meetings of the Human Rights Committee when their reports are examined. Such representatives are expected to answer the questions put by the Committee. The Committee may also request State parties to submit additional information. The Committee considers the report in public meetings. A summary of the consideration of each State report is included in the Committee's annual report which is submitted to the General Assembly through the Economic and Social Council (ECOSOC). The Committee also elaborates general comments to various articles of the Covenant and their implementation and progress made towards achieving observance of the rights recognized in the Covenant.

Under article 41 of the Covenant, a State party may bring a complaint that another State party is not fulfilling its obligations under the Covenant. Should such a communication be received, and provided that both parties — the complaintant and the State complained against — have recognized the Committee's competence, the Committee can perform certain functions in settling the dispute concerning the application of the Covenant, with a view to a friendly solution of the matter on the basis of respect for the Covenant.

Under its Optional Protocol, individuals who claim that any of their rights enumerated in the Covenant have been violated, and who have exhausted all available domestic remedies, may submit written petitions to the Human Rights Committee for consideration. However, no such petition or communication by the individual can be considered by the Committee, if it concerns a State party to the Covenant, which is not also a party to the Optional Protocol. The Committee considers communication in the light of all written informations made available to it by the individual and by the State party concerned, and forwards its views to the State party concerned and to the individual.

2. *Committee on Economic, Social and Cultural Rights* is composed of 18 experts, with recognized competence in the field of human rights, nominated by State parties to the Covenant and elected by the Council (ECOSOC) for a term of four years. They serve in their personal

capacity. It has been established by the Economic and Social Council (ECOSOC) and held its first session from 9-27 March, 1987, and since then meets annually for a period of upto three weeks, at Geneva.

The International Covenant provides for the progressive realization of the rights embodied in the Covenant without discrimination of any kind and calls for periodic report to the Secretary General for consideration by the ECOSOC. These reports are passed on to the Committee which discusses its contents with representatives of the governments concerned. Its general comments on the reports are intended to help State parties in their task of implementation as well as to bring to their attention, deficiencies in reports.

The Committee's mandate is to assist the Council to fulfil its responsibilities under articles 21 and 22 of the Covenant, which call upon the Council to submit to the General Assembly "reports with recommendations of a general nature and a summary of the information received from the States parties... and the specialized agencies on the progress made in achieving general observance of the rights recognized" in the Covenant; and to "bring to the attention of other organs of the United Nations, their subsidiary organs and specialized agencies concerned with furnishing technical assistance any matters arising out of the reports...which may assist such bodies in deciding, each within its field of competence, on the advisability of international measures likely to contribute to the effective progressive implementation" of the Covenant.

It should be noted here that United Nations have adopted several resolutions emphasizing the need for equitable management of world economy — pre-requisite for the realization of economic, social and cultural rights which are intertwined with civil and political rights.

3. *Committee on the Elimination of Racial Discrimination* monitors the implementation of the International Convention on the elimination of All Forms of Racial

Discrimination and is composed of 18 members elected by States parties to the Convention for a four-year term. The Committe examines reports submitted by States parties on measures taken and success achieved in relation to the provisions of the Convention. The Committee is also authorized to establish permanent working groups and/or ad hoc conciliation commissions to consider communications from individuals and inter-State disputes relating to obligations contained in the Convention.

4. *Committee on the Elimination of Discrimination Against Women* was established to oversee the implementation of the Convention on the Elimination of All Forms of Discrimination against Women. It is composed of 23 experts elected by secret ballot from a list of persons of high moral standing and competence in the field of the human rights of women nominated by States parties to the Convention. The Committee meets regularly to examine reports and any other information submitted by States parties. This examination forms the basis of suggestions and recommendations made by the Committee. The Committee may also make general recommendations on steps which might be taken by States to fulfil their obligations under the Convention.

5. *Committee Against Torture* is composed of 10 experts elected for a four-year term to consider reports submitted by States parties to the Convention against Torture and Other Cruel, Inhuman or Degrading Treatment or Punishment on measures taken to honour their undertakings under the Convention. In addition to considering these reports, investigating them and forwarding them to the States parties and to the General Assembly with comments, the Committee is authorized to make confidential inquiries. These may include on-the-spot inquiries, in aggreement with the State party concerned, when the Committee receives reliable

information indicating that torture is being systematically practised in the territory of that State party.

The United Nations Voluntary Fund for Victims of Torture was set up in 1981 to receive voluntary contributions for distribution through established channels of assistance as humanitarian, legal and financial aid to persons who have been tortured and to members of their families. The Fund depends entirely on voluntary contributions from Governments, private organizations, institutions and individuals. It is administered by the Secretary-General of the United Nations with the assistance of a board of trustees composed of a chairperson and four members with wide experience in the field of human rights. Most of the subsidies are used to finance therapy and rehabilitation projects and training programmes. The purpose of these projects is to enable victims and their families to lead productive, normal lives within their community.

6. *Committee on the Rights* of the Child first met in 1991. It is composed of 10 experts and is entrusted with the task of generating a permanent dialogue involving all parties concerned with the promotion of children's rights. The Committee will identify dangers to the well-being of the world's children; look for practical answers to specific problems; mobilize the human and financial resources needed to solve them; and raise the level of public awareness and concern for the protection and promotion and promotion of the rights of the child. In this task, the Committee will be open to collaboration with other organizations active in the same field. The Committee will monitor the progress made by States which ratify or accede to the 1989 Convention on the Rights of the Child to comply with their obligations. States parties to the Convention accept the duty to submit regular reports directly to the Committee on the steps they have taken to put the Convention into effect and on progress in securing the enjoyment of childrens rights. These reports are to be made public and given

wide national distribution.

(iv) **Other Instruments (Declarations etc.)**

Declaration on the Elimination of All Forms of Intolerance and Discrimination Based on Religion or Belief. Universal Declaration as well as International Covenants, specifically calls elimination of discrimination of all forms of intolerance based on religion or belief.

Religious tensions and conflicts have often led to genocide and denial of human rights, the United Nations has, therefore, devoted special attention to the elimination of all forms of religious intolerance and have carried out detailed studies on the subject. However, it has not yet been possible to adopt a separate convention (multilateral treaty) obligating states eliminate this social evil.

As a prelude to the Convention, the General Assembly in its resolution adopted and proclaimed in November 1981, the "Declaration on the Elimination of All Forms of Intolerance and Discrimination based on Religion or Belief' and resolved to take all necessary measures for the speedy elimination of such intolerance in all its forms and manifestation and to prevent and combat discrimination on the grounds of religion or belief.

The Declaration defines the expression "intolerance and discrimination" as meaning "any distinctive exclusion, restriction or preference based on religion or belief and having as its purpose or as its effect or impairment of the recognition, enjoyment or exercises of human rights and fundamental freedoms on equal basis".

Article 4 states:

1. All States shall take effective measures to prevent and eliminate discrimination on the grounds of religion or belief in the recognition, exercise and enjoyment of human rights and fundamental freedoms in all fields of civil, economic, political, social and cultural life.

2. All States shall make all efforts to enact or rescind legislation where necessary to prohibit any such discrimination, and to take all appropriate measures to combat intolerance on the grounds of religion or other beliefs in this matter.

Right to Development

One of the concepts set out by the UN General Assembly, in 1977, to guide future work within the United Nations system, with respect to human rights question, was the realization of a more equitable and just international economic order; such an order would permit the achievement of balanced developmental levels in all countries, thus turning into reality the principles contained in the Universal Declaration of human Rights, which recognized equal rights for all human beings to enjoy an adequate standard of living (Article 25).

Following this guideline, the Commission on Human Rights took up intensive study regarding the affects of the existing international economic order, on the economies of the developing countries and the obstacles that it represented for the implementation for the human rights and fundamental freedom. These studies by experts and various reports that followed, led to the concept of the Right to Development.

In 1981, the Commission established a working group of 15 governmental representatives to set the scope and content of the Right to Development and the most effective means to ensure the realization, in all countries, all the economic, social and cultural rights with particular attention to the obstacles encountered by the developing countries in their efforts to secure the enjoyment of human rights.

After working on the subject for 4 years (1981-84). The working group adopted a report which the Commission transmitted to the General Assembly, through the ECOSOC, enabling the Assembly to adopt the Declaration on the Right to Development in its resolution 41/128 of 4 December 1986.

The Declaration proclaims, in its articles 1 and 2:

Article 1

1. The Right to Development is an inalienable human right by virtue of which every human person and all peoples are entitled to participate in, contribute to, and enjoy economic, social, cultural and political development, in which all human rights and fundamental freedoms can be fully realized.

Article 2

1. The human person is the central subject of development and should be the active participant and beneficiary of the right to development.

2. All human beings have a responsibility for development, individually and collectively, taking into account the need for full respect for their human rights and fundamental freedoms as well as their duties to the community, which alone can ensure the free and complete fulfillment of the human being, and they should therefore promote and protect an appropriate political, social and economic order for development.

3. States have the right and duty to formulate appropriate national development policies that aim at the constant improvement of the well-being of the entire population and of all individuals, on the basis of their active, free and meaningful participation in development and in the fair distribution of the benefits resulting therefrom.

Declaration on the Protection of Women and Children in Emergency and Armed Conflict (1974)

It should be noted that while development in science and technology has brought immense benefit to mankind, it has, at the same time, led to development of ghastly weaponry which is used to kill innocent non combatant civilians.

During the First World War, only 5 per cent of the casualties were civilians; today the proportion in wars and armed conflicts have reached 75 per cent to 90 per cent. It is also estimated that among the civilian casualties, 80 per cent are women and children.

In 1974, the General Assembly proclaimed the Declaration on the Protection of Women and Children in Emergency and Armed conflicts. The Declarations states that bombings and attacks in any form on civilians, especially on women and children who are the most vulnerable members of the population shall be prohibited and condemned and that states involved in armed conflicts shall make all efforts "to spare women and children from the ravages of war".

The reality, as we all know, is very different. Notwithstanding the ending of the Cold War (which was held responsible for 'proxy wars', insurgencies etc.), there has been no respite from wars and armed conflicts which are more widely spread all over the world than ever before. A recent study by P.I.O.O.M. A Netherland-based human rights research organization, has listed 84 on-going wars and armed conflicts in different parts of the world which have resulted in killing of more than 9 million people, including women and children, during the last five years. The on-going armed conflicts have also resulted in surging increase of refugees estimated to be 19 million with another 39 million displaced within their own homeland.

From time to time, the United Nations bodies have adopted resolutions linking the enjoyment of human rights with the maintenance of international peace and security. Mention, in particular, should be given to the General Assembly Resolution of 12 November 1994, expressing the conviction "that life without war serves as the primary international pre-requisite for the material well-being, development and progress of countries, and for the full implementation of the human rights and fundamental freedoms proclaimed by the United Nations.

The resolution solemnly proclaims "that the peoples of

our planet have a sacred right to peace", and declares that the preservation of that right and the promotion of its implementation constitute a fundamental obligation of each State. It emphasizes that ensuring the exercise of that right demands that the policies of the States be directed towards the elimination of the threat of war, particularly nuclear war, the renunciation of the use of force in international relations and the settlement of international disputes by peaceful means on the basis of the Charter.

Declaration on the Rights of the Mentally Retarded Persons

In 1971, the General Assembly proclaimed the Declaration on the Rights of the Mentally Retarded Persons and called for national and international action to ensure that the Declaration would be used as a common basis and frame of reference for the protection of the rights setsforth therein. The Declaration specifically emphasizes that all necessary assistance should be given to mentally retarded persons to develop their abilities in various field of activity and of promoting their integration, as far as possible, in normal social life. It also sets out the principles that the mentally retarded person has, to the maximum degree of feasibility, the same rights as other human-beings and as enshrined in various international instruments. It aslo calls upon member states to undertake special protective measures to ensure necessary education, training, rehabilitation, medical care, economic security and standards of living.

Declaration on the Rights of the Disabled Persons

In December 1975, the General Assembly proclaimed a Declaration on the Rights of the Disabled Persons and called for national and international action to ensure that it should be used as a common basis and frame of reference for the protection of the rights setforth therein. The Declaration specifically emphasizes the necessity of preventing physical and mental disabilities and of assistance to disabled persons to develop their abilities in the most varied fields of activities and of promoting their integration, as far as possible, in normal social life.

The Declaration defines the term "disabled persons" as meaning "any person" unable to ensure by himself/herself, wholely or partly, the necessities of a normal individual and/ or social life, as a result of a deficiency, either congenital or not, in his/her physical or mental capabilities. It provides that full encouragement be given to disabled persons to form their organizations which could be usefully consulted in all matters regarding the rights of such persons.

In its 11 articles, the Declaration setsforth the basic principles which includes all the rights enshrined to any other individual and also some special rights for their protection and measures designed to enable them to become as self-reliant as possible.

Standard Minimum Rules for the Treatment of Prisoners

In 1955, the First United Nations Congress on the Prevention of Crime and Treatment of Offenders (Geneva, 1955), adopted a set of Standard Minimum Rules for the Treatment of Prisoners. In July 1957, the Economic and Social Council approved those rules and recommended them to member states, for observance. These Rules calls for complete prohibition of corporal punishment, punishment by placing in a dark cell and all cruel, inhuman or degrading punishments.

In 1977, the General Assembly drew the attention of member states to the Standard Minimum Rules and recommended that they should be effectively implemented and incorporated in national legislation. The General Assembly made additional recommendations on the subject, in 1984.

In December 1990, the General Assembly, on the recommendations of the Eighth United Nations Congress on the Prevention of Crime and the Treatment of Offendors, further elaborated the Basic Principles on the Treatment of Prisoners. The Principles confirm certain fundamental prisoners' rights and stipulate *Inter alia*, that all prisoners should be treated with due respect for their inherent dignity and value as human beings, without discrimination of any kind. Except for the necessary limitations of the freesom of movement, all prisoners should be afforded the human rights and fundamental freedoms, set out in universally recognized international instruments. By declaring those rights, the Principles complement the provisions of the Standard Minimum Rules for the Treatment of Prisoners and the body of Principles for the Protection of All Persons under Any Form of Detention or Imprisonment, adopted by the General Assembly in December 1988.

Principles of Medical Ethics

In its resolution of 31/85 of 13 December 1976, the General Assembly invited WHO to prepare a draft code on medical ethics relevant to the protection of persons subjected to any form of detention or imprisonment against torture and other cruel, inhuman or degrading treatment or punishment.

The Executive Board of WHO, at its sixty-third session, in January 1979, decided to endorse the principles set forth in a report entitled "Development of Codes of Medical Ethics" containing, in an annex, a draft body of principles prepared by the Council for International Organizations of Medical Sciences and entitled "Principles of medical ethics relevant to the role of health personnel in the protection of persons against torture and other cruel, inhuman or degrading treatment or punishment".

The Economic and Social Council, in its resolution 1981/27 of 6 May 1981, reccommended that the General Assembly should take measures to finalize the draft Code of Medical Ethics. The Principles of Medical Ethics were adopted by the General Assembly in its resolution 37/194 of 18 December 1982.

The Assembly went on to set further standards in this field by adopting the Principles of Medical Ethics relevant to the Role of Health Personnel, particularly Physicians, in the Protection of Prisoners and Detainees against Torture and Other Cruel, Inhuman or Degrading Treatment or Punishment, as set out in the annex to its resolution 37/194. It called upon all

Governments to give Principles of Medical Ethics the widest possible distribution, in particular among medical and paramedical associations and institutions of detention or imprisonment; and invited all relevant intergovernmental organizations; in particular WHO, and non-governmental organizations concerned, to bring the Principles to the attention of the widest possible group of individuals, especially those active in the medical and paramedical field.

Principle 1 of the Principles of Medical Ethics Provides:

Health personnel, particularly physicians, charged with the medical care of prisoners and detainees have a duty to provide them with protection of their physical and mental health and treatment of disease of the same quality and standard as is afforded to those who are not imprisoned or detained.

Principle 2 States:

It is a gross contravention of medical ethics, as well as an offence under applicable international instruments, for health personnel, particularly physicians, to engage, actively or passively, in acts which constitute participation in, complicity in, incitement to or attempts to commit torture or other cruel, inhuman or degrading treatment or punishment.

A cross-reference is made in the principle, by a footnote, to article 1 and 7 of the Declaration on the Protection of All Persons from Being Subjected to Torture and Other Cruel, Inhuman or Degrading Treatment or Punishment, where torture is defined as and declared to be a criminal offence.

Standard Minimum Rules for the Administration of Juvenile Justice

On the recommendation of the VIIth United Nations Congress on the Prevention of Crime and Treatment of Offenders, the General Assembly adopted (in November 1985), the Standard Minimum Rules for the Administration of Juvenile Justice. The

Rules relate to such matters as the minimum age of criminal responsibility, the objectives of juvenile justice and administration and the human rights principles to be applied. They also cover matters relating to investigation and prosecution of crimes committed by juveniles, including the question of detention, pending trial. They also lay down essential protection covering juvenile offenders placed in institutions. The General Assembly recommeded that states apply these Standard Minimum Rules wherever necessary and bring them to the attention of the relevant authorities and the public, in general.

In December 1990, the General Assembly on the recommendation of the VIIIth United Nations Congress on the Prevention of Crime and the Treatment of Offenders adopted the United Nations Rules for the Protection of Juvenile Deprivation of their Liberty. The Rules advocate the least possible rules of deprivation of liberty, especially in prison and other closed institutions. They provide specific Principles which apply to all juveniles held in any form of detention and call for the separation of juveniles from adults in detention and the classification of juveniles according to their sex, age, personality and type of offence, with a view to ensuring their protection from harmful influences and risk-situations. They setforth special provisions covering various aspects of institutional life, such as the physical environment and accommodation, education, recreation, religion, medical care, contacts with the outside world, inspection, complaints and return to the community.

Code of Conduct for Law Enforcement Officials

In its resolution 34/169 of 17 December 1979, the General Assembly adopted a Code of Conduct for Law Enforcement Officials and transmitted it to Government with the recommendation that favourable consideration should be given to its use within the framework of national legislation or practice as a body of principles for observance by law enforcement officials

Article 5 of the Code reads:

> No law enforcement official may inflict, instigate or tolerate any act of torture or other cruel, inhuman or degrading treatment or punishment or punishment, nor may any law enforcement official invoke superior orders or exceptional circumstances such as a state of war or a threat of war, a threat to national security, internal political instability or any other public emergency as a justification of torture or other cruel, inhuman or degrading treatment or punishment.

In its commentary on article 5, the Assembly points out:

> This prohibition derives from the Declaration on the Protection of All Persons from Being Subjected to Torture and Other Cruel, Inhuman or Degrading Treatment or Punishment, according to which [such an act is] an offence to human dignity and shall be condemned as a denial of the purposes of the Charter of the United Nations and as a violation of the human rights and fundamental freedoms proclaimed in the Universal Declaration of Human Rights [and other international human rights instruments].

The term "crual, inhuman or degrading treatment or punishment" had not been defined by the General Assembly, but should be interpreted so as to extend the widest possible protection against abuses, whether physical or mental.

Basic Principles on the Use of Force and Firearms by Law Enforcement Officials.

The Eighth United Nations Congress on the Prevention of Crime and the Treatment of Offenders adopted the Basic Principles on the Use of Force and Firearms by Law Enforcement Officials, which were welcome by the General Assembly in its resolution 45/116 of 18 December 1990.

The Basic Principles establish guidelines for the use of firearms and set out standards for the policing of unlawful assemblies and of persons in custody or detention. Special consideration is given to the use of force and firearms as a last resort; ethical issues; new technologies for developing non-lethal incapacitating weapons and ammunition; responses by law enforcement officials in proportion to the seriousness of the offence and the legitimate objective to be achieved; qualification and training in the use of force and firearms by law enforcement officials; stress counselling for law enforcement officials required to use force or firearms in the course of their duties; and effective reporting and review procedures.

The Eighth Congress recommended the Principles for national, regional and international action and implementation and called upon the Committee on Crime Prevention and Control to consider their effective implementation as a matter of priority. The Congress requested the Secretary-General to take appropriate steps to ensure the widest possible dissemination of the Principles and invited Member States to inform the Secretary-General every five years on the progress achieved in the implementation of the Principles.

(v) Regional Human Rights Instruments

Three regional inter-governmental organizations the Council of Europe, the Organization of African Unity (OAU) and the Organization of American States(OAS) — have adopted international instruments relating to human rights, including Conventions, establishing special organs to promote the recognition and observance of human rights within their respective regions.

Europe

European Convention on Human Rights

Under the auspices of the Council of Europe, the European Convention for the Protection of Human Rights and Fundamental Freedoms was concluded at Rome 4th November 1950 and entered into force on 3rd September 1953.

The Convention guarantees a wide range of rights, such as the right to life, the right not to be subjected to torture, and freedom from slavery, among others. This range has been expanded by additional Protocols to add the right to property and the right to education (first Protocol). Protocols 4 and 5 expand the list further by prohibiting deprivation of liberty for failure to comply with contractual obligations and guaranteeing the right to liberty of movement. Protocol 6 requires abolition of the death penalty, and Protocol 7 requires that aliens must be accorded various due procedural safeguards in determining whether they may be expelled from a country where they are residing. This instrument also provides for the right of appeal in criminal proceedings, compensation in cases of miscarriage of justice, the right not to be subjected to double jeopardy, and equal rights and responsibilities between spouses.

European Social Charter

Like the European Convention, the European Social Charter (1961) was prepared under the auspices of the Council of Europe. It complements the Convention, which guarantees civil and political rights, by establishing a regional European system for the protection of economic and social rights. More than half the member States of the Council of Europe are parties to the Charter. The Charter establishes a reporting system designed to monitor whether States are complying with their obligations.

The European Convention for Prevention of Torture and Inhuman or Degrading Treatment or Punishment concluded at Strasbourg (France) on 26 November 1987 which entered into force on 1st February 1995.

European Court of Human Rights

Initially, the European Convention conferred only limited jurisdiction to the European Court of Human Rights. The Court obtained advisory jurisdiction in 1970, with the entry into force of Protocol 2 to the Convention. The Convention empowers only

States and the European Commission of Human Rights, not individuals, to file cases with the Court. However, the Individual claimant has gradually acquired a more important status before the Court. The Court can be said to have become the constitutional court for civil liberties in Western Europe. Its case-law is vast in terms of the range of subjects the Court has addressed, and its impact is increasing. In the 40 year period (1953-93) since its creation, the Court has delivered 307 judgements; most of them (numbering 229) concerned solely or principally, the question of the existence of a violation ("on the merits"). In more than two third of these judgements, the Court found a failure to comply with the Convention or an additional Protocol.

The European Commission of Human Rights and the European Court of Human Rights are based in Strasbourg (France).

Africa

African Charter on Human And Peoples' Rights

Under the auspices of the Organization of African Unity (OAU), the African Charter on Human and Peoples' Rights was concluded at Nairobi (Kenya), on 27th June 1981 and entered into force on 21st October 1986. The African Charter is the first International Convention dealing with human rights which guarantees in a single Convention, the civil and political rights of individuals as well as their economic, social and cultural rights, and rights of individuals as well as peoples' rights.

It comprises a preamble and three substantive parts containing 68 articles. Part I, dealing with rights and duties, is sub-divided into two chapters on human and peoples' rights (arts. 1-26) and duties (arts. 27-29). Part II, containing measures of safeguard, is subdivided into four chapters dealing with the creation of the African Commission on Human and Peoples' Rights (arts. 30-44) the mandate of the Commission, its procedures and functions.

The main functions of the Commission are promotional and standard-setting. The Commission also receives and considers inter-State and "other communications". The latter term includes communications from individuals or groups of individuals and from organizations or institutions dealing with human rights issues.

The Commission is based in Banjul. (Gambia).

The Americas

The Charter of the Organization of American States (OAS) adopted at Chapultepec, Mexico, in 1948, entered into force in 1951. The Charter declared members commitments for the promotion of the fundamental rights of the individual without distinction as to race, nationality, creed or sex. The same Conference that adopted the OAS Charter also promulgated the *American Declaration of the Rights and Duties of Man*, which proclaims a list of 27 human rights and 10 duties.

American Convention on Human Rights was concluded at San Jose, Costa Rice, on 22 November, 1969 and entered into force on 18 July, 1978. The Convention guarantees a dozen broad categories of civil and political rights, such as the right to judicial personality and the right to life, to humane treatment, to a fair trial, to property, and to freedom of association, among others.

An additional Protocol to the Convention, relating to economic, social and cultural rights and known as the San Salvador Protocol, was adopted in 1988.

In accordance with the provisions of the Convention, the Inter American Commission on Human Rights and the Inter-American Court of Human Rights were established. The Commission is based in Washington, D.C., and the Court in San Jose. States parties to the Convention may take declarations, under article 45, accepting the right of other States parties to submit a complaint to the Commission. Under article 62 of the Convention, a State party may declare that it recognizes as binding the jurisdiction of the Court in all matters relating to the interpretation and application of the Convention. At present, 19 of the 24 States parties to the Convention have accepted the competence of the Court. In 1988-1989, the Court issued its first three judgements, all of them involving disappearances. As at 31 December 1991, the Court had also issued 12 advisory opinions.

The functions of the *Inter-American Commission on Human Rights* are spelled out in article 41 of the American Convention on Human Rights. It codifies the Commission's pre-existing functions as an OAS organ and mandates it "to take action on petitions and other communications pursuant to its authority" under articles 44-51 of the Convention. The Convention empowers the Commission to deal with individual petitions and inter-State communications. The admissibility of a petition is conditional, *inter alia*, on the exhaustion of domestic remedies, in accordance with the generally recognized principles of international law. There is a requirement that the petition be submitted to the Commission within a period of six months from the date on which the victim of the alleged violation was notified of the final domestic judgement in the case. When a complaint is admissible, the Commission examines the allegations, seeks information from the Government concerned and investigates the facts. As part of this process, the Commission may hold hearings in which the Government and the petitioner(s) participate.

The Inter-American Court of Human Rights has contentious jurisdiction, which is jurisdiction to adjudicate cases involving charges that a State party has violated the American Convention on Human Rights. It also has jurisdiction to render advisory opinions concerning the Convention and certain human rights treaties. Once a case has been referred to it, the Court has the powerfully to review the findings of fact and law of the Inter-American Commission on Human Rights. The Court is empowered to award money damages and render declaratory judgements specifying not only what rights have been violated, but also how States should remedy the violation.

Appendix - II

International Human Rights Instruments : Ratifications, Accessions Etc.

(As of I January, 1995)

International Instruments (date of entry into force)	Total No. of states Parties	Total No. of Asian States	Ratification accession notification of succession acceptance etc by Asian States.
(1)	(2)	(3)	(4)
1. International Covenant on Economic, Social and Cultural Rights (3 January 1976)	128	18	Afghanistan, Democratic (North) Korea, Democratic Yemen, India, Iran, Iraq, Japan, Jordan, Lebanon, Mangolia, Nepal, Sri Lanka, The Philippines, Syria, Vietnam, Cambodia, Israel, Republic of Korea.
2. International Covenant on Civil and Political Rights (23 March 1976*)	130	18	Afghanistan, Cambodia, Democratic (North) Korea, democratic yemen, India,

				Iran, Japan, Jordan, Lebanon, Mangolia, The Philippines, Republic of Korea, Sri Lanka, Syria, Vietnam, Israel, Nepal.
3.	Optional Protocol to the International Covenant On Civil and Political Rights (23 March 1979)	78	4	Republic of Korea, Mangolia, Nepal, The Philippines.
4.	Second Optional Protocol to the International Covenant on Civil and Political Rights aiming at the abolition of the death penalty	24	Nil	
5.	Convention on the Prevention and Punishment of the Crime of Genocide (12 January, 1951)	111	27	Afghanistan, China Cambodia Democratic Yemen, Fiji, India, Iran, Iraq Israel, Jordan Laos, Lebanon, Maldives, Mangolia, Mynamar, Nepal, Pakistan, Papua New Guinea, Republic of Korea, South Vietnam, The Philippines, Saudi Arabia, Sri Lanka, Syria, Vietnam, Democratic Republic of Korea,
6.	Convention on the Non applicability of Statutory Limitations to War Crimes and Crime against Humanity (11 November 1970)	38	8	Afghanistan, Democratic Yeman, India, Laos, Mongolia, The Philippines, Vietnam, Democratic Republic of Korea,
7.	International Convention on the Elimination of All Forms of Racial Discriminations	141	27	Afghanistan, Behrain, Bangladesh, China, Cambodia, Democratic

* Following 39 State parties have so far made declarations recognizing the competence of Human Rights Committee under article 41 of the Covenant: Algeria, Argentina, Austria, Australia, Belarus, Belgium, Bosnia-Herzegovina, Canada, Chile, Congo, Denmark, Ecuador, Finland, Gamcia, Germany, Guyana, Hungary, Iceland, Italy, Luxemburg, Malta, The Netherlands, New Zealand, Norway, Peru, The Philippines, Poland, Republic of Korea, Senegal, Slovenia, Spain, Sri Lanka, Sweden, Switzerland, Tunisia, Ukraine, USA, UK & Zimbabwe.

	(4 January 1969)*			Yemen, Fiji, India, Iran, Iraq, Israel, Jordan, Kuwait, Laos, Lebanon, Maldives, Mongolia, Nepal, Pakistan, Papua, New Guinea, The Philippines, Qatar, Republic of Korea, Sri Lanka, Syria, United Arab Emirates, Vietnam.
8.	Convention relating to The Status of Refugees (22 April 1954)	122	11	China, Cambodia, Fiji, Iran, Israel, Japan, The Philippines, Yemen, Papua New Guinea, Republic of Korea.
9.	Protocol Relating to the Status of Refugees. (4 October 1967)	119	11	China, Cambodia, Fiji, Iran, Israel, Japan, Papua New Guinea, The Philippines Yeman, Republic of Korea.
10.	Convention Relating of the Status of Stateless persons (6 June 1960)	42	3	Fiji, Israel, Republic of (South) Korea.
11.	Convention on the Reduction of Statelessness (13 December 19750	18	Nil	Nil
12.	Convention on the Political Rights of Women (7 July 1954)	104	17	Afghanistan, Democratic Yeman, Indonesia, Israel Japan, Jordan, Laos, Lebanon, Mangolia, Fiji Nepal, Pakistan, India, The Philippines, Papua New Guinea, Republic of Korea, Thailand.
13.	Convention on the Nationality of Married Women (11 August, 1958)	64	6	Fiji, Israel, Malaysia, Singapore, Sri Lanka, Jordan.
14.	Convention on the Consent	41	4	Democratic Yemen, Fiji,

* Following 19 State parties have so far made declarations recognising the competence of the Committee on the Elimination of Racial discrimination under Article 14 of the Convention:Algeria, Australia, Bulgaria, Coasta Rica, Denmark, Eduador, France, Hungary, Iceland, Italy, Netherlands, Norway, Peru, Russian Federation, Senegal, Sweden, Ukrain, Uruguay, Cyprus.

	to Marriage, Minimum Age for Marriage, and Registration of Marriages (9 December, 1954)			The Philippines, Jordan.
15.	Slavery Convention of 1926	73	11	Afghanistan, Bangladesh, Fiji, India, Iraq, Israel, Lebanon, Myanmar, Nepal, Syria, Yemen.
16.	Protocol Amending The Slavery Convention (7 December, 1953)	56	8	Afghanistan, Bangladesh, Fiji, India, Iraq, Israel, Myanmar, Syria.
17.	Slavery Convention of 1926 as commended in 1953 (7 July 1955)	90	18	Afghanistan, Bangladesh, Fiji, India, Iraq, Israel, Jordan, Kuwait, Mangolia, Myanmar, Nepal, The Philippines, Papua new Guinea, Pakistan, Saudi Arabia, Sri Lanka, Syria, Yeman.
18.	Supplementary Convention on the Abolition of Slavery the Slave Trade and Institutions and practices similar to slavery (30 April 1957)	112	20	Afghanistan, Bangladesh, Cambodia, Fiji, India, Iran, Iraq, Israel, Jordan, Kuwait, Laos, Malaysia,
19.	Convention for the Suppression of the Traffic in Person and of the Exploitation of the prostitution of others (25 July 1951)	70	16	Afghanistan, Bangladesh, India, Iraq, Israel, Japan, Jordan, Kuwait, Laos, Pakistan, Republic of Korea, The Philippines, Singapore, Sri Lanka, Syria, Yeman.
20.	International Convention on the Suppression and Punishment of the Crime of Apartheid (18 July 1976)	99	21	Afghanistan, Bangladesh, Cambodia, China, India, Iran, Iraq, Kuwait, Laos, UAE, Maldives, Mangolia, Pakistan, Nepal, The Philippines, Qatar, Sri Lanka, Syria, Vietnam, Jordan, Yeman.
21.	Convention on the Elimination of all Forms of Discrimination against Woman (3 September, 1981)	138	21	Bangladesh, Bhutan, China, Cambodia, Democratic Yeman, Indonesia, Iraq, Japan, Jordan, Kuwait, India, Israel, Laos, Maldives,

				Mangolia The Philippines, Republic of (South) Korea, Sri Lanka, Thailand, Vietnam, Nepal.
22.	Convention against Torture and other Cruel, Inhuman or or Punishment Degrading Treatment (26 June 1987)*	85	9	Afghanistan, Cambodia, China, Israel, Jordan, Nepal, Yeman, The Philippines, Sri Lanka
23.	International Convention against Apartheid in Sports (3 April 1988)	57	9	India, Iran,. Iraq, Jordan, Nepal, Mangolia, The Philippines, Qatar, Syria
24.	Convention on the Rights of the Child (2·September, 1990)	168	34	Afghanistan, Behrain, Bangladesh, Bhutan, Cambodia, China, Fiji, India, Indonesia, Iran, Iraq, Israel, Jordan, Japan, Kuwait, Lebanon, Laos, Republic of Korea, Maldives, Mongolia Myanmar, Nauru, Nepal, Pakistan, Papua New Guinea, The Philippines, Samoa, Seychelles, Sri Lanka, Syria, Thailand, Vietnam, Yeman,

* Following 36 State Parties have, so far made declaration recognizing the competence of the Committee against torture under Article 21 and 22 of the Convention. Algeria, Argentina, Austria, Australia, Bulgaria, Canada, Crotior, Cyprus, Denmark, Ecuador, Finland, France, Germany, Greece, Hungary, Italy, Liechtenstein, Luxembarg, Malta, Monaco, Netherlands, New Zealand, Norway, Portugal, Poland, Russian Federation, Spain, Sweden, Switzerland, Slovenia, Togo, Tunusia, Turkey, UK. Uruguay, Yugoslavia.

Appendix - III

Protection of Human Rights:
Salient Provisions in the
Constitution of India and Criminal Laws *

Human Rights	Constitution/Law	Article/ Section	Gist of Provisions
1	2	3	4
Equality before laws	Constitution of India (Constitution)	Art. 14	The State shall not deny to any person equality before the law of the equal protection of the laws within the territory of India.

* All India Police Science Congress. MPA, Nashik.

1	2	3	4
Protection of life and personal liberty	- do -	Art. 21	No person shall be deprived of his or personal liberty except according to procedure established by law.
Right against arbitrary or illegal arrest	- do-	Art. 22	No person who is arrested shall be detained in custody without being information of the ground for such arrest, not shall be denied the right to consult and to be defended by, a legal practitioner of his choice.
	Code of Criminal Procedure (Cr. P.C)	Sec.57	Every person who is arrested shall be produced before the nearest Magistrate within a period of 24 hours of such arrest, excluding the time necessary for the journey from the place of arrest to the court of the Magistrate.
Rights against arbitrary or illegal arrest	Code of Criminal Procedure (Cr. P.C)	Sec. 41	A police officer can arrest a person without warrant only when he is concerned in a congnizable offence.
	- do -	Sec. 151	A police officer can arrest a person without warrant to prevent the commission of cognizable offence, which cannot be other-wise prevented. The arrested person is to be produced before the Magistrate within 24 hours.
	- do -	Sec. 46	The police officer is authorised to touch or confine the body of the person to be arrested only if the person does not submit himself to the custody.

1	2	3	4
			It is only when a person forcibly resists the endeavour to apprehend him or attempts to evade arrest that a police officer can use "all means necessary to effect the arrest." Only that much force can be used which is necessary to overcome the resistance of person concerned. This Section denies the power to cause the death of the person sought to be arrested, even if he resisting or evading arrest, unless, the person concerned is accused of an offence punishable with death or imprisonment for life.
	Cr. P.C.	Sec. 49	The person of arrested shall not be subjected to more restraint than is necessary to prevent his escape.
Right to be released on bail	*Cr. P.C.*	Sec. 50	The person arrested has to be informed of the grounds of his arrest of his right to bail in non-bailable offences. In bailable offences, bail is a matter of right. While in non-bailable offences, it is left to the court to decide whether the person should be released on bail.
Right against arbitrary or unreasonable searches and seizures	Cr. P.C.	Sec. 47	A police officer is entitled to ask for free ingress into any place or building where the person wanted in a congnizable offence is suspected to be hiding to evade arrest. It is only when such ingress or opportunities of search are not afforded that he is authorised to break open and make a forcible entry.

1	2	3	4
	Cr. P. C.	Sec. 51	The police officer has the power to search the arrested person and seize articles, but a receipt of the seized articles has to be given to the concerned person. Whenever it is necessary to cause a female to be serched, the shall be made by another female with strict regard to decency.
	Cr. P.C.	Sec. 100	Whenever search of a place is to be carried out, the officer conducting the search is required to do so in the presence of two respectable inhabitants of the locality. A list of all things seized in the course of such, search and of the places in which they are respectively found has to be prepared by the officer and signed by the witnesses. A copy of the list has to be delivered to the occupant of such place or to some person on his behalf. The occupant must be permitted to remain present during the search.
Protection against cruel or inhuman treatment during investigation	Cr. P.C.	Sec. 54	This section confers upon the arrested person the right to get himself medically examined. He can make a request to the Magistrate for his examination by a medical practitioner, where such examination by a medical practitioner will disprove the commission of any offfence by him or will establish the commission by any other person of any offence against his body.

1	2	3	4
	Cr. P.C.	Sec. 162	No Statement of a witness recorded by a police officer can be used for any purpose other than that of contradicting his statement before the court. This section forbids the police officer to obtain the signature of a person on the statement made by him.
	The Indian Evidence Act	Sections 25 and 26	Any confession made to a police officer is inadmissible in evidence.
	The Indian Evidence Act	Sec. 24	Confession must be made voluntarily and if it is made under any inducement threat or promise, it is irrelevant in criminal proceedings.
	Cr. P.C.	Sec. 164	It is for the Magistrate to ensure that the confession or statement is being made by the accused voluntarily. If at any time before the confession is recorded, the person appearing before the Magistrate states that he is not willing to make the confession, the Magistrate shall not authorise the detention of such person in police custody.
	The Indian Panal Code (IPC)	Sections 330 and 331	Voluntarily causing hurt or grievous hurt to extort confusion or to compel restoration of property are serious penal offences. According to Sec. 331, whoever voluntarily causes grievous hurt for the purpose of extorting any confession or any information which may lead to the detection of an offence, or for the purpose of compelling or causing the restoration of any

1	2	3	4
			property shall be punished with imprisonment for a term which may extend to 10 years and shall also be liable to fine.
	Cr. P.C.	Sec. 176	In cases of deaths in police custody, inquiry into the cause of death by a Magistrate is mandatory under this provision of law. This section requires an inquiry to be conducted into the cause of death by a Magistrate either instead of, or in addition to, the investigation held by the police officer. While holding such inquiry, the Magistrate shall , wherever practicable, in form the relatives of the deceased and allow them to remain present at the inquiry.
Protection against Conviction/enhanced punishment under ex post facto law	Constitution	Art. 20 (1)	No person shall be convicted of any offence except for violation of a law in force at the time of the commission of the offence, nor shall he be subjected to a penalty greater than what is prescribed under the law in force at the time of the commission.
Protection against double jeopardy	Constitution and Cr. P.C.	Art. 20 (2) and Sec. 300	No person shall be prosecuted and punished for the same offence more than once. A person once convicted or acquitted not to be tried against for the same offence.
Protection against self incrimination	Constitution and Cr. P.C.	Art. 20 (3) and Sec. 161	No person accused of any offence shall be compelled to be a witness against himself. A person examined by the police officer during the course of investigation is bound to answer truly all questions relating to the case other than the questions

1	2	3	4
			the answers to which would have a tendency to expose him to a criminal charge or to a penalty or forfeiture.
Right to benefit of doubt	Indian Evidence Act	Sections 101 to 104	These Sections of law stress on the right of the accused to be presumed innocent till the guilt is proved beyond a shadow of reasonable doubt. It is for the prosecution to produce evidence to prove that the accused is guilty beyond doubt.
Right to Assemble	Constitution	Art. 19	The Right to assemble peacefully and without arms is one of the six important rights mentioned in this Article.
	Cr. P.C.	Sections 129-131	It is only when the assembly becomes unlawful that the police can use force to disperse it. The main principle underlying these provisions of law is that only minimum force must be used to disperse the unlawful assembly.
Prohibition of excessive use of force by police instructions	Police Manuals		In addition to legal provisions, Police Manuals of different States/UTs contain detailed instructions either prohibiting or restricting the use of force by the police while effecting arrest, interrogating suspects, and accused or during any other stage of investigation of the case or during law and order disturbances. In case any illegitimate use of force by the police for any purpose what soever comes to notice, the instructions require an immediate inquiry to be conducted into the circumstances of the case. If any *prima facie* evidence or excessive or

1	2	3	4
			illegitimate use of force is found, the delinquent officer is liable for severe punishment.
Protection of Human Rights	Code of Conduct for the police	Clause 1	The Police must bear faithful allegiance to the Constitution of Indian and respect and uphold the rights of the citizens as guaranteed by it.
	Code of Conduct for the police	Clause 3	The Police should recognise and respect the limitations of their powers and functions. They should not usurp or even seem to usurp the functions of the judiciary and sit in judgement on cases to avenge individuals and punish the guilty.
		Clause 4	When the application of force becomes inevitable, only the irreducible minimum of force require in the circumstances should be used.
	Code of Behaviour for Police Officers	Clause 7	This clause lays down that no police officer shall commit abuse of authority. He shall be deemed to have committed abuse of authority if he "(a) without good and sufficient cause makes an arrest, or (b) uses any unnecessary violence towards any prisoner or other person with whom he may be brought into contact in the execution of his duty, or (c) is uncivil to any member of the public".
Right to remedies for	Constitution	Art. 32	This Article guarantees the right to move the Supreme Court for the enforcement of Fundamental Rights.

1	2	3	4
enforcement of human rights			It empowers the Supreme Court to issue directions or orders or writs for the enforcement of any Fundamenal Rights.
	Constitution	Art. 226	This Article empower the High Courts to issue to any person or authority or Government within its territory, directions, orders or writs, or any of them, for the enforcement of any of the Fundamental Rights.

Appendix - IV

The Protection of Human Rights Act, 1993 (10 of 1994)

An Act provide for the Constitution of a National Human Rights Commission, State Human Rights Commissions in State and Human Rights Courts for better protection of human rights and for matters connected therewith or incidental thereto.

Be if enacted by Parliament in the Forty-fouth Year of the Republic of India as follows:

I

PRELIMINARY

1. Shout title, extent and commencement.

(1) This Act may be called the Protection of Human Rights Act, 1993.

(2) It extends to the whole of India: Provided that it shall apply to the State of Jammu and Kashmir only in so far as it pertains to the matters relatable to any of the entries

enumerated in List I of List III in the Seventh Schedule to the constitution as applicable to that State.

(3) It shall be demed to have come into force on the 28th day of September, 1993.

2. Definitions.

(1) In this Act, unless the context otherwise requires:

(a) "Armed Forces" means the navel, military and air forces and includes any other armed forces of the Unions;

(b) "Chairperson" means the Chairperson of the Commission or of the State Commission, as the case may be;

(c) "Commission" means the National Human Rights Commission constituted under section 3;

(d) "Human Rights" means the rights relating to life, liberty, equality and dignity of the individual guaranteed by the Constitution or embodied in the International Covenants and enforceable by courts in India;

(e) "Human Rights Courts" means the Human Rights Court specified under section 30;

(f) "International Covenants" means the International covenant on Civil and Political Rights and the International Covenant on Economic, Social and Cultural Rights adopted by the General Assembly of the United Nations on the 16th December, 1966;

(g) "Member" means a Member of the Commission or of the State Commission, as the case may be, and includes the Chairperson;

(h) "National Commission for Minorities" means the National Commission for Minorities Act, 1992 (19 of 1992)

(i) "National Commission for the Scheduled Castes and Scheduled Tribes" means the National Commission for the Scheduled Castes and Scheduled Tribes referred to in Article 338 of the Constitution;

(j) "National Commission for Women" means the National Commission for Women constituted under section 3 of the National Commission for Women Act, 1990 (20 of 1990);

(k) "Notification" means a notification published in the Official Gazette;

(l) "Prescribed" means prescribed by rule made under this Act;

(m) "Public servant" shall have the meaning assigned to it in Section 21 of the Indian Penal Code (45 of 1860);

(n) "State Commission" means a State Human Rights Commission constituted under section 21.

(2) Any reference in this Act to a law, which is not in force in the State of Jammu and Kashmir, shall, in relation to that State, be construed as a reference to a corresponding law, if any, in force in that State.

II

THE NATIONAL HUMAN RIGHTS COMMISSION

3. Constitution of a National Human Rights Commission.

(1) The Central Government shall constitute a body to be known as the National Rights Commission to exercise the powers conferred upon and to perform the functions assigned to it under this Act.

(2) The Commission shall consists of:

(a) Chairperson who has been a Chief Justice of the Supreme Court;

(b) One Member who is, or has been, a Judge of the Supreme Court;

(c) One Member who is, or has been the Chief Justice of High Court;

(d) Two Members to be appointed from amongst persons having knowledge of, or practical exprience in, matters relating to human rights.

(3) The Chairperson of the National Commission for Minorities, the National Commission for the Scheduled Castes and Scheduled Tribes and the National Commission fro Women shall be deemed to be Members of the Commission for the discharge of functions specified in clauses(b) to (f) of section 12.

(4) There shall be a Secretary General who shall be the Chief Excutive Officer of the Commission and shall exercise such powers and discharge such functions of the Commission as it may delegate to him.

(5) The headquarters of the Commission shall be at Delhi and the Commission may with the previous approval of the Central Government, establish offices at other places of India.

4. Appointment of Chairperson and other Members.

(1) The Chairperson and other members shall be appointed by the President by warrant under his hand and seal:

Provided that every appointment under this sub-section shall be made after obtaining the recommendations of a Commission consisting of:

(a) The Prime Minister - Chairperson

(b) Speaker of the House of the people - Member

(c) Minister in charge of the Ministry of Home Affairs in Government of India - Member,

(d) Leader of the Opposition in the House of the people - Member.

(e) Leader of the opposition in the Council of States — Member.

(f) Deputy Chairman of the Council of State - Member:

Provided further that no sitting Chief Justice of the Supreme Court or sitting Chief Justice of a High Court shall be appointed except after consultation with the Chief Justice of India.

(2) No appointment of a Chairperson or a Member shall be invalid merely by reason of any vacancy in the Committee.

5. Removal of a Member of the Commission.

(1) Subject to the provision of sub-section (2) the Chairperson or any other Member of the Commission shall only be removed from his office by order of the President on the ground of proved misbehaviour or incapacity after the Supreme Court on reference being made to it by the President, has, on inquiry held in accordance with the procedure prescribed in that behalf by the Supreme Court, reported that the Chairperson or such other Member as the case may be ought on any such ground to be removed.

(2) Notwithstanding anything in sub-section (1) the President may by order remove from office the Chairperson or any other Member if the Chairperson or such other member as the case may be:

(a) is adjudged an insolvent; or

(b) engaged during his term of office in any paid employment outside the duties of his office; or

(c) is unfit to continue in office by reason of infirmity of mind or body; or

(d) is of unsound mind and stands so declared by a competent court; or

(e) is convicted and sentenced to imprisonment for an offence which in the opinion of the President involves moral turpitude.

6. Term of Office of Members.

(1) A person appointed as Chairperson shall hold office for a term of five years from the date on which he enters upon his office or until he attains the age of seventy years, whichever is earlier.

(2) A person appointed as a Member shall hold office for a term of five years from the date on which he enters upon his office and shall be eligible for re-appointment for another term of five years; provided that no Member shall hold office after he has attained the seventy years.

(3) On ceasing to hold office, a Chairperson or a Member shall be ineligible for further employment under the Government of India or under the Government of any State.

7. Member to act as Chairperson or to discharge his functions in certain circumstances.

(1) In the event of the occurrence of any vacancy in the office of the Chairperson by reason of his death, resignation or otherwise the President may, by notification authorise one of the Members to act as the Chairperson untill the appointment of a new Chairperson to fill such vacancy.

(2) When the Chairperson is unable to discharge his functions owing to absence on leave or otherwise, such one of the Members as the President may, by notification authorise in this behalf, shall discharge the functions of the Chairperson until the date on which the Chairperson resumes his duties.

8. Terms and conditions of service of Members.

The salaries and allowances payable to any other terms and conditions of service of Members shall be such as may be prescribed:

Provided that neither the salary and allowances nor the other terms and condition of services of a Member shall be varied in to his disadvantages after his appointment.

9. Vacancies etc., no to invalidate the proceedings of the Commission.

No act or proceeding of the Commission shall be questioned or shall be invalidated merely on the ground of existence of any vacancy or defect in the Constitution of the Commission.

10. Procedure to be regulated by the Commission.

(1) The Commission shall meet at such time and place as the Chairperson may think fit.

(2) The Commission shall regulate its own procedure.

(3) All orders and decisions of the Commission shall be authenticated by the Secretary General or any other Officer or the Commission duly authorised by the chairperson in this behalf.

11. Officers and other staff of the Commission.

(1) The Central Government shall made available to the Commission.

(a) an officer of the rank of the Secretary to the Government of India who shall be the Secretary-General of the Commission; and

(b) such police and investigative staff under an officer not below the rank of a Director General of Police and such other officers and staff as may be necessary for the efficient performance of the functions of the Commission.

(2) Subject to such rules as may be made by the Central Government in this behalf the Commission may appoint such other administrative, technical and scientific staff as it may consider necessary.

(3) The Salaries, allowances and conditions of service of the officers and other staffs appointed under sub-section (2) shall be as may be prescribed.

III

FUNCTION AND POWERS OF THE COMMISSION

12. Function of the commission.

The Commission shall perform all or any of the following functions, namely

(a) inquiry, *suo motu* or on a petition presented to it by a victim or any person on his behalf into complaint of:

(i) violation of human rights or abetment thereof;

(ii) negligence in the prevention of such violation, by a public servant;

(b) intervene in any proceeding involving any allegation of violation of human rights pending before a court with the approval of such court;

(c) visit under intimation to the State Government any jail or any other institution under the control of the State Government where person are detained or lodged for purposes of treatment, reformation or protection to study the living conditions of the immates and make recommendations thereon;

(d) review the safeguards provided by or under time being in force for the protection of human rights and recommended measures for their effective implementation;

(e) review the factors, including acts of terrorism, that inhibit the enjoyment of human rights and recommend appropriate remedial measures;

(f) study treaties and other international instruments on human rights and make recommendations for their effective implementation;

(g) undertake and promote research in the field of human rights;

(h) spread human rights literacy among various sections of society and promote awareness of the safeguards available for the protection of these rights through publications, the media, seminars and other available mean;

(i) encourage the efforts of non-governmental organizations and institutions working in the fields of human rights:

(j) encourage the efforts of non-governmental organizations and institutions working in the fields of human rights.

13. Powers relating to inquiries.

(1) The Commission shall, while inquiring into complaint under this Act, have all the powers of a civil court trying a suit under the Code of Civil Procedure, 1908 (5 of 1908), and in particular in respect of the following matters, namely.

(a) summoning and enforcing the attendance of witnesses and examining them on oath:

(b) discovery and production of any document;

(c) receiving evidence on affidavits:

(d) requisitioning any public record or copy thereof from any court of office;

(e) issuing Commissions for the examinations of witnesses or documents

(f) any other matters which may be prescribed.

(2) The Commission shall have power to require any person, subject to any privilage which may be claimed by that person under any law for the time being in force to furnish information and such points or matters as, in the opinion of the Commission may useful for, or relevant to the subject matter of the inquiry and any person so required shall be deemed to be legally bound to furnish such information within the meaning of sect ion 176 and section 177 of the Indian Penal Code (45 of 1860).

(3) The Commission or any officer, not below the rank of a Gazetted Officer, specially authorised in this behalf by the Commission may enter any building or place where the Commission has reason to believe that any document relating to the subject matter of the inquiry may be found and may seize any such document or take extract or copies therefrom subject to the provisions of section 100 of the Code of Criminal Procedure, 1973 (2 of 1974) in so far as it may be applicable.

(4) The Commission shall be deemed to be a civil court and when any offence as is described in section 175, section 178, section 179, section 180 or section 228 of the Indian Penal Code (45 of 1860) is committed in the view or presence of the Commission / the Commission may, after recording the facts constituting the offence and the statement of the accused as provided for in the Code of Criminal Procedure, 1973 (2 of 1974) forward the case to a Magistrate having jurisdiction to try the same and the magistrate to whom any such case is forwarded shall proceed to hear the complaint against the accused as if

the case has been forwarded to him under section 346 of the Code of Criminal Procedure, 1973.

(5) Every proceedings before the Commission shall be deemed to be a judicial proceeding within the meaning of sections 193 and 228; and for the purposes of section 196, of the Indian Penal Code (45 of 1860) and the Commission shall be deemed to be a civil court for all the purposes of section 195 and Chapter XXVI of the Code of Criminal Procedure, 1973 (2 of 1974).

14. Investigation.

(1) The Commission may for the purpose of conducting any investigation pertaining to the inquiry, utilise the services of any officer of investigation agency of the Central Government or any State Government with the concurrence of the Central Government or the State Government, as the case may be.

(2) For the purpose of investigating into any matter pertaining to the inquiry, any officer or agency whose services are utilised under sub-section (1) may, subject to the direction and control of the Commission

(a) summon and enforce the attendance of any person and examine him;

(b) require the discovery and production of any document; and

(c) requisition any public record or copy thereof from any office.

(3) The provisions of section 15 shall apply in relation to any statement made by a person before any office or agency whose services are utilise under sub-section (1) as they apply in relation to any statement made by a person in the course of giving evidence before the Commission.

(4) The officer or agency whose services are utilised under

subsection (1) shall investigate into any matter pertaining to the inquiry and submit a report thereon to the Commission within such period as may be specified by the Commission in this behalf.

(5) The Commission shall satisfy itself about the correctness of the facts stated and the conclusion, if any, arrived at in the report submitted to it under sub-section and for this purpose the Commission may make such inquiry (including the examination of the person or person who conducted or assisted in the investigation) as it thinks fit.

15. Statement made by persons to the Commission.

No statement made by a person in the course of giving evidence before the Commission shall subject him to, or be used against him in any civil or criminal proceeding except a prosecution for giving false evidence by such statement: Provided that the statement.

(a) is made in reply to the question which he is required by the Commission to answer; or

(b) is relevent to the subject matter of the inquiry.

16. Persons likely to be prejudicially affected to be heard.

If, at any stage of the inquiry, the Commission:

(a) considers it necessary to inquiry into the conduct of any person; or

(b) is of the opinion that the reputation of any person is likely to be prejudicially affected by the inquiry.

It shall give to that person a reasonable opportunity of being heard in the inquiry and to produce evidence in his defence:

Provided that nothing in this section shall apply where the credit of a witness is being impeached.

IV

PROCEDURE

17. Inquiry into complaints.

The Commission while inquiring into the complaints of violations of human rights may;

(1) call of information or report from the Central Government or any State Government or any other authority or organisation subordinate thereto within such time as may be specified by it:

Provided that —

(a) If the information or report in not received with the time stipulated by the Commission, it may proceed to inquiry into the complaint on its own;

(b) If, on receipt of information or report, the Commission is satisfied either that no further inquiry is required or that the required action has been initiated or taken by the concerned Government or authority it may not proceed with the complaint and inform the complaint accordingly;

(2) without prejudice to anything contained in clause (1) if it considers necessary, having regard to the nature of the complaint, initiate an inquiry.

18. Steps after inquiry.

The Commission may take any of the following steps upon the completion of an inquiry held under this Act, namely;

(1) Where the inquiry disclose to the commission of violation of human rights or negligence in the prevention of violation of human rights by a public servant, it may recommend to the concerned Government or authority the initiation of proceedings for prosecution or such other action as the

Commission may deem fit against the concerned person or persons.

(2) approach the Supreme Court or the High Court concerned for such direction, orders or writs as that court may deem necessary;

(3) recommend to the concerned Government or authority for the grant of his family as the Commission may consider necessary;

(4) subject to the provisions of clause (5) provide a copy or the inquiry report to the petitioner or his representative;

(5) the Commission shall sent a copy of its inquiry report together with its recommendations to the concerned Government or authority and the concerned Government or authority shall within a period of one month, or such further time as the Commission may forward its comments on the report including the action taken or proposed to be taken thereon, to the Commission;

(6) the Commission shall publish its inquiry report together with the comments of the concerned Government or authority, if any, and the action taken or proposed to be taken by the concerned Government or authority, on the recommendations of the Commission.

(7) the Commission shall publish its inquiry report together with the comments of the concerned Government or authority, if any, and the action taken or proposed to be taken by the concerned Government or authority, on the recommendations of the Commission.

19. Procedure with respect to armed forces.

(1) Notwithstanding anything contained in this Act, while dealing with complaints of violation of human rights by members of the armed forces, the Commission shall adopt

the following procedure, namely,

(a) it may, either on its motion or on receipt of a petition, seek a report from the Central Government;

(b) after the receipt of the report, it may either not proceed with the complaint or as the case may be, make its recommendations to that Government.

(2) The Central Government shall inform the Commission of the action taken on the recommendations within three months or such further times as the Commission may allow.

(3) The Commission shall publish its report together with its recommendations made to the Central Government and the action taken by the that Government on such recommendations.

(4) The Commission shall provide a copy of the report published under sub-section (3) to the petitioner or his representative.

20. Annual and Special Reports of the Commission

(1) The Commission shall submit an annual report to the Central Government and to the State Government concerned and may at any time submit special reports on any mater which, in its opinion, is of such urgency or importance that it should not be referred till submission of the annual report.

(2) The Central Government and the State Government, as the case may be shall cause the annual and special reports of the Commission to be laid before such House of Parliament or the State Legislature respectively, as the case may be along with a memorandum of action t aken or proposed to be taken on the recommendations of the Commission and the reason for non acceptance of the recommendations, if any.

V

STATE HUMAN RIGHTS COMMISSIONS

21. Constitution of State Human Rights Commissions

(1) A State Government may constitute a body to be knows as the ....(name of the State) Human Rights Commission to exercise the powers conferred upon, and to perform the functions assigned to a State Commission under this Chapter.

(2) The State Commission shall consist of -

(a) a Chairperson who has been a Chief Justice of a High Court;

(b) one Member who is, or has been a judge of a High Court;

(c) one Member who is, or has been a District judge in the State;

(d) two members to be appointed from amongst persons having knowledge of, or practical experience in matters relating to human rights.

(3) There shall be a secretary who shall be the Chief Executive Officer of the State and shall exercise such powers and discharge such functions of the State Commission as it may delegate to him.

(4) The headquarters of the State Commission shall be at such place as the State Government may, be notification specify.

(5) A State Commission may inquire into violation of human rights only in respect of matters relatable to any of the entries enumerated in List II and List III in this Seventh Schedule to the Constitution:

Provided that if any such matter is already being enquired

into by the Commission or any other Commission duly constituted under any law for the time being in force, the State Commission shall not inquire into the said matter:

Provided further that in relation to the Jammu & Kashmir Human Rights Commission, this sub-section shall have effect as if for the words and figures "List II and List III in the Seventh Schedule to the Constitution", the words and figures "List III in the Seventh Schedule to the Constitution as applicable to the State of Jammu and Kashmir and in respect of matters in relation to which the Legislature of that State has power to make Laws" had been substituted.

22. Appointment of Chairperson and other Members of State Commission.

(1) The Chairperson and other Members shall be appointed by the Governor by warrant under his hand and seal:

Provided that every appointment under this sub-section shall be made after obtaining the recommendation of a Committee consisting of —

(a) The Chief Minister — Chairperson

(b) Speaker of the Legislative Assembly—Member

(c) Minister in-charge of the Department of— Member Home in the State

(d) Leader of the Opposition in the—Member Legislative Assembly

Provided further that where there is a legislative Council in a State, the Chairman of that Council and the Leader of the Opposition in that Council shall also be members of the Committee:

Provided also that no sitting Judge of a High Court or a sitting District Judge shall be appointed except after consultation with the Chief Justice of the High Court of the Concerned State.

(2) No appointment of a Chairperson or a Member of the State Commission shall be invalid merely by reason of any vacancy in the Committee.

23. Removal of a Members of the State Commission.

(1) Subject to the provision of sub-section (2), the Chairperson or any other Member of the State Commission shall only be removed from his office by order of the President on the ground of proved misbehaviour or incapacity after the Supreme Court, on a reference being made to it by the President, has, on inquiry held in accordance with the procedure prescribed in that behalf by the Supreme Court, reported that the Chairperson or such other Member, as the case may be ought on any such ground to be removed.

(2) Notwithstanding anything in sub-section (1), the President may by order remove from office the Chairperson or any other member if the Chairperson or such other member, as the case may be:

(a) is adjudged an insolvent; or

(b) engages during his term of office in any paid employment outside the duties of his office; or

(c) is unfit to continue in office by reason of infirmity of mind or body; or

(d) is of unsound mind and stands so declared by a competent court; or

(e) is convicted and sentenced to imprisonment for an offence which in the opinion of the President involves moral turpitude.

24. Term of office of Member of the State Commission.

(1) A Person appointed as Chairperson shall hold office for term of five years from the date on which he enters upon

his office or until he attains the age of seventy years, whichever is earlier.

(2) A person appointed as a member shall hold office for a term of five years from the date on which he enters upon his office and shall be eligible for re-appointment for another term of five years:

Provided that no Members shall hold office after he has attained the age of seventy years.

(3) On ceasing to hold office, a Chairperson or a Member shall be ineligible for further employment under the Government of a State or under the Government of India.

25. Member to act as Chairperson or to discharge his functions in certain circumstances.

(1) In the event of the occurrence of any vacancy in the office of the Chairperson, by reason of his death, resignation or otherwise, the Governor may, by notification, authorise one of the Members to act as the Chairperson until the appointment of a new Chairperson to fill such vacancy.

(2) When the Chairperson is unable to discharge his functions owing to absence on leave or otherwise, such one of the Members as the Governor may, by notification, authorise in this behalf, shall discharge the functions of the Chairperson untill the date on which the Chairperson resumes his duties.

26. Terms and conditions of service of Members of the State Commission.

The salaries and allowances payable to, and other terms and conditions of service of, the Members shall be such as may be prescribed by the State Government:

Provided that neither the salary and allowances nor the other terms and conditions of service of a Member shall be varied to his disadvantage after his appointment.

27. Officers and other staff of the State Commission.

(1) The State Government shall make available to the Commission,

(a) an officer not below the rank of a Secretary to the State Government who shall be the Secretary of the State Commission; and

(b) such police and investigative staff under an officer not below the rank of an Inspector General of Police and such other officers and staff as may be necessary for the efficient performance of the functions of the State Commission.

(2) Subject to such rule as may be made by the State Government in this behalf, the State Commission my appoint such other administrative, technical and scientific staff as it may consider necessary.

(3) The salaries, allowances and conditions of service of the officers and other staff appointed under sub-section (2) shall be such as may be prescribed by the State Government.

28. Annual and Special Reports of State Commission.

(1) The State Commission shall submit an annual report to the State Government and may at any time submit special reports on any matter which, in its opinion, is of such urgency or important that it should not be deferred till submission of the annual report.

(2) The State Government shall cause the annual and special reports of the State Commission to be laid before each House of State Legislature where it consists of two Houses or where such Legislature consists of one house, before that House along with a memorandum of action taken or proposed to be taken on the recommendations of the State Commission and the reasons for non-acceptance of the recommendation, if any.

29. Application of certain provisions relating to National Human Rights Commission to State Commission.

The provisions of sections 9, 10, 12, 13, 14, 15, 16, 17 and 18 shall apply to a State Commission and shall have effect, subject to the following modifications, namely;

(a) reference to "Commission" shall be constructed as reference to "State Commission".

(b) in section 10, in sub-section (3) for the word "Secretary General", the word "Secretary" shall be substituted:

(c) in section 12 clause (1) shall be omitted;

(d) in sectin 17, in clause (f), the words "Central Government or any" shall be omitted.

VI

HUMAN RIGHTS COURTS

30. Human Rights Courts.

For the purpose of providing speedy trial of offences arising out of violation of human rights, the State Government may, with the concurrence of the Chief Justice of the High Court, by notification, specify for each district a Court of Session to be a Human Rights Court to try the said offences:

Provided that nothing in this section shall apply if:

(a) a Court of Session is already specified as a special court;

(b) a special court is already constituted, for such offences under any other law for the time being in force.

31. Special Public Prosecutor.

For every Human Rights Court, the State Government shall, by notification, specify a Public Prosecutor or appoint an advocate who has been in practice as an advocate for not less than seven years, as a Special Public Prosecutor for the purpose of conducting cases in that Court.

VII

FINANCE, ACCOUNTS AND AUDIT

32. Grants by the Central Government

(1) The Central Government shall, after due appropriation made by Parliament by law in this behalf, pay to the Commission by way of grant such sums of money as the Central Government may think fit for being utilised for the purpose of this Act.

(2) The Commission may spend such sums as it thinks fit for performing the functions under this Act, and such sums shall be treated as expenditure payable out of the grants referred to in sub-section (1).

33. Grants by the State Government.

(1) The State Government shall, after due appropriation made by Legislature by law in this behalf, pay to the State Commission by way of grants such sums of money as the State Government may think fit for being utilised for the purposes of this Act.

(2) The State Commission may spend such sums as it thinks fit for performing the functions under Chapter V, and such sums shall be treated as expenditure payable out of the grants referred to in sub-section (1).

34. Accounts and audit.

(1) The Commission shall maintain proper accounts and other relevant records and prepare an annual statement of accounts in such form as may be prescribed by the Central Government in consultation with the Comptroller and Auditor-General of India.

(2) The accounts of the Commission shall be audited by the Comptroller and Auditor General at such intervals as may be specified by him and any expenditure incurred in connection with such audit shall be payable by the Commission to the Comptroller and Auditor General.

(3) The Comptroller and Auditor General and any person appointed by him in connection with the audit of the accounts of the Commission under this Act shall have the same rights and privileges and the authority in connection with such audit as the Comptroller and Auditor General, generally has in connection with the audit of Government accounts and in particular, shall have the right to demand the production of books, accounts, connected vouchers and other documents and papers and to inspect any of the offices of the Commission.

(4) The accounts of the Commission, as certified by the Comptroller and Auditor General or any other person appointed by him in this behalf, together with the audit report thereon shall be forwarded annually to the Central Government by the Commission and the Central Government shall cause the audit report to be laid, as soon as may be after it is received, before each House of Parliament.

35. Accounts and audit of State Commission.

(1) The State Commission shall maintain proper accounts and other relevant records and prepare an annual statement of accounts in such form as may be prescribed by the State Government in consultation with the Comptroller and Auditor-General of India.

(2) The accounts of the State Commission shall be audited by the Comptroller and Auditor-General at such intervals as may be specified by him and any expenditure incurred in connection with such audit shall be payable by the State Commission to the Comptroller and Auditor.

(3) The Comptroller and Auditor-General and any person appointed by him in connection with the audit of the accounts of the State Commission under this Act shall have the same rights and privileges and the authority in connection with such audit as the Comptroller and Auditor-General generally has in connection with the audit of Government accounts and in particular, shall have same rights and privileges and the authority in connection with such audit as the Comptroller and Auditor-General, generally has in connection with such audit as the Comptroller and Auditor-General, generally has in connection with the audit of Government accounts and in particular, shall have the right to demand the production of books, accounts, connected vouchers and other documents and papers and to inspect any of the offices of the State Commission.

(4) The accounts of the State Commission, as certified by the Comptroller and Auditor-General or any other person appointed by him in this behalf, together with the audit report thereon, shall be forwarded annually to the State Government shall cause the audit report to be laid, as soon as may be after it is received before the State Legislature.

VIII

36. Matters not subject to jurisdiction of the Commission.

(1) The Commission shall not inquire into any matter which is pending before a State Commission or any other Commission duly constituted under any law for the time being in force.

(2) The Commission or the State Commission shall not inquire into any matter after the expiry of one year from the data on which the act constituting violation of human rights is alleged to have been committed.

37. Constitution of special investigation teams.

Notwithstanding anything contained in any other law for the time being in force, where the Government considers it necessary so to do, it may constitute one or more special investigation teams, consisting of such police officers as it thinks necessary for purposes of investigation and prosecution of offences arising out of violations of human rights.

38. Protection of action taken in good faith.

No suit or other legal proceeding shall lie against the Central Government, State Government, Commission or any Member thereof or any person acting under the direction either of the Central Government, State Government, Commission or the State Commission in respect of anything which is in good faithe done or intended to be done in pursuance of this Act or of any rules or any order made thereunder or in respect of the publication by or under the authority of the Central Government, State Government. Commission or the State Commission of any report, paper or proceedings.

39. Members and officers to be public servants.

Every Member of the Commission, State Commission and every officers appointed or a uthorised by the Commission or the State Commission to exrcise functions under this Act shall be deemed to be a public servant within the meaning of section 21 of the Indian Penal Code (45 of 1860).

40. Power of Central Government to make rules.

(1) The Central Government may, by notification, make rules to carry out the provision of this Act.

(2) In particular and without prejudice to the generality of the foregoing power, such rules may provide for all or any of the following matters namely:

(a) the salaries and allowances and other terms and conditions of service of the Members under section 8;

(b) the conditions subject to which other administrative, technical and scientific staff may be appointed by the Commission and the salaries and allowances of officers and other staff under sub-section (3) of section 11;

(c) any other power of a civil court required to be prescribed under clause (f) of sub-section (I) of section 13;

(d) the form in which the annual statement of account is to be prepared by the Commission under sub-section (I) of section 34; and

(e) any other matter which has to be, prescribed.

(3) Every rule made under this Act shall be laid, as soon as may be after it is made, before each House of Parliament, while it is in session, for a total period of thirty days which may be comprised in one session or in two or more successive sessions, and if, before the expiry of the sessions immediately following the sessions or the successive sessions aforesaid, both Houses agree in making any modification in the rule or both Houses agree that the rule should not be made the rule shall thereafter have effect only in such modified form or be of no effect as the case may be: however, that any such modification or annulment shall be without prejudice to the validity of anything previously done under that rule.

41. Power of State Government to make rules.

(1) The State Government may, by notification, make rules to carry out the provisions of this Act.

(2) In particular and without prejudice to the generality or the foregoing power, such rules may provide for all or any of the following matters namely;

(a) the salaries and allowances and other terms and conditions of service of the Members under section 26;

(b) the conditions subject to which other administrative, technical and scientific staff may be appointed by the State Commission and the salaries and allowances of officers and other staff under sub-section (3) of section 7;

(c) the form in which the annual statement of accounts is to be prepared under sub-section (1) of section 35.

(3) Every rule made by the State Government under this section shall be laid, as soon as may be after if is made, before each House of the State Legislature where it consists of two Houses, or where such Legislature consists of one House, before that House.

42. Power to remove difficulties.

(1) if any difficulty arises in giving effect to the provisions of this Act, the Central Government may by order published in the Official Gazette, make such provisions not inconsistent with the provisions of this Act as appear to it to be necessary or expedient for removing the difficulty:

Provided that no such order shall be made after the expiry of the period of two years from the date of commencement of this Act.

(2) Every order made under this section shall, as soon as may be after it is made, be laid before each house of Parliament;

43. Repeal and savings.

(1) The Protection of Human Rights Ordinance, 1993(Ord. 30 of 1993) is hereby repealed.

(2) Notwithstanding such repeal, anything done or any action taken under the said Ordinance, shall be deemed to have been done or taken under the corresponding provisions of this Act.

Appendix-V

Amnesty International's Observations on Violation of Rights in India: Pattern and Sources

The victims of human rights violations and abuses are not just statistics; they are people with names, families, friends and aspirations, whose lives are irrevocably affected when state officials or opposition groups abuse their rights. Amnesty International tells their stories and condemns those who have abused them—often men in uniform who have been entrusted to protect the very rights they violate—and urges that they be brought to justice and that steps be taken to end the violations.

The human rights situation in India is full of contradictions. Form the discussions of rights that underpinned the Constitution, to the recent establishment of the National Human Rights Commission (NHRC), Indian leaders have acknowledged the need for enforceable rights and monitoring of their implementation. The government and courts have indicated their support for attempts to establish legal aid schemes and judicial initiatives such as public interest litigation, which intend to ensure that access to justice is more freely available. Similarly, by defining categories of people in need of special protection, the particular vulnerabilities of groups with little political social, of economic power have been recognized.

However, the rights of all Indian citizens are inherently limited. The "Fundamental Rights" in Part III of the *Constitution of India*. 1950 are subject to conditions which have enabled successive governments to enact laws that violate India's obligations as a signatory to the *International Covenant on Civil and Political Rights* (ICCPR), for example in the acceptance of preventive detention implicit in Article 22 of the Constitution. Nonetheless, the right to approach the courts for the enforcement of rights provides remedies, including that of *habeas corpus* when rights are violated. Despite the existence of remedies in the constitution and in law, poor implementation of laws and court orders provide the context in which violations of human rights continue.

It is not just the legal framework that supports the continuing violence and denial of basic rights that are endemic throughout India, local, regional and national power structures perpetuate corrupt practices and provide virtual impunity for those who violate human rights. Most often it is those with little power. disadvantaged by poverty or status, who suffer the consequences of the widespread abuse of power. In 1992, whilst documenting the incidence of torture, rape and deaths in custody in India, Amnesty International observed that half of India's population were poor and illiterate, and a quarter of them were officially recognized as being in need of special protection.

> *"People from this most vulnerable section of the population form the majority of torture victims: members of the scheduled castes and scheduled tribes, tribal women in the northeast, migrant workers, landless labourers........"*

Other types of victims were observed, such as:

> *"People arrested for their political convictions or people arrested in connection with the situations of armed conflict that prevail in the northeast, Jammu and Kashmir, and Punjab."*

All the factors contributing to the widespread violation of human rights in India are linked. Provisions in the legislative framework that do not conform to international standards permit human rights violations by the forces of law and order to go unpunished. Protective measures, where they exist, are unevenly implemented, compounding the violations of the rights of individuals, many of whose rights are breached simply because of the ethnic, religious or social group to which they belong. The vulnerabilities of specific communities are clear in the large scale human rights violations and abuses seen in situations of internal armed conflict, such as in Jammu & Kashmir, where there is an armed opposition and where the security forces are extensively deployed. It is also clear in the pervasive endemic violence throughout the country, for example the continuing incidence of custodial deaths as documented extensively by Amnesty International in recent years, as well by the NHRC.

This summarizes the patterns of violations and abuses of rights in India that fall within Amnesty International's mandate, before examining some of the shortcomings of the legal and judicial system facilitating the continuing violations. The perpetrators and victims are then discussed.

Patterns of violations and abuses

Amnesty International has several long-standing concerns about violations by government forces in India. These include torture and ill-treatment of detainees and prisoners, and unfair trials for political prisoners.

Over the years, the patterns of violations have changed. Increasingly, the forces of law and order have used extrajudicial methods to exercise control, particularly in regions experiencing internal armed conflict. Many people have "disappeared" after apparently being taken into custody by agents of the state. Legal safeguards for the protection of detainees are thus ignored with impunity. Records of detention are not adequately maintained, the lawful role of the judiciary in the detention process is ignored and there is little access to judicial remedies for the relatives of the "disappeared".

Extrajudicial executions, carried out by state agents, or with their acquiescence, are common, particularly in situations of armed conflict. While the Government dismisses the majority of these as deaths during "encounters" with armed opposition groups, full and impartial investigations into the circumstances of these deaths are rate, and there is little effort to substantiate claims that an "encounter" has taken place.

Whatever imperatives the Indian state has to maintain internal peace and security, the violation of rights protected by the *Constitution of India* as well as by international human rights standards is avoidable. Yet in recent years Amnesty International has reported the following patterns of human rights violations:

* Preventive detention provisions have meant that thousands of political prisoners have been held without charge or trial. An NHRC report to the government stated that 3,007 people were in detention in Jammu & Kashmir in 1994, while local civil liberties groups estimated the number of detainees was 20,000. Fair and prompt trials are compromised by routine delays in the legal system throughout the country. Thousands of people remain detained under the provisions of the now lapsed *Terrorist and Disruptive Activities (Prevention) Act.*

* Torture of detainees in police and military custody remains endemic, often in an effort to extract confessions or information. The most common method of torture is beating with *lathis*(canes). Other methods include suspension by the wrists and ankles and electric shocks. Reports of rape indicate that it is used as a method of torture by state agents as well as armed opposition groups. In 1995 at least 100 people died in the custody of the police or security forces throughout India, as a result of torture and medical neglect. The NHRC itself documented 130 deaths in custody in a 10-month period in 1995. Those tortured were both criminal suspects and political detainees.

* Within prisons and other places of detention, poor conditions amounting to cruel, inhuman and degrading treatment is widespread and fails to meet the requirements of the UN *Standard Minimum Rules for the Treatment of Prisoners.*

* Dozens of political detainees have "disappeared", most of whome are young men suspected of links with armed opposition groups. The lack of adequate redress runs counter to the provisions of the UN *Declaration on the Protection of All Persons from Enforced Disappearance.*

* The excessive use of force in counter-insurgency and law enforcement has led to the reported extrajudicial execution of hundreds of people by the security forces.

* The death penalty is still applied. At least three people were judicially executed during 1995.

Amnesty International has also recorded human rights abuses by armed opposition groups, which have continued to be common in the past year. Hostages were taken, many were tortured and killed, and civilians and members of the security forces were deliberately and arbitrarily killed. Such abuses are strictly prohibited by Indian law and by common Article 3 of the four Geneva Conventions which establish minimum humanitarian standards in situations of internal armed conflict.

Legislation that contravenes international human rights standards

A complex web of legal norms governs all aspects of life in India, with differing bodies of civil and personal laws governing specified regions and communities. Many of Amnesty International's concerns relate to the body of criminal law as applied throughout the country. Some of these laws, like the *Indian Penal Code and Indian Evidence Act,* were enacted in the colonial period, while others such as the *Code of Criminals* procedure were introduced or re-enacted after independence. Jurists in India have for many years maintained that certain laws need to be updated and amended. However, the lengthy process of introducing new legislation or amendments has not been extensively undertaken for the criminal law. An example is the *Code of Criminal Procedure (Amendment) Bill* which has been pending before the *Lok Sabha* (parlimentary 'House of People') in its present form since 1994.

Arrest, Detention, Trial and the Legal Process

Amnesty International is particularly concerned about existing measures for the protection of detainees against illtreatment and torture and for ensuring that political prisoners are given a fair trial. Protection for detainees is extensively provided for in Indian law. For example:

* Sections 46-58 of the *Code of Criminal Procedure* provide for arrest and detention procedures, including that the arrested person be informed of the grounds of the arrest, and that a medical examination, if requested by the police or the arrested person, can be held.
* Section 56 and 167 of the *Code of Criminal Procedure* state that a person arrested is not to be detained for more than 24 hours before being brought before a magistrate, who can then order detention in police custody for a further 15 days, and thereafter in judicial custody for up to 60 or 90 days (depending on the seriousness of the alleged offence).

However, Amnesty International is concerned that these measures do not provide adequate safequard against human rights violations. For example, police do not have to inform relatives promptly of an arrest. The absence of this simple procedure facilitates "disappearances". Similarly, the absence of mandatory procedures to ensure that all detainees are given a prompt medical examination following arrest facilitates deaths in custody. The UN Body of *Principles for the Protection of All Persons under Any Form of Detention or Imprisonment* sets out comprehensive guidelines for arrest and detention, but many of these guidelines are not followed either in law or in practice in India.

Amnesty International welcomes the intention behind the proposed amendments to the criminal law which seek to strengthen the provisions for the protection of detainess, but notes that many of these amendments were first introduced in the *Lok Sabha* in 1988 and are yet to be legislated. For example, included in the *Code of Criminal Procedure (Amendment) Bill*, 1994, are:

* an amendment to Section 176 of the *Code of Criminal Procedure* to provide for judicial inquiries into every case of death in custody, "disappearance" and rape;

* an amendment that would empower the detaines to inform a nominated person of their arrest (see above):

* an amendment prohibiting the arrest of a woman "after sunset and before sunrise" except in "exceptional circumstances", a qualification which Amnesty International fears would leave the provision open to misuse.

Moreover, the legal safeguards that do exist are not implemented by the police and the security forces. Arrest and interrogation procedures are routinely flouted. Detainees are not always brought before a judicial magistrate within 24 hours of arrest. Inquests into deaths in custody are not always held. These problems are compounded by lengthy delays and flaws in the legal process (see below).

Impunity

Sanctions against public officials for human rights violations exist in the general criminal law. These include:

* Article 21 of the Constitution of India protects the right to life, and Articles 32 and 226 of the Constitution provide for the enforcement of all fundamental rights;

* Section 330 and 331 of the *Indian Penal Code* forbid torture;

* Section 376 of the *Indian Penal Code* provides for the punishment of a police officer who commits rape;

* Section 176 of the *Code of Criminal Procedure* states that

a magisterial inquiry must be held when there is a death in police custody;

* A civil suit for damages can be brought under Section 79 of the *Civil Procedure Code*;
* A criminal prosecution can be brought against a public servant under Section 197 of the *Code of Criminal Procedure*. This provision cannot be used against a member of the armed forces. Amnesty International is concerned to note that the *Code of Criminal Procedure (Amendment) Bill*, 1994 seeks to extend this impunity to other public servants acting for the maintenance of public order.

Amnesty International has also welcomed the provision included in the *Criminal Law Amendment Bill* 1995 which states, in Section 24(2), that any police officer who "corruptly or maliciously proceeds or threatens to proceed against any person for an offence" under the proposed bill would be prosecuted.

Amnesty International is concerned about the effect upon human rights of the large body of law enacted to administer regions of the country where political violence is widespread. Impunity for the armed forces in general criminal law is extended by **special legislation**, and can be further extended when a state of emergency is declared by the President in any part or the whole of India. Similarly, regions of the country continue to be placed under President's rule where the powers extended increase the ability of police and security forces to act with impunity.

An example of special legislation is the *Armed Forces (Special Powers) Act*, which is enforced in Jammu & Kashmir, parts of the northeast, and Punjab & Chandigarh. It has been criticized by the UN Human Rights Committee for providing the security forces with broadly defined powers to shoot to kill, with virtual impunity from prosecution. Amnesty International's concerns include that:

* the power to shoot to kill violates Article 6 of the ICCPR which guarantees the right to life, and Article 3 of the UN *Code of Conduct for Law Enforcement Officials*. As Article 6 of the ICCPR is a non-derogable article, the right to life must be respected at all times and in all circumstances. This special legislation is therefore of particular concern as it indicates that India has not fully taken on its obligation under international human rights law.

* that Section 6 of the special legislation protects people operating under the Act from prosecution, giving the impression that the security forces can act with impunity, and facilitating torture, extrajudicial executions and "disappearances".

Other special legislation confers similar impunity on the armed forces, including the *Jammu and Kashmir Public Safety Act* (see below) and the *Assam Disturbed Areas Act*. Impunity is further ensured as the NHRC cannot examine reports of violations by members of the armed forces.

Preventive detention

Special legislation, as outlined above, provides for preventive detention, thereby separating the detainees from the normal judicial process and the safeguards attached to it (see below).

In the past Amnesty International has expressed concern about the use of the *Maintenace of Internal Security Act*, which is no longer in force, and the numerous arrests made under it during the emergency rule of 1975 to 1977 Similarly, the extensive public criticism and government review of the use of the *Terrorist and Disruptive Activities (Prevention) Act(TADA)*, the legislation most widely used for preventive detention, led to its lapse in May 1995. However, Amnesty International is concerned about reports of the continuing application of TADA for offences committed before its lapse as well as the continued detention of hundreds of people under its provisions who have not yet been brought to trial and who, Amnesty International believes, will not receive a fair trial.

The Jammu & Kashmir Public Safety Act is extensively used for preventive detention. Other legislations including the *National Security Act* and the *Prevention of Balckmarketering and Maintenance of Supplies of Essential Commodities Act*, continue to provide for prolonged periods of detention without trial. The proposed extension of provisions similar to those which existed in TADA in to the general criminal law, through the *Criminal Law (Amendment) Bill*, 1995, is of particular concern. It would mean that the provisions of this special legislation, previously limited in its application to specific regions and activities, would be extended to the whole of India. Amnesty International routinely monitors proposed legislations, for example, the organization is concerned to note the provisions in the *Conservation of Forests and Natural Eco-Systems Bill* which would provide forest officials with powers to arrest on the suspicion that a forest is being encroached upon, and could lead to arbitrary arrests and detentions.

The death penalty

Amnesty International opposes the death penalty in all circumstances because it violates the right to life and the right not to be subjected to cruel, inhuman or degrading treatment or punishment. These rights are spelled out in the ICCPR as well as in the *Constitution of India*. Imposition of the death penalty also carries a risk of killing an innocent person and has not been proven to have any unique deterrent effect.

Despite India's ratification of the ICCPR which states, in Article 6 (5), that the death penalty shall not be imposed for crimes committed by person below the age of 18, the *Juvenile Justice Act,* which provides a uniform legal framework for the treatment of children, defines a juvenile as "a boy who has not attained the age of sixteen years or a girl who has not attained the age of eighteen years". This means that the availability of the death penalty in the general criminal law is applicable to any male aged 16 or over, in contravention of the ICCPR and the *Convention on the Rights of the Child*, ratified by India in 1992.

The circumstances in which the death penalty is used have benn narrowed by Indian courts; the penalty is now applied only in the "rarest of rare" cases, as decided by the Supreme Court Nonetheless, in a detailed examination of the death penalty in 1989, Amnesty International noted that those who are judicially executed tend to come from disadvantaged and vulnerable sectors of society. Moreover, the number of offences carrying the death penalty has increased. Offences carrying the death penalty are found in numerous laws, including:

* the *Indian Penal Code; the Code of Criminal Procedure*; the *Army Act*; the *Air Force Act*; the *Navy Act*; the *Commission of Sati (Prevention) Act*; the *Scheduled Castes and Scheduled Tribes (Prevention of Atrocities) Act*; the *Narcotics, Drugs and Psychotropic Substances Act*; the *Arms Act*; the *Explosives Act*; the *Inflammable Substances Act*.

A legal process that facilitates violations

The lengthy delays in the conclusion of legal proceedings and the inherent problems in using the law for those suffering political, social and economic disadvantage in themselves facilitate violations. The implementation of those laws which do conform to international standards for the protection of human rights is compromised by a legal system that is unable to cope with its docket, and does not provide easy access to justice. The problems include proceedings in the Supreme Court are only conducted in the English language, which effectively excludes the majority of the population from seeking judicial redress in this forum; the ineffectiveness of the judicial system in many areas; the high costs involved; the difficulties inherent in accessing judicial fora discourage the registration of cases, for example, when a relative has "disappeared".

Amnesty International welcomes the intention behind the *Legal Services Authorities Act* which aims at the provision of legal aid to those unable to afford legal redress. However, as with other legislations, Amnesty International is concerned that it is not comprehensively applied throughout the country and therefore does not provide universal right to call upon a lawyer of one's choice, as called for in UN *Basic Principles on the Role of Lawyers*. Similarly, public interest litigation, a legal mechanism that emerged in response to the need for greater access to justice, is also subject to the delays of the whole legal system, and to the poor implementation of the orders that are given.

International standards place the onus on the State to ensure that the legal system provides adequate mechanisms to provide redress and full, fair and impartial investigations, in cases of human rights violations. Amnesty International has raised its concerns with the Indian authorities about the failure of the legal system to ensure that all violations are redressed that existing safeguards are implemented, and that full investigations are carried out.

The perpetrators of human rights violations and abuses

Amnesty International's concern for the protection and promotion of human rights within its mandate, leads to specific concerns relating to the conduct of the forces of law and order, and of armed opposition groups.

Although many legal sanctions do exist,in practice state agents are able to act with little fear of being held accountable. However, initiatives, for example by the NHRC, to introduce training in human rights, have acknowledged the need for greater sensitivity to human rights issues throughout the forces of law and order. Similarly, whilst there have been few instances of criminal action taken against state agents, awards for compensation have been made by the courts to the families of some victims, acknowledgeing the lasting effect of the violation of human rights.

The police

There is wide scope for the abuse of power within the confines of police stations in India. As acknowledged by successive

National Police Commissions within India, resort to torture and other forms of cruel, inhuman and degrading treatment is encouraged by many factors. These include: the lack of investigatory machinery available to police; pressure on police to mete out instant punishment because of the inability of the criminal justice system to deliver justice promptly and effectively; corruption; poor wages. The sense of impunity generated by the infrequency with which police officials have been held publicly accountable for their actions, the rare convictions of those responsible for rape or deaths in custody, and the length of legal proceedings, further encourage the perception that resort to torture is acceptable.

Police are given wide powers under a variety of legislation which allows them to arrest, detain and investigate. Detainees can be kept in police custody for long periods, particularly under legislation permitting preventive detention, during which they are at risk of torture and ill-treatment. In violation of Indian law and police procedure, the practice of unrecorded police detentions is common and there is little doubt that it facilitates police abuse such as beatings and other forms of ill-treatment or torture, such as rape. Moreover, lawyers and relatives are routinely denied access by police to people held in custody. Most torture and illtratment in India occurs during the first stage of detention in police custody, when access to outsiders is routinely denied. Indian law is virtually silent on the procedures for questioning suspects in police custody, and no provisions exist detailing safeguards in the *Code of Criminal Procedure.*

The methods used by the police during law enforcement are also of concern. Amnesty International has documented discriminatory practices in policing that militates against the rights of specific communities, and is investigating reports that the police use violent methods during routine procedures, for example in evictions from illegal settlements, or when land is acquired by the government. In addition, Amnesty International has documented cases where the police have acted in collusion with other power brokers in civil society, facilitating the torture and ill-treatment of people. Amnesty International has documented the illegal actions of police officers outside their home state, and is investigating reports which suggest that the police act in collusion with other non-state actors, to violate the rights of Indian citizens.

The police are rarely required to give a public account of their actions. No independent groups or agencies have the authority to visit police stations or inspect police records, and it appears that the judiciary seldom undertakes this function. There is no independent police complaints mechanism to encourage transparency and accountability in day-to-day policing. Although the NHRC has investigated complaints against the police, it cannot enforce its findings.

The army

As with the police, the unpunished recourse to extra-legal methods prevents the active recognition of human rights by members of the armed forces, although recent initiatives to introduce human rights training could nurture a concern for human rights. Some violations occur when the army is deployed in civilian areas, particularly at times of civil disturbances. However, it is when it is called upon to deal with situations of internal armed conflict that most of the violations take place. The existence of special legislation granting the army wide powers (see above) leaves civilians including political activists and suspected supporters of armed opposition groups, particularly vulnerable to violation. These include arbitrary arrest and detention, incommunicado detention in unofficial interrogation centres, torture and ill treatment, "disappearance" and killings in "encounters."

While the NHRC has been vocal in its criticism of many police procedures and practices, the army and paramilitary forces do not come under its remit. There is therefore very little scope for the independent investigation of army practices, procedures or violations, nor for bringing those responsible for violations to justice. Again, the lack of transparency in the internal disciplinary proceedings and court martials protects army officials from being held publicly accountable for their actions.

Paramilitary groups

There are several paramilitary forces in India, including the Central Reserve Police Force (CRPF). the Border Security Force (BSF), the Rashtriya Rifles and the Provincial Armed Constabulary (PAC), and these operate with even fewer safeguards than the armed forces. Amnesty International has documented a number of occasions when members of these forces have committed gross violations of human rights. As with the armed forces, the NHRC is not empowered to examine reports of violations by paramilitary forces, and, again, with notable exceptions, few of the forces have ever been held publicly accountable for their actions.

Prison administration

Amnesty International has been concerned at the conditions in prisons throughout India for many years and first documented these in a report published in 1974. The *Prison Act* of 1894, which has been regularly criticized, remains in force. Repeated calls, most recently by the NHRC, for the standardization of prison manuals, which set out guidelines on the management of prisons, have not yet been heeded. Despite the concern expressed about the prison system by the judiciary in India, Amnesty International continues to receive many reports of conditions in prisons which contravene the UN *Standard Minimum Rules for the Treatment of Prisoners* and the UN *Body of Principles for the Protection of All Persons under any Form of Detention or Imprisonment*.

Although prison officials can be identified as the perpetrators of human rights violations, many of the problems in prisons emanate from the slow legal proceedings which mean that detainees await trial for many years, and from the inadequate facilities provided to house detainees. Whatever the cause, the effect is undisputed. In November 1995 the NHRC expressed concern at the "dismal" conditions in many prisons all over the country, including the inadequate diet lack of sanitation and poor medical facilities, and called for urgent action to improve them. The Commission described an almost 300% increase in the number of reported deaths in judicial custody in 1995, caused by poor nutrition, lack of medical care, overcrowding and in some cases, torture.

Overcrowding in prisons is endemic throughout the country. For example, Tihar Jail in Delhi, built for 2,500 detainess, now houses 9.000 inmates, 8,000 of whome were reported to be awaiting trial. As a direct result of overcrowding, many detainees in Jammu & Kashmir are sent to jails outside their home state, and procedures for informing relatives of such moves are often disregarded. Some states, including Arunachal Pradesh, do not have a state prison, so detainees are sent to other state prisons to await trial or serve their sentence, in this case to Assam. This distancing of detainees from their family and legal counsel contravenes principles set out by the UN.

In addition to lawful prisons and detention centres, unofficial interrogation and detention centres have been established by the police and security forces. These are not subject to any legal regulation and therefore provide those in positions of control with impunity to violate the human rithts of those detained.

Armed opposition groups

Noting the increase in the incidence of human rights abuses by armed political entities other than governments, which contravene minimum standards of human behaviour, as expressed in a number of international instruments, Amnesty International, in 1991, began to campaign against torture, the killing of prisoners, other deliberate and arbitrary killings and the taking of hostages by these groups.

Amnesty International is concerned at the number of reports from all over India of abuses by armed opposition groups, including by armed militias and private armies. It has condemned the deliberate killing of thousands of civilians in Punjab. In Jammu & Kashmir, armed separatist groups have captured and killed civilians, taken hostages, tortured and raped women in their custody. In Andhara Pradesh, groups have killed or mutilated alleged "informers", and in the northeast of India, many armed opposition groups have committed abuses including torture and deliberate killings on the civilian population. Amnesty International has repeatedly called on such groups to observed the basic principles of humanitarian law and to immediately halt such abuses.

The victims of human rights violations and abuses

The victims of human rights violation in India come from every community and every region. The complexity of Indian society and its inclusion of many different ethnic, cultural, religious, social and political groupings, mean that trends can only be used as a general indication of patterns that have emerged. From its work over the past few decades Amnesty International has been able to identify those most vulnerable political and social activists, scheduled castes, scheduled tribes and other disadvantaged communities, minorities, women, children and refugees. State agents have also been the victims of human rights abuses: they have been tortured and killed in the captivity of armed opposition groups acting in situations of internal armed conflict. Similarly, civilians, in the context of sporadic disturbances, and, in particular, in regions where there is on-going conflict, have become victims of abuse, regardless of their group or personal identities.

Political and Social Activists

Political and social activists are targeted for human rights violations across the country. The victims represent a wide spectrum of political views and a diversity of interests and opinions. Over the years Amnesty International has documented violations against non violent activists, such as J.P.Narayan, other political leaders, such as L.K. Advani, and social activists, such as Mrinal Gore. All three were arrested during emergency rule between 1975 and 1977 and were amongst the dozens adopted by Amnesty International as prisoners of conscience.

Many others exercising their rights to freedom of expression in an non-violent manner have had their rights violated, particularly in the context of internal armed conflict. They include journalists and human rights activists, abused by the security forces as well as armed opposition groups. Among other targeted groups are "Naxalities" active in different parts of the country and suspected members of armed opposition groups active in Jammu & Kashmir, Punjab and the northeast areas.

Amnesty International has also highlighted violations of the rights of activists working with specific communities, or in the context of land, labour and property struggles. From the large metropolitan centres located throughout the country, to the vast rural areas, land is at the centre of many of the tensions within India that lead to pervasive violations of human rights. Similarly, Amnesty International is investigating reports of ill-treatment in the context of evictions from squatter or slum settlements with the collusion or complicity of the police. Violations in the context of environmental activism, much of which is concerned with the displacement of people from their land and the destruction of the natural habitat, also take place. For example, in 1992 Amnesty International expressed concern at the shooting of a woman who was protesting at her eviction from land that was to be used for resettlement as a result of the Sardar Sarovar dam project.

Scheduled castes, scheduled tribes and other disadvantaged communities

Many of the dalit and adivasi communities, designated as "scheduled castes" and "scheduled tribes" by the Constitution, together with other socially and economically disadvantaged communities, some of which are designated as "other backward classes" by the Constitution, are especially vulnerable to the types of human rights violations prevalent throughout India. In some instances, the desire for autonomy expressed by indigenous communities, for example in northeast India, has resulted in acute tensions resulting in violations by the armed forces and abuses by armed opposition groups.

Amnesty International is also concerned that failure to resolve land conflicts appears to have fuelled human rights violations. Moreover, Amnesty International is concerned that the perception amongst disadvantaged communities that a high level of violations is normal reinforces the vulnerability of these people withing the criminal justice system.

Minority groups

The "minority" status of a group of people can be difficult to define because ethnic, religious and cultural differences suffuse the country. Some communities are national minorities, such as Muslims, Sikhs and Christians. But at a local and regional level, even the majority can be in a minority situation. Similarly, local power structures can mean that a community that is disadvantaged in one region may not be so in another.

Politics in India are increasingly being defined on communal grounds. The resultant intercommunal tension puts an onus on the State to provide communities under threat with protection, and to ensure the peaceful co-existence of people with ethnic, religious or cultural differences. However, it is in situations where state interference has been called for that some of the worst violations have occurred. In the past Amnesty International has responded to reports of communal bias in policing in Bombay and in the activity of the armed forces in Jammu & Kashmir. Also reported has been the abuses directed against Muslim communities, for example by the Provincial Armed Constabulary in Uttar Pradesh.

Women

The rights of women cannot be separated from the rights of all Indian citizens, and therefore relate to all the issues discussed in this document. As an individual, as participant in civil society as, for example, a contract worker or a lawyer, or as a mother, daughter or wife, every human rights violation impacts on women. Recognizing this, Amnesty International's 1995 global campaign 'Human Rights are Women's Rights,' highlighted the cases of individuals and groups of women who have often been the "invisible" victims of human rights violations. The Government of India has also recognised the particular vulnerabilities of women by its ratification of the UN *Convention on the Elimination of Discrimination Against Women*, in 1993, and earlier, of the UN *Convention of the Political Rights of Women*, in 1961, and by passing numerous laws and amendments to legislations that seek to address specific violations of the rights of women.

Amnesty International has documented the violations of women's rights in the context of international armed conflict, for example, rape and torture by the armed forces and in the custody of the police. In addition, Amnesty International is concerned that systematic practices in society which are detrimental to the rights of women go unaddressed by the forces of law and order. Concern remains that the few convictions of police officers for crimes against women, the delay in introducing legal safeguards to protect women detainess, and the problems of the legal process exacerbate the specific vulnerabilities of women.

Children

As an especially vulnerable group, children tend to have less defence against human rights violations than adults, and are unable directly to access the legal system to seek remedy for violations. Amnesty International has reported many violations of the rights of children, or of close relatives, in India, despite the government having acceded to the UN *Convention on the Rights of the Child in 1992.*

Children, defined by the Convention as anyone below the age of 18 years, have been imprisoned and detained, have been tortured and have died in custody. They have been extrajudicially killed, and as already noted, boys between the ages of 16 and 18 can be judicially executed because of the definition of a child in the *Juvenile Justice Act*. In situations of internal armed conflict, children have been directly targeted and have been affected by the violations against members of their families. Delays in the legal process exacerbate the violations against children, many of whom remain in custody for long periods awaiting the pendency of trials. Amnesty International has also documented instances of rape of girls by members of the police, the armed forces and armed opposition groups.

Refugees

Amnesty International opposes any person being forcibly returned to a country where there is a risk of imprisonment as a prisoner of conscience, of torture, "disappearance", or execution. India has not ratified the 1951 Geneva *Convention Relating to the Status of Refugees*, which protects refugees against forcible return (*refoulement*) to the country from which they fled persecution. Nonetheless, India is bound by the principle of *non-refoulement*, which is a norm of customary international law.

Additionally, Amnesty International notes the internal movement of people within India as a result of human rights violations in particular regions. For example, large numbers of residents of Kashmir, from Hindu communities, have been compelled to leave their homes to avoid being targeted by armed opposition groups. Amnesty International has also expressed its concern for the sefety of members of the Chakma and Hajong communities in Arunachal Pradesh, who had been displaced from Bangladesh.

Appendix - VI

India's Third Report to the UN Human Rights Committee and Amnesty's Proposals For Improving the Situation in the Country

In pursuance of the requirement under article 40 of the International Covenant on Civil and Political Rights (ICCPR), India's third report which was due in 1992 was submitted by the Government on 29 Nov. 1995 to the UN Human Rights Committee, which is the main monitoring body on observance of human rights by signatory memberstates. The Indian report presents an idealised picture of the state of human rights scene in the country.

We express our concern at the real state of things and reproduce below some of the proposals submitted to the Human Rights Committee by the Amnesty International - Ed.

* The shortcomings of India's implementation of safeguards to prevent human rights violations — contained in the Indian Constitution, the criminal law and in court orders;
* The absence of adequate mechanisms to ensure full redress (including investigation, prosecution and compensation) for all victims of human rights violations;
* The continuing state of impunity for the majority of perpetrators of human rights violations — particularly in areas of armed conflict;
* The existence of special legislation which grants security forces

wide powers to arrest and detain, shoot to kill and escape prosecution for violations, provisions of which suspend safeguards to protect the fundamental rights of citizens in India;

* The existence of a raft of legislation which provides for preventive detention which has been used to detain people not only in areas of armed conflict but has also been used against those defending the full range of human rights as set out in the Universal Declaration of Human Rights;
* The particular vulnerabilities of economically and socially disadvantaged groups in India, including women, *dalit* and tribal peoples, to a whole range of human rights violations and the particular problems they have in obtaining redress.

RECOMMENDATIONS TO THE GOVERNMENT OF INDIA

Amnety International calls on the Government of India to take steps to ensure the realisation of the rights specified in the ICCPR. In order to achieve this Amnesty International urges the Government of India to

* Withdraw the declarations made at the time of accession to the covenant with respect to articles 9 and 13
* Review Article 22 of the Constitution of India to bring it in line with international standards. With a view to this, implement the changes to Article 22 of the Constitution as required by the Constitution (Forty-Fourth) Amendment Act, 1978
* Review the Protection of Human Rights Act, 1993 as a matter of urgency to strengthen the mandate and operation of the National Human Rights Commissions, the State Human Rights Commissions and the Human Rights Courts
* Review the Armed Forces (Special Powers) Act, 1958, to ensure there are strict legal limitations on the use of force and firearms by law enforcement officials
* Ensure that UN standards concerning the conduct of law enforcement officials, including the Code of Conduct for Law Enforcement Officials and the Basic Principles on the Use of Force and Firearms by Law Enforcement Officials, are reflected in legislation, guidelines and training for police, paramilitary and armed forces in India
* Review all legislation at the central and state level, including the

National Security Act, 1980, which provide for preventive / administrative detention, with a view to the removal of such provisions

* Amend the definition of a juvenile given in the Juvenile Justice Act to remove the possibility that a juvenile boy can be sentenced to death. This would bring Indian law in consonance with article 37(a) of the Convention on the Rights of the Child and with article 6(5) of the covenant
* Take steps to abolish the death penalty in law and practice and ratify the second optional protocol to the ICCR
* Ratify the first optional protocol to the ICCPR to allow for individual complaints to the Human Rights Committee
* Ratify the Convention against Torture and Other Cruel, Inhuman and Degrading Treatment or Punishment.*

Amnesty International urges the Government of India to take the following measures to ensure the safety of those defending the whole range of rights as set out in the Universal Declaration of Human Rights

* Give a commitment that human rights defenders will be permitted to document human rights violations, and protest and campaign against such violations, in freedom and back this up in law and administrative guidelines
* Ensure that the freedom to peacefully protest is granted throughout India and that excessive force will not be used against protesters
* Ensure the protection from harassment and attacks of those defending the rights of others who may be under threat from vested interests
* Order prompt and impartial investigations into all attacks on human rights defenders and bring those responsible to justice
* Ensure the free and unhindered flow of information to and from human rights organizations in India
* Grant free access to international human rights organi- zations and United nations human rights mechanisms to all parts of India.

Amnesty International urges the Government of India to take the following measures to end discriminatory practices

* Review the implementation of the Scheduled Castes and Scheduled

---

* The Convention has been ratisfied by the Govt. of India 1997-ed.

Tribes (Prevention of Atrocities) Act, 1989 and the Protection of Civil Rights Act, 1955 to ensure that they are fulfilling the purpose for which the Acts were passed — that is, to grant protection to members of vulnerable communites;

* Review the Code of Criminal Procedure and the implementation of existing safeguards to enhance the protection provided to women detainees
* Ensure that any woman who bring charges of rape or sexual abuse against law enforeoment personnel is effectively protected from harassment or reprisals.
* Provide training in the basic principles of international human rights law to government officials, including all members of the security forces

Amnesty International urges the Government of India to take the following measures to provide redress and end impunity

* Ensure meticulous adherence to laws which already exist in India which have been enacted to safeguard human rights
* Review all provisions protecting public servants from arrest and prosecution. To this end, amend sections 45 and 197 of the Code of Criminal Procedure, 1973 to remove the requirement of the sanction of the central or state government for the prosecution of members of the police or armed forces
* Ensure the accountability of members of the praramilitary and armed forces for human rights violations which take place in the context of situations of armed conflict in India
* Review the Code of Criminal Procedure to ensure that mandatory judicial inquiries are carried out into all allegations of torture, death in custody, rape in custody, "disappearance", extrajudicial executions and into attacks on human rights defenders
* Take measures to ensure that investigations into human rights violations are fully independent and impartial and that victims, their relatives and witnesses are granted protection from harassment and intimidation
* Provide an effective machinery for prompt and adequate redress and compensation for victims of human rights violations which includes assurances that those found responsible for violations are prosecuted in accordance with law.

Index